Photo of Vladimir Djuro DEGAN

武大国际法讲演集

第二卷

Wuhan University Lectures on International Law Ⅱ

Vladimir Djuro DEGAN

WUHAN UNIVERSITY PRESS
武汉大学出版社

图书在版编目(CIP)数据

武大国际法讲演集.第二卷/Vladimir Djuro DEGAN. —武汉：武汉大学出版社,2010.9
ISBN 978-7-307-07829-1

Ⅰ.武… Ⅱ.D… Ⅲ.国际法—演讲—文集—英文 Ⅳ.D99-53

中国版本图书馆 CIP 数据核字(2010)第106800号

责任编辑:罗晓华　　责任校对:刘　欣　　版式设计:支　笛

出版发行：武汉大学出版社　(430072　武昌　珞珈山)
(电子邮件：cbs22@whu.edu.cn　网址：www.wdp.com.cn)
印刷：武汉中远印务有限公司
开本：720×1000　1/16　印张:19.5　字数:354千字
版次：2010年9月第1版　2010年9月第1次印刷
ISBN 978-7-307-07829-1/D·1021　定价:32.00元

Contents

Preface

Wuhan University Institute of International Law has been fortunate to receive various distinguished scholars of international law from time to time. In the Autumn Semester of 2009, we had Professor Vladimir Djuro DEGAN here as our Expert in Residence.

During his stay on campus, Professor DEGAN participated in the teaching of "Advanced Studies in Public International Law", a course given in English for graduate students. Both the staff members of our institute and the students benefited greatly from his lectures, our conversations with him, and generally, his presence.

Some time ago, Wuhan University Institute of International Law started a series of publications under the title of "Wuhan University Lecutres on International Law", collecting lectures given by distinguished visitors both in English and in Chinese. Volume one of this series was published in 2006. The Lectures given by Professor Vladimir Djuro DEGAN present us with the opportunity to produce Volume 2 of this series, completely in English.

Readers of these Lectures will find that while attempting to provide teaching materials to the graduate students of international law, Professor DEGAN has given us a great deal of his personal insights. We are certain that Professor DEGAN's Lectures will be of great value to students and researchers alike. We are pleased that these Lectures now feature as Volume 2 of our Wuhan University Lectures series.

Yu Mingyou, Acting Director
Sienho Yee, Chief Expert
Wuhan University Institute of International Law

Biographical Note

Vladimir Djuro DEGAN was born on 2 July, 1935 at Bosanski Brod (Bosnia-Herzegovina). He is now Vice-president of the Institute of International Law; Head of the Adriatic Institute of the Croatian Academy of Sciences and Arts in Zagreb; Marco Polo Fellow of the Silk Road Institute of International Law, Xi'an Jiaotong University (China); and Emeritus Professor of the University in Rijeka.

Having finished his studies at the Faculty of Law in Sarajevo, he lectured between 1969 and 1981 Comparative Government and Public International Law at the Faculty of Political Sciences of the Sarajevo University. Since 1981 until his retirement in 2005 he was Professor of International Law at the Faculty of Law, University of Rijeka (Croatia).

During the period between 1979 and 1991 he organized three-week courses in International Law and International Relations at the Inter-University Centre in Dubrovnik, each year alternately in English and French.

In 1984, he was professeur associé to l'Université du Maine (Le Mans); and in 1990 and 1993 professeur invité to l'Université de Nanterre (Paris XIII) and l'Université Panthéon-Assas (Paris II).

In 1988 and 1992, he lectured at the Helsinki Summer School of International Law.

In 1999, he lectured at the Hague Academy of International law on the topic of "Création et disparition de l'Etat (à la lumière du démembrement de trois fédérations multiethniques en Europe)".

In 2006 he presented a course on "The Scope and Patterns of Erga Omnes Obligations in International Law" at the Bancaja Euromediterranean Courses of International Law in Castellon (Spain).

In 2008 he has done postgraduate courses on various topics of international law at the Silk Road Institute of International Law, Xi'an Jiaotong University in China.

In 2009 he was invited as "Expert in Residence", and took part in the teaching of "Advanced Studies in Public International Law" within the Wuhan University Institute of International Law.

In 1983 he was elected associé, and since 1989 he has been full member of the Institute of International Law.

Between 1991 and 1995, he was a Croatian member at the Expert Groups on Human and Minority Rights, and on State Succession at the International Conference on the Former Yugoslavia. Between 1996 and 2001, he was Member of Croatian delegation at the negotiations on Succession issues of the former Yugoslavia.

Decorations: by the French Republic, dans l'Ordre des Palmes Académiques chevalier in 1988; officier in 1997; commandeur in 2004. No decorations or prizes received in Croatia or the former Yugoslavia.

Chapter I
On Sources of International Law in General

Bibliography: Max SOERENSEN: *Les sources du droit international*, Copenhague 1946, 274 pages; Clive PARRY: *The Sources and Evidences of International Law*, Manchester Univ. Press 1965, 122 pages; G. J. H. VAN HOOF: *Rethinking the Sources of International Law*, The Hague 1983, 314 pages; Gennadi Mikhailovich DANILENKO: *Law-Making in the International Community*, Martinus Nijhoff Publishers 1992, 343 pages; Julio A. BARBERIS: *Formación del derecho internacional*, Buenos Aires 1994, 324 pages; V. D. DEGAN: *Sources of International Law*, The Hague 1997, 564 pages.

I. Introduction

The notion of sources of international law seems to be of utmost importance for proper understanding of this entire discipline. Although no author of treaties on international law can avoid its explanation, in some books the treatment of it is limited and simplified. Their authors give otherwise excellent explication of most of other problems of this discipline, but they did not treat the complex problem of sources of international law quite properly. That is the origin of much confusion on this subject matter.

However, the sources of international law, including here the law of treaties, customary law, general principles of law, and unilateral acts of States—together with responsibility of States for internationally unlawful acts—form the core of this entire discipline. They form as to say "the lawyer's law". To students who understand these problems well, all other topics such as the law of the sea, law of diplomatic and consular relations, etc., are much simpler to grasp.

"principal judicial organ", as is provided in Article 92. Therefore, the law applied by the principal judicial organ of the UN is the law obligatory to almost all States in the world.

It can therefore be presumed that Article 38(1) determines sources of that international law which is generally accepted by States. This conclusion applies even to the parties of the Statute that have not accepted the compulsory jurisdiction of the Court, either by their unilateral commitments on the basis of its Article 36(2), or on behalf of some bilateral or multilateral treaties.

*

Let us now give an explanation of the content of Article 38. Its paragraph 1 displays the existence of two kinds of sources of international law. Conventions, custom and general principles of law, qualified by Briggs and Schwarzenberger as "law-creating processes", are for the Court itself the main sources of this law. Judicial decisions and doctrine are its subsidiary sources (or according to Schwarzenberger "law-determining agencies"), being according to the wording of this provision: "subsidiary means for the determination of rules of law."

Besides this distinction, Article 38 does not provide any ground for a hierarchy as between the main sources of international law. Such a hierarchy, based on the general principle of law *lex specialis derogat generali*, does not seem to be admissible at the present time.

Article 53 of the *1969 Vienna Convention* on the *Law of Treaties* (the *1969 Vienna Convention*) avows the existence of peremptory norms of general international law (*jus cogens*), as being accepted and recognized "*by the international community of States as a whole*". Practically all norms of this kind are general customary rules. This means that general norms of this character and scope make void or terminate any special rules conflicting with them. ① When the matter is of operation of these norms, the general principle *lex specialis derogat legi generali* does not apply.

---

① See an interesting approach to this problem in Sienho Yee: "Strategies for Settling the Hierarchy of the Sources of International Law", V. CRNIĆ-GROTIĆ, M. MATULOVIĆ(Ed): *International Law and the Use of Force at the Turn of Centuries*, Essays in honour of V. D. DEGAN, Rijeka 2005, pp. 341-375.

*

However, in spite of the highly authoritative character of Article 38 of the ICJ Statute, its wording can no longer be considered as exhaustive and all-embracing, when the matter is either of main or of subsidiary sources of international law.

(i) First of all, its sub-paragraph (b) describes international custom as evidence of "a general practice", accepted as law. This could mean that only general customary international law is provided in it. However the State practice, some Judgments of the Court itself and the doctrine have for a long time ago ascertained the existence of *particular customary law.* Although not frequent in practice, the rules of this kind are very much similar to non-written agreements. They are in many other important aspects dissimilar to the general customary law.

(ii) Next to them, *unilateral acts* by which a State assumes certain new legal obligations, or relinquishes its actual rights (waiver), or even acquires new rights, can no longer be denied as a principal and autonomous source of international law. The legal effects of unilateral acts of this kind are not dissimilar to the effects of treaties or of particular customary rules.

(iii) There is a tendency in the practice within some international organizations to give rise to another autonomous source of international law. Some UN specialized agencies—namely the World Health Organization, the World Meteorological Organization and the International Civil Aviation Organization—issue within their competencies some *standard rules.* Formally, they are not obligatory for their member States as such. Nevertheless, all the respective States almost invariably conform themselves with these the so-called "non-obligatory" rules, which are the product of high technical expertise and knowledge. That is because member States are usually not able to impose the alternatives, and because their refusal by them might harm their own interests. These are for instance numerous regulations concerning the safety of airports.

In case that some new intergovernmental organizations were established with similar competencies, and in case of proliferation of rules of this kind, one could discuss of the appearance of this new main source of international law. But it seems still to allege that.

A tendency in this respect seems to be some provisions of the *1982 UN Law of the Sea Convention* which refer to "generally accepted international rules and standards" in the domain of protection of marine environment. ① The competent organization for issuing these rules and standards is the International Maritime Organization, a UN specialized agency.

The legal scope of these "rules and standards" is still uncertain. There is not enough of State practice in order to demonstrate that some of them have transformed into customary rules of general international law. Still less can be proved that all State parties to the *1982 Convention* have committed themselves in advance to respect them as a kind of treaty obligations. However, in case of new grave accidents at seas with disastrous consequences such a law-creating by the I. M. O. could acquire in a short period of time universal approval by States.

(iv) Furthermore, there have been views in the doctrine ascribing to *the UN General Assembly resolutions* the role of a source of direct obligations for its member States. That would be tantamount to assign at least to some of these resolutions the character of an autonomous source of international law, distinct from others. That allegation does not seem to be justified. Neither is it, however, correct to deny a legal importance of any of these resolutions. Some of them can play an important role as a material source or documentary evidence of customary international law. The same can be claimed for some portions of the *1975 Helsinki Final Act* in respect to European States.

(v) Finally, Article 38 of the Court's Statute is not all embracing any more in its *enumeration of subsidiary means for the determination of legal rules.* The matter is in practice mainly of subsidiary means (or "law-determining agencies"), for determination of customary legal rules. On the contrary, when the matter is of a treaty in written form, its own text is the main agency for the determination of the rights and duties of its parties.

Besides judicial decisions and doctrine, that role can play in customary process: multilateral and bilateral treaties, and especially conventions on codification of international law; concordant unilateral acts of a larger number of States; or some non-conventional instruments like the UN General Assembly resolutions, final acts of

① That was an attempt to harmonize the protection of the marine environment with the preservation of the freedom of navigation. The matter is mainly of paragraphs 2, 5 and 6 of Article 211, paragraph 1 (a) of Article 226, and paragraph 2 of Article 21.

diplomatic conferences, joint statements of heads of State and Government, etc.

Ⅳ. Law-creating processes and law-determining agencies

After ascertaining the distinction between the main and the subsidiary sources of positive international law, we can now return to the controversy on the meaning of the term of "sources of international law". It seems that this legal term has several and distinct meanings in practice.

In its simplest sense, the term "source of law" means the source of legal rights and obligations of parties to a legal instrument. In this sense a treaty is the source of rights and obligations for its parties. The same can be said for these unilateral acts of States, which are a genuine source of international law.

Such a narrow interpretation of this term is correct but not sufficient. When discussing some specific sources we associate at the first glance to the form and origin of a particular legal norm. Thus, when speaking of treaty rules we imply written legal norms, although, there are agreements not in written form, which are infrequent in practice.

When we speak of customary rules we mean unwritten norms that appear in practice of States and are accepted by them as law (*opinio juris*). However, the most important customary rules are today codified in conventions, or they can arise from other treaty provisions, or from some resolutions of the UN General Assembly, or even from judicial decisions. Strictly speaking, in these cases customary rules are not "unwritten".

Finally, under general principles of law are usually meant principles common to the municipal civil, criminal or constitutional legal orders, which are, subject to circumstances, applicable as legal norms in international relations, but are distinct from customary rules. There is however no convincing reasons why a norm of that kind should not operate both as a customary legal rule and as a general principle of law at the same time.

*

Nevertheless, the meaning of the main sources cannot be reduced to their bare form or to their origin only. Like Schwarzenberger and Briggs, we understand under this term primarily *the law-creating processes*. And we shall also take into account the respective law-determining agencies in the sense: how an alleged rule is to be verified as a norm of positive international law.

The main agency of conclusion and operation of a treaty is a concordance of wills of two or more subjects of international law (i. e. international persons), intended to achieve an effect in international law by creating a legal relationship of their mutual rights and duties. In absence of that concordant will there is no treaty.

In the same sense, a source of international law is the will of one State issuing a unilateral act, intended to achieve an effect in international law by assuming a new legal obligation, or by waiving its actual legal rights, or in some circumstances by acquiring new rights. In absence of such a will the matter is not of a source, i. e. of a law-creating process.

The customary process is of a more complex nature. Normally, a uniform practice of several international persons precedes *opinio juris*. ① Their practice and *opinio juris* can be manifested in their conduct, but also in various written acts such as treaties, acts of diplomatic conferences, declarations of political organs of international organizations, or concordant unilateral acts of legislative, executive, military or judicial organs of a number of States. In this customary process of importance can be, in addition, some other pronouncements which can influence future practice of States, namely decisions of international courts or tribunals, and sometimes even writings of publicists (doctrine).

Subject to circumstances, some of these acts can be evidence of a practice, or constitute the practice itself. At a later stage of customary development they can be a catalyst for creation of *opinio juris*, or they can simply be declaratory of a customary rule already in force. Therefore, the law-determining agencies can be material sources (i. e. factors) in a customary process in progress. In case of a final and successful transformation of these acts into new legal rules, they can serve *ex post facto* as documentary evidences of its contents and scope in law. Hence, the very role of these acts in customary process can change in time.

Specific problems can arise in regard to general principles of law. Operation of some principles of this kind, like that of *pacta sunt servanda*, ② is a prerequisite to

① *Opinio juris sive necessitatis* is the conviction of participating States that their actual practice has become legally obligatory.

② The rule *pacta sunt servanda* means that all their parties in good faith must perform treaties.

the existence of a legal order of any kind. The respect of some procedural principles like that of the equality of parties throughout the procedure, or that of *res judicata*,① is a prerequisite of a judicial procedure in whatsoever legal order.

Nevertheless, under the resort to general principles of law sometimes is understood the implied power of an international judge to have recourse by analogy to rules of municipal law, in order to fill the gaps in international law. Hence, these two concepts of this term of general principles of law are dissimilar.

V. Notion of the "international legal order"

We must finally introduce in our present explanation another concept. By the term of "*international legal order*" we understand rules of positive international law in force at a given time, arising from all the main sources of international law. The matter is therefore of the sum of rules from all treaties in force, whatever their parties may be, of all general and particular customary rules, of all applicable general principles of law, and of relevant unilateral acts of States.②

In case that parties to a dispute refer to this legal order as the basis of its settlement by an independent judicial organ, or if they simply refer to Article 38(1) of the Statute of the ICJ, it is the most likely that the international judge or arbitrator will be able to find a legal solution to their case. He will then not be compelled to resort to his equitable considerations *praeter legem*, or to a simple analogy with municipal law, in order to avoid declaring *non liquet* (incompetence) for lack of applicable legal rules. Like in municipal legal orders, an international judge or arbitrator should not declare *non liquet* in contentious procedures.

---

① The principle *res judicata* means that the parties to a dispute in good faith must perform a final judgment and that on the case decided by it there cannot be new proceedings.

② This notion of international legal order should not be confused with that of "transnational law". However, probably the rules from both legal orders were encompassed by the larger notion of the "Common Law of Mankind", suggested by C. Wilfred JENKS: *The Common Law of Mankind*, London 1958, *passim*.

Chapter II
Customary Process in International Law

Bibliography: Karol WOLFKE: *Custom in Present International Law*, Wroclaw 1964, 185 pages; Michael AKEHURST: "Custom as a Source of International Law", *The British Year Book of International Law 1974-1975*, pp. 1-53; Maurice MENDELSON: "The Subjective Element in Customary International Law", *The British Year Book of International Law 1995*, pp. 177-208; V. D. DEGAN: *Sources of International Law*, The Hague 1997, pp. 142-252.

I. Common features of custom in international law

It is sometimes asserted that custom, i. e. the process of creation, modification and abrogation of legal rules of this kind, is a mysterious phenomenon. The present chapter aims to remove mysteries from it so that it becomes clear to students.

Unlike general principles of law, which are common to all legal systems, international customary rules are peculiar to international law alone. All of them appear in the practice of States and of other international persons and have as their purpose the regulation of actual inter-State and other international relations. On the same ground, a general principle of law which is actually absorbed in customary international law (like for instance that *pacta sunt servanda*) is also confirmed in State practice and has as its purpose the regulation of actual inter-State relations.

Article 38 (1b) of the *ICJ Statute* defines international custom "as evidence of a general practice accepted as law". However it was already stressed that this qualification did not prevent the rise of particular customary rules, generated from the particular practice of a few States only, and not from the general practice.

This wording was the object of much criticism. It was said that it puts the cart before the horse, because it is practice which evidences the custom, and not *vice versa*. So, one might have expected to find a general practice which is being accepted as law, as evidence of the existence of international customary rules.

In spite of the above objection this definition accurately indicates two elements of customary international rules of law — a material element: practice, which can be general or common to two or more international persons in their mutual relations only;— and a psychological element: *opinio juris sive necessitatis*, i. e. the fact that a uniform, consistent and durable practice (or "usage") has been "accepted as law" by its participants.

We shall first deal with problems of practice, then with *opinio juris*. Finally we shall draw some conclusions on acts that can influence custom as a continuous social process.

II. Practice

(a) Continuation or repetition of the practice over a considerable period of time usually precedes the psychological element of *opinion juris*. It is clear that the practice of subjects of international law (i. e. of "international persons") is only relevant in generating customary rules. They are first of all sovereign States, then intergovernmental organizations, but can also be recognized insurgents within their limited capacity to act.

Authors are inclined with good reason to ascribe the practice of political organs of intergovernmental organizations — such as the UN General Assembly or Security Council — to States whose representatives act in these bodies, rather than to the organization itself. This means that most customary rules are created by the practice of States and they regulate relations between States. Sovereign States are in this capacity at once the main creators and the addressees of customary rules of international law.

This does not, however, exclude the practice of administrative organs in the name of an intergovernmental organization within its own capacity, as relevant in customary process. It is, nevertheless, hard to assert that this kind of practice of administrative organs of organizations can affect rights and duties of States. On the other hand, applicable customary rules created by States are binding on international organizations as well.

As a general rule, the practice of private persons acting on their own, as well as of non-governmental organizations, is not relevant in customary process. There is nevertheless an important exception in this respect. The International Committee of the Red Cross, a non-governmental organization under Swiss law, has, by virtue of the *Geneva Conventions* on humanitarian law and the *Additional Protocols* thereto, some "public functions". Its practice within these rules could be creative of customary law. But because this branch of international law is codified in detail by written rules, this kind of practice does not seem susceptible of playing a big role in a gradual customary process.

(b) In customary process the practice of organs competent to bind a State internationally — thus having at the same time treaty-making capacity — is capable of forming the basis of customary rules. But this is not all. Besides that, customary rules can emerge from concordant legislative or other unilateral acts of a number of States. Even some decisions of municipal courts can influence customary process. In the case that the national armed forces are stationed on a foreign territory on whatever basis, their conduct can also be relevant in the customary process. On the other hand, their conduct can sometimes consist in internationally wrongful acts, or even in international crimes. Then such a practice is obviously not of custom-creative character.

The proper practice of intergovernmental organizations consists primarily in the practice of its administrative organs (secretary general, director, and their deputies), when they act within their competencies in the name of the organization as a particular international person.

(c) According to some pronouncements by the ICJ, which we cannot elaborate here in details, the practice of relevant State organs must in general terms be "settled" (or consistent), uniform, and continuous (i. e. without important brakes). ①

(d) The next question is that of the passage of time in order that a settled, uniform and continuous practice transforms into a customary rule of law. In this respect there are no commonly accepted criteria.

The British scholar of Chinese origin Bin Cheng spoke about "instant custom",

---

① See the details—V. D. DEGAN: *Sources of International Law*, pp. 147-162, in particular pp. 150-152.

without precedents. The accelerating developments in technology in the 20th century, such as the discovery of the air-plane, of the submarine, space flights, the possibility of exploitation of the sea-bed etc. , have created new objective situations to which the existing customary law adapted almost spontaneously, although not without important exceptions.

In such circumstances a relatively short period of time may be sufficient for the creation of new customary rules, such as these on the air law, on the law of outer space, or on the continental shelf. However, in other domains of international relations, which are not affected by the revolutions in technology, such as for instance in the domain of human rights, a longer period of time is still necessary for a uniform and continuous practice to transform into new customary law.

(e) The last question is that of the quality of State practice. The matter can be of positive acts and of passivity.

International courts and tribunals were in this respect not always clear. It should be stressed that positive actions of competent State organs, as well as legislative acts which are actually put into practice, have more probative value than laws that remain a dead letter, or contradictory verbal statements of its representatives. Nevertheless, all normative acts and conventional engagements are certainly acts of the will of the respective State, which it cannot deny, in a judicial procedure.

Even voting in the UN General Assembly in favour of a resolution embodying legal principles fundamental for maintenance of international peace and security, are acts that a State cannot easily deny, if it is accused for their violation. ① Finally, verbal statements of representatives of a State — others than by the Head of State or Government — can have also a probative value as being that State's practice, in particular if other acts are lacking.

It must nevertheless be acknowledged that circumstances of a case can overwhelm all the above abstract considerations that belong to this author. A very large margin of discretionary power of judges cannot be neglected, especially when they are faced with different kinds of manifestation of a State's practice.

---

① Hence, the ICJ has stressed in its 1986 Judgment in *Nicaragua* case that: "*opinio juris* may, though with all due caution, be deduced from, *inter alia*, the attitude of the Parties and the attitude of States towards certain General Assembly resolutions..." *Cf. I. C. J. Reports 1986*, pp. 99-100, para. 108.

On the other hand, especially in the process of creation of customary rules of general international law, the relevant practice of States does not only consist in positive actions, but passivity, tolerance, or failure to protest against acts by others, can also be of law creative value. It can then be presumed that passivity of a State means its acquiescence to the practice of other States, which in these circumstances becomes opposable to the passive State.

Ⅲ. *Opinio juris sive necessitatis*

It can happen that a certain practice of States and of other international persons is constant and uniform, that it is of long duration and emanates from competent organs, but that it is still not transformed into a new rule of law. Important are motives of such a practice.

The International Court has sometimes ascribed "extra legal motives" to a certain practice, which are not creative of customary legal rules. In its *Judgment of 1969 on the North Sea Continental Shelf* the Court has emphasized that: "There are many international acts, e. g., in the field of ceremonial and protocol, which are performed almost invariably, but which are motivated only by considerations of courtesy, convenience or tradition, and not by any sense of legal duty."①

The criterion that divides a simple usage from a customary rule of law is the second essential element of custom: *opinio juris sive necessitatis*, i. e. the conviction of States that a social habit is according to international law obligatory or right. As was already emphasized, that subjective or psychological element of custom is embodied in the definition laid down in Article 38(1b) of the *Statute of the ICJ*—with the reference to a general practice "accepted as law".

Ⅳ. Custom as a social process

The correlation of the two elements of customary rules: practice and *opinio juris*, can primarily be understood if custom is taken in its sense of a source of law, as a continuous, gradual and progressive social process.

---

① *I. C. J. Reports 1969*, p. 44, para. 77.

Normally, this customary process begins with the particular practice of one or of a few States to which is aggregated the practice or acquiescence of a larger number of other States, until it attains the necessary generality, uniformity, density, continuity and duration.

It is normal that at an unknown moment such a practice crystallizes into an obligatory rule of law due to the conviction of its participants that just such an attitude is in accordance with law, and that its disregard could provoke international responsibility for violation of a legal obligation.

Nevertheless, if *opinio juris* fails to appear, the actual practice remains at the level of a social habit, or usage, or a political principle. Disregarding it then does not amount to the violation of a legal obligation, although it can sometimes entail important political consequences.

V. Generation of customary rules of general international law

As was already stressed, custom remains the main process in which rules of general international law arise, modify and terminate. Practically no other law-creating process in this domain exists today. The international community of States does not possess a legislative organ that could enact laws directly obligatory on all States and other international persons.

In this respect we can distinguish between gradual and articulated customary process.

In gradual process, which was already described as slow, continuous and progressive, and which never ends, practice of States precedes *opinio juris.* However here it is almost impossible to ascertain the precise moment in which a settled practice crystallizes into a new legal rule.

Generally speaking, due to its fluctuating and unstable character it is much more difficult to establish responsibility for breach of a customary rule of international law than responsibility for violation of an obligation from a written treaty. Again and again it is necessary to prove the very existence of a customary rule and the fact that the State that is charged with its infringement did not succeed in exempting itself from the general scope of its validity.

The ascertainment of all these facts may in the last resort be one of impression. And all these complexities of the rise of binding customary law and its application,

(ii) *Some UN resolutions*. The next way of willfully influencing general customary process is by the adoption of some resolutions or declarations by the UN General Assembly, formulating general and abstract rules of conduct for States. Without further developing this topic, one could mention here the *Declaration on Principles of International Law Concerning Friendly Relations and Co-operation among States in Accordance with the Charter of the United Nations*. This large text, which codifies and further develops the principles of the United Nations from Article 2 and Article 1(2) of its *Charter*, was adopted by the General Assembly resolution 2625 (XXV) of 1970 without vote, i. e. by consensus. It will be referred to as the *1970 Declaration on Principles Concerning Friendly Relations*.

To this list should be added the Definition of Aggression, also adopted by the *General Assembly Resolution 3316 (XXIX) of 1974*. This resolution will be applicable as a statement of general international law until States agree on a general convention on this subject matter, and until it enters into force. This cannot be expected in a foreseeable future.

(iii) *Judicial decisions*. Certain judgments and advisory opinions of the International Court of Justice resolved some important dilemmas in general international law, where pending customary process was indecisive. They crystallized hitherto uncertain, vague or contradictory practice into new rules of law.

Notwithstanding the principle: *sententia jus facit inter partes* (that no judicial decisions have binding force except between the parties to a dispute), which is embodied in Article 59 of the *Court's Statute*, every statement of the Court on customary law will be accepted as law in force at least by these States whose national interests correspond with it. And on States with different interests will fall the heavy burden to prove the opposite. That is sometimes impossible, especially when the previous practice of States was sparse, vague or contradictory.

Among other examples in this respect, here could be mentioned the 1951 Judgment in the *Anglo-Norwegian Fisheries* case. The Court enunciated a number of general rules on drawing straight baselines for measuring the territorial sea in localities where the coastline is deeply indented and cut into, or where there is a fringe of islands along the coast. ①

---

① *I. C. J. Reports 1951*, pp. 133, 135, 142. The matter is of coastlines of Norway, Croatia, Greece, etc.

Only seven years later these rules were incorporated in Article 4 of the *Geneva Convention on the Territorial Sea and Contiguous Zone*, codifying customary rules of general international law that nobody denied. With very slight innovations Article 7 of the *1982 UN Law of the Sea Convention* confirmed these rules. Hence, there is no opposition to such rules enunciated in judicial decisions if they provide rights for coastal States at the expense of the areas of the high seas.

(iv) *Opinio juris* can in addition be expressed in *Unilateral and Joint Statements of Heads of State and Government*, such as within the Organization of African Unity (nowadays the African Union), or the Non-aligned movement.

Here should be stressed in particular the five principles of peaceful coexistence, first defined in the joint statement by Zhou Enlai and Jawaharlal Nehru in New Delhi in April 1954, and the principles adopted by the Bandung Conference of Asian and African countries in April 1955, in which China had also a prominent role. ①

Ⅵ. Particular customary legal rules

As was said, customary rules of this kind are not very frequent in international practice. The reason is that the treaty making remains the main process of creation of legal rules in relations between a limited number of international persons.

Like all other customary rules, particular custom consists of two elements: (a) a constant, uniform and durable practice of a restrained number of States only, and (b) conviction of competent State organs that such a practice became obligatory as legal rules for the States in question (*opinio juris*).

However, in spite of these similarities with general customary law, particular customary rules are in their substance close to treaties. Customary rules of this kind always provide rights and duties for a limited number of international persons. Like treaties, they cannot legally bind third States that did not take part in practice or did not express a form of assent to them.

For this very reason, unlike general customary rules, particular custom is essentially a kind of tacit agreement (*tacitus consensus*), very similar to agreements not in written form.

---

① Also with his participation at the 1954 Geneva Conference on Indochina, Zhou Enlai proved to be an important figure in international politics of the 20th century.

Chapter III
Treaties and Unilateral Acts as Sources of Particular International Law; Opposable Situations

Bibliography: Lord McNAIR: *The Law of Treaties*, Oxford 1961, 789 pages; *Reports of the International Law Commission* on the second part of its seventeenth session 3-28 January, 1966 and on its eighteenth session 4 May-19 July, 1966. General Assembly Official Records: Twenty-first Session, Supplement No. 9 (A/6309/Rev. 1); also, *American Journal of International Law 1966*, No. 1, pp. 248-470; T. O. ELIAS: *The Modern Law of Treaties*, Oceana, Dobbs Ferry 1974, 272 pages; Sir Ian SINCLAIR: *The Vienna Convention on the Law of Treaties*, Second Revised and Enlarged Edition, Manchester University Press 1984, 260 pages; Suzanne BASTID: *Les traités dans la vie internationale*, Conclusion et Effets, Paris 1985, 303 pages; Paul REUTER: *Introduction au droit des traités*, 3e édition revue et augmentée par Philippe Cahier, Paris 1995, 211 pages.

Treaties

I . Preliminaries

There is no doubt that treaties are the most important practical mode of regulation of rights and duties of States and other international persons, in their mutual i. e. particular relations.

Among all other law-creating agencies that have been discussed or just mentioned in previous chapters, treaty has some undisputable practical advantages. Because most of them are concluded in written form, their parties can express in their text their mutual interests in very precise terms. They can thus establish better than by other means the desired balance of their rights and obligations. Relations between sovereign and equal subjects are essentially based on equilibrium and reciprocity.

Although there have always been unequal treaties, imposed on one party by some kind of constraint, the continuous process of negotiations, followed by signature, ratification and reservations if any, is an assurance that all parties of a treaty, carefully assess their particular interests. Thus, they can assure the equality of their rights and obligations in respect to other negotiating States more than by any other means of law-creating. That continuous treaty-making process reduces the risk of irresponsible and hasty decisions, that what could harm confidence and stability in legal relations.

Some modalities of international co-operation can be realized and maintained only by written treaties. Intergovernmental organizations, including the composition and competencies of their organs, can be established only by written treaties. The same is with commercial relations and all kinds of communications between States, including reduction of armaments, etc. Specific commitments of States on compulsory procedures on settlement of their disputes are mainly provided by treaties. Thus, customary rules and unilateral declarations are useless in these domains of international cooperation. They cannot replace treaties.

Of particular importance seems to be the fact that the largest number of treaties is concluded in written form. Unlike customary rules, legal obligations assumed by parties are provided in a written instrument, which in the most cases does not create problems of its interpretation.

*

The *Law of Treaties*, as a particular branch of international law, has largely been codified by several conventions. The most important is the *Vienna Convention on the Law of Treaties of 23 May, 1969*, (from now the *1969 Convention*) which entered into force on 27 January, 1980.

This *Convention* is applicable on the treaties in written form and it has resolved some previous doctrinal dilemmas. It should be mentioned here that the law of treaties as a whole is based on some general principles of law common to all agreements between whatever parties.

Before 1969, these general principles were recognized and generally adopted in the State practice and doctrine, but there was no unanimous agreement on the conditions of their applicability to treaties entered by States. The matter of long debates was for instance the scope of the *clausula rebus sic stantibus* in regard of the time of the conclusion of a treaty. What is applicable now are very restrictive conditions concerning fundamental change of circumstances stipulated in Article 62 of this *Convention*. These changes can only empower an interested State to ask formal modification (revision) of the treaty in question, but not its unilateral revocation by any of its parties.

Following its adoption, most provisions from this *Convention* acquired an objective character. Almost all of them are now admitted as declaratory of the customary rules of general international law, contested by nobody. Its written provisions apply today, or are considered to be applicable, to parties to all the treaties, even those concluded by the States which have not ratified the *Vienna Convention*, such as France. It is exactly for this reason that this *Convention* is probably the most important convention on the codification of international law today.

Other conventions on this subject-matter are not of equal importance. The *Vienna Convention on Succession of States in Respect of Treaties of 23 August, 1978* binds only a small number of its State parties (see Chapter IX bellow). The *Vienna Convention on the Law of Treaties Between States and International Organizations or Between International Organizations, of 21 March, 1986*, has almost no chances to formally enter into force. Its essential rules are the same as these stipulated in the *1969 Vienna Convention* so that its very conclusion proved to be unnecessary.

Ⅱ. The concept of treaties

Article 2, paragraph 1 (a) of the *1969 Vienna Convention* provides, for its own purposes, the meaning of "treaty" in following terms:

> "(a) '*Treaty*' *means an international agreement concluded between States in written form and governed by internationai law, whether embodied in a single instrument or in two or more related instruments and whatever its particular designation...*"

Article 3 states, in addition, that the fact that this *Convention* does not apply to international agreements concluded between States and other subjects of international law, or between such other subjects, or "to international agreements not in written form", shall not affect the legal force of such agreements. This means that general principles of law as codified in the *1969 Vienna Convention* are applicable on all these agreements.

For the purposes of the present explanation of sources of international law, a more generic definition of treaty seems to be necessary. It must, however, be in perfect harmony with the above explained meaning.

A treaty consists *in a concordance of wills of two or more subjects of international law* (i. e. international persons), *intended to achieve an effect in international law by creating a legal relationship of rights and duties for its parties.* It can be embodied in a single instrument, or in two or more related instruments. It can be concluded in written or in other form. Hence, in case of absence of such a concordance of wills, there is not a treaty.

In order to achieve an effect in international law, this concordance of wills — i. e. consent of all parties to a treaty to this end — implies the operation of the general principle of law *pacta sunt servanda.* Its content and scope will be discussed latter on.

In order that a treaty achieves the intended effect in international law, several conditions must be satisfied:

(i) All parties to a treaty must be international persons, i. e. States, intergovernmental organizations, or recognized insurgents. On the other hand, contracts concluded by a State with a foreign private financial institution, or with a political sub-division of a foreign State which is itself deprived of international personality, are not treaties on which directly apply the rules of the *1969 Vienna Convention.* But they are not devoid of obligatory character for their parties, because they too are subject to the general principle of law *pacta sunt servanda.*

(ii) With regard to the object of regulation, a materially impossible act, or an act forbidden by law, or even an immoral act, is deprived of legal effect. According to Article 53 of the *1969 Vienna Convention*: "A treaty is void if, at the time of its conclusion, it conflicts with a peremptory norm of general international law" (*jus cogens*).

(iii) As regards the third prerequisite, the law starts from the hypothesis of the full correspondence of declared will with genuine will of authors of a treaty. Various causes and circumstances produce differences in this respect. They are of two kinds.

There are absolute causes of invalidity of a treaty. These are: coercion of a representative of a State to agree on an unequal treaty (Article 51); coercion exercised on a State to the same end by the threat or use of force (Article 52), and the already mentioned *jus cogens* (Article 53).

Other causes of invalidity, such as error in a treaty (Article 48), fraud by its other party (Article 49) and corruption of a representative of a State to conclude a treaty (Article 50), are of relative character. If a State has not invoked such a defect in its consent in a due time, and proceeds to apply the treaty as it is, it has acquiesced on it.

(iv) General international law does not impose any particular form of a treaty. For this reason, oral agreements are not excluded, although they are extremely scarce in actual practice. Agreements can be concluded even by signs, as these made in armed conflicts by flags of truce. ①

III. The fundamental principle: *pacta sunt servanda* and its scope of application

Article 26 of the *Vienna Convention*, entitled: "*Pacta sunt servanda*", declares:

> "*Every treaty in force is binding upon the parties to it and must be performed by them in good faith.*"

Each element of this normative stipulation needs a short comment. First is the principle of good faith (*bona fides*) which is a part of the principle *pacta sunt servanda* itself. Its scope of application is, however, much larger. The principle of good faith applies not only in execution of treaties but also in their interpretation. Article 31 (1) of the Vienna Convention has embodied it in its "general rule of interpretation", stating *inter alia*, that: "*A treaty shall be interpreted in good faith...*" The same principle applies also in execution of final judgments rendered by international courts and tribunals by all parties to the dispute.

Turning back to Article 26, important are restrictions implied in its wording.

---

① See Articles 32 to 34 of the *Hague Regulations Respecting the Laws and Customs of War on Land*, annexed to the *1907 Fourth Hague Convention*.

Most of these restrictions of the principle *pacta sunt servanda* consist in fact in other general principles of law. They are as such codified by other provisions of the *1969 Vienna Convention*.

Article 26 stresses that every treaty in force "*is binding upon the parties to it...*" Consequently, and as a matter of principle, the principle *pacta sunt servanda* does not apply to third States and other international persons which a not parties to a treaty. The second restriction resulting from the said provision is that the principle *pacta sunt servanda* relates only to treaties which are *in force at a given time*. It does not apply on treaties which terminated or are temporarily suspended.

This principle does not also apply on treaties which are, according to the respective provisions of the *1969 Convention*, void. There was already the word of some causes of invalidity of treaties.

The principle *pacta sunt servanda* applies, within the above restrictions, on treaties which are *provisionally in force*. Article 25 of the *1969 Vienna Convention* provides that a treaty or a part of it is applied provisionally pending its entry into force, if the treaty itself so provides, or the negotiating States have in some manner so agreed. During its provisional application the treaty is binding like all other treaties which have entered into force definitely.

The most important recent application of Article 25 is Article 7 (1) (c) of the *1994 Agreement* relating to the implementation of Part XI of the *UN Law of the Sea Convention of 1982*.① States and entities which have not so far become parties to the said *1982 Convention*, and which have only signed the said *Agreement*, got the privilege to consent to its provisional application which could not last latter than 16 November, 1998. But this provisional application is lasting until the present date, because the United States has not as yet ratified the *1982 Convention* (see the details in Chapter VII bellow).

Almost all other important rules on the law of treaties are codified in the *1969 Vienna Convention*. There is already a considerable practice of States and judicial bodies in its application and interpretation. These rules relate to the conclusion of treaties (Articles 6 to 18); to reservations on them (Articles 19 to 23); to their

---

① Adopted by the UN General Assembly Resolution 48/263 of 28 July, 1994. *Cf.*, *International Legal Materials*, *1994*, (ILM) No. 5, pp. 1309-1327.

(1) Their author, i. e. creator must be a sovereign State or another subject of international law such as intergovernmental organization or recognized belligerents in a civil conflict.

(2) Their content ought not to be inadmissible by law. This means that it must be materially possible and not forbidden by a peremptory norm of general international law (*jus cogens*).

(3) The expressed will of its author must be identical with its authentic or actual will, i. e. it must not have faults or vices. Therefore, some provisions from the 1969 Vienna Convention on the Law of Treaties, especially its Articles 46 to 53, are *mutatis mutandis* applicable to unilateral acts. It was already proved that some of them consist in fact in general principles of law.

Finally, (4) as regards to their form, on most unilateral acts international law does not impose any special or strict requirements. ① However in regard to some particular unilateral acts in the law of the sea, sometimes is required their notification to competent international agencies, or giving due publicity to domestic regulations or maps.

Opposable Situations in International Law

Bibliography: I. C. MacGIBBON: "The Scope of Acquiescence in International Law", *The British Year Book of International Law 1954*, pp. 143-186; V. D. DEGAN: *Sources of International Law, The Hague 1997*, pp. 339-354.

"Opposability" and "inopposability" are outcomes of recent developments in international law. It is likely that the International Court of Justice has adopted them from the French municipal law and procedure. The Court has gradually adjusted them in its practice to special requirements of positive international law.

Opposability mainly refers to acts or conduct of third States. It is not quite

① *Cf.*, *Nuclear Tests case*, *I. C. J. Reports 1974*, p. 267, para. 45.

precise to speak that a treaty in force is opposable to its parties, because it is legally obligatory on them. On the same account, a treaty providing for rights or obligations for third parties subject to conditions laid down in Articles 35 to 37 of the *1969 Vienna Convention*, equally does not become "opposable" to third States. In these circumstances it is creative of legal rights or obligations for third States to such a treaty.

But the question arises: does a third State have at least a duty passively to respect legal consequences of a treaty concluded between its parties, even if it does not confer some rights or duties on that State? It is similar to the effects of a judicial judgment on States which are not parties to a case decided by it.

Opposability is a notion which does not imply a duty on the part of a third State to take any active action. But it implies at least its duty passively to respect all legal consequences of such an act. On the other hand, it is said that an act is inopposable to a third State, in a situation when it does not contest its validity, but is entitled to decline all its legal effects in its own regard.

Opposable situations for thirds appear the most often as a consequence of their explicit or implied recognition of the act in question, or by the way of acquiescence. By contrast, a State can prevent an opposable situation in its own respect, if it protests against an act or practice of others.

However, by operation of estoppel an act becomes opposable even to its author. The matter is in international law of a special kind of estoppel by conduct (or equitable estoppel). A person who, by his words or conduct, willfully causes another person to believe in existence of certain state of things, and induces him to act on that belief, so as to alter his position for the worse, is estopped from setting up against the latter person a different state of things as existing at the time of question. Therefore, in such a singular situation, the words or deeds of a person acting in bad faith become opposable against itself.

We shall proceed now to acts and attitudes of States which either create opposable situations or preclude them. The matter is of recognition, protest and acquiescence.

(i) **Recognition** is a unilateral act of a State, or a collective act of a group of States, for purpose of making a situation opposable to recognizing States. It can be expressed either by a formal declaration or notification in written; or can be implied from another act; or it can be acquiesced.

Recognition is tantamount to waiver, if a State recognizing other's claim relinquishes its own actual right. Only in this situation recognition is a unilateral act producing legal rights and duties in international law. In other circumstances it merely produces opposable situations.

Recognition is also tantamount to withdrawal of previous protests and disapprovals of acts or situations which became recognized.

With the same effects recognition can be implied from a State's own illegal practice. If such a State makes an unlawful claim in its own favour, asserting that actual legal norms suffered changes, it is implied that it recognizes by its own attitude the admissibility of similar claims by all other States within the limits of its own pretensions. Therefore, such a State becomes impeded by its own act to deny the same advantages to others.

This implied recognition, resulting from somebody's own conduct, is based on the broad general principle of law: *non concedit venire contra factum proprium*, that is to say — nobody is in right to ask of others different conduct than is his own.

The said implied recognition of the same initially unlawful practices or claims by others as to be valid, accelerates the process of generation of new customary rules in general international law, as well as of modification or abrogation of existing ones. A certain initially unlawful practice, if followed by a large number of other States, can in a short period of time generate into a new general customary rule, provided that it was not opposed by considerable number of other States. On this basis in the law of the sea appeared the concept of the exclusive economic zone, or of the zone of exclusive fishing rights up to 200 miles from the baselines.

(ii) **Protest** has the opposite effects to recognition. It precludes any inference which might otherwise be drawn from silence, including acquiescence. Its purpose is to prevent a situation from becoming opposable to a State which protested against it, and may thus deprive it of any legal effect in respect of the protesting State.

Protest can have, in particular, a negative effect on the formation of historic titles, such as acquisitive or extinctive prescription. It interrupts the lapse of time which is deemed necessary that an adverse possession of a part of land or sea transforms into a valid title (acquisitive prescription). It has the same negative effect to the extinction of the right to raise a claim against wrongful acts by others (extinctive prescription).

There is however no general rule of international law as regards the length of time and of other circumstances which are necessary either for acquisitive or extinctive prescription.

(iii) **Acquiescence** is probably the most delicate question and of the greatest importance in practice. The absence of protest can in certain circumstances be interpreted as implied or tacit recognition, especially if a situation calls for protests. The very notion of acquiescence consists in this: it is silence in situations which call for protests, from which can be implied tacit recognition.

An opposable situation created by acquiescence is of particular importance for a State which enjoys a right on the basis of a customary rule which has not yet been fully consolidated or received in general international law, or when all aspects of its application on individual situations are still a matter of dispute. If enjoyment of its presumed rights is not opposed by protests it can be presumed that it was acquiesced by all other States.

The doctrine of acquiescence embodies however important limitations. The party to which implied consent is imputed must first of all be in knowledge of facts in regard to which it abstained to protest. The formal notification is not necessary unless provided by a treaty. But silence in regard to a notified claim makes a presumption of existence of tacit consent stronger.

Nevertheless, in some circumstances even knowledge is not sufficient to create acquiescence. Failure to protest can be justified by the fact that the question has been kept open by the disputing parties, either because of protracted negotiations, or by establishment of a *modus vivendi*, i. e. of an agreement of temporary character.

Lastly, Swiss Emerich de Vattel suggested two centuries ago that a State claiming title by prescription could not impute acquiescence to a State which "sets forth valid reasons for (its) silence such as impossibility of speaking of a well founded fear".

Alike situations are perfectly possible today. In case that they happen, acquiescence is rebutted on the basis of the general principle of law which invalidates a State's consent to a treaty that has been procured either by coercion of its representative, or by the threat or use of force against it, in violation of the principles of international law embodied in the *UN Charter*.

Chapter IV The Scope and Patterns of *Erga Omnes* Obligations in International Law

Bibliography: "Obligations and Rights *Erga Omnes* in International Law", *Annuaire de l' Institut de droit international*, Session de Cracovie, Vol. 71-I, Paris 2005, pp. 119-212. In particular the first report by Giorgio Gaja and the literature indicated therein.

Like opposable situations themselves, the concept of *erga omnes* obligations was also an outcome of the practice of the International Court of Justice (ICJ). However, everything in this respect started with an improper and indecent judgment of that Court. It is necessary to give a short explanation of the situation that happened.

Two former member States of the League of Nations — Ethiopia and Liberia — instituted the proceedings before the Court in 1960 against South Africa on the basis of Article 7 of the Mandate for South West Africa of 1920. ① Their main complaint was that, especially by its practicing of *apartheid*, South Africa has violated the terms of its Mandate over the territory of South West Africa, which is now called

① Paragraph 2 of Article 7 has provided the following: "The Mandatory (The Union of South Africa) agrees that, if any dispute whatever should arise between the Mandatory and another Member of the League of Nations relating to the interpretation or the application of the provisions of the Mandate, such dispute, if it cannot be settled by negotiation, shall be submitted to the Permanent Court of International Justice provided for by Article 14 of the *Covenant of the League of Nations.*" Since 1946, in application of Article 37 of its *Statute* and Article 80(1) of the *UN Charter*, that jurisdiction was replaced by the newly-established International Court of Justice. This fact was later confirmed in the Court's *Advisory Opinion on International Status of South-West Africa* of 11 July, 1950. *Cf.*, *I. C. J. Reports 1950*, pp. 138 and 143.

"Namibia".

Quite surprisingly, by its *Judgment of 18 July, 1966* in the Second Phase of these proceedings, by the President's casting vote, (the votes being equally divided seven to seven), the Court found that Ethiopia and Liberia could not be considered to have established any legal rights or interests appertaining to them or to their citizens in the subject-matter of their claim. On that ground the Court rejected their applications.

Because of that Judgment the Court had no work for several years. It was boycotted for a time by many States. It also endured strong criticism by the doctrine, including some writings of this author. ①

However the new majority in the Court by an *obiter dicta* statement in its *Judgment of* 1970 *in Barcelona Traction Case* drew "an essential distinction" (which is now well-known to all scholars in International Law):

> "*... between the obligations of a State towards the international community as a whole, and those arising vis-à-vis another State in the field of diplomatic protection. By their very nature the former are the concern of all States. In view of the importance of the rights involved, all States can be held to have a legal interest in their protection; they are obligations erga omnes.*"
>
> *The Court continued: "Such obligations derive, for example, in contemporary international law, from the outlawing of acts of aggression, and of genocide, as also from the principles and rules concerning the basic rights of the human person, including the protection from slavery and racial discrimination. Some of the corresponding rights of protection have entered into the body of general international law...; others are conferred by international instruments of a universal or quasi-universal character.*"

---

① *Cf.*, "Attempts to Codify Principles of Treaty Interpretation and the South-West Africa Case", *The Indian Journal of International Law 1968*, (New Delhi), No. 1, pp. 9-32; "Preliminary Objections in The Hague Court's Contentious Procedure: A Re-Examination", *Ibid. 1970*, No. 4, pp. 425-458; *L'équité et le droit international*, (Martinus Nijhoff), La Haye 1970, Preface and pp. 227-238; and also some writings published in Croatian language.

In the spirit of the above dictum, South Africa's practice of *apartheid* in its Mandate territory was obviously not only the question of legal rights or interests by Ethiopia and Liberia and their citizens in the field of diplomatic protection. That practice of racial discrimination runs counter South Africa's *erga omnes* obligation which is by its very nature the concern of all States in the world.

The term "international crimes" was not expressly mentioned in that context. But it is undisputable that almost all obligations described there by the Court are obligations derived from peremptory norms of general international law (*jus cogens*), as being *erga omnes* obligations relating to all States in the world.

*

For the further development of the concept of *erga omnes* obligations important was the work of the International Law Commission in preparation of its *Draft Articles on State Responsibility for Internationally Wrongful Acts.* This important subject-matter was on the agenda of the Commission between 1956 and 2001, when it adopted its final text. Hence, the Commission studied and analyzed this problem for 45 years.

Substantial progress during that long period of time was achieved since 1976 under the Special Rapporteur Roberto Ago from Italy. He proposed, and the Commission adopted, a division into primary and secondary rules of State responsibility. *Primary rules* relate to the very content of international obligations of States, or their interpretation, whatever their origin can be: conventional, customary, or other.

However, these primary rules were put aside and were not the subject-matter of the Commission's codification. Its emphasis was on the so-called *secondary rules*, i. e. the general conditions under international law for States for their wrongful actions or omissions, and the legal consequences which flow from there, whatever the origin of the primary rules at stake.

Since then this division has been universally recognized and was also endorsed in the final draft articles of the Commission. However justified, it sometimes raises serious problems in respect of primary rules, that what is the topic of our explanation here.

Another contribution by Roberto Ago, which was not of a lasting effect in the Commission itself, was his proposed division of all internationally wrongful acts into *international crimes* and ordinary *international delicts.* It was obviously made under the impact of the statement by the Court on *erga omnes* obligations in the 1970 *Barcelona Traction Judgment.* Paragraph 2 of draft Article 19, proposed by Roberto Ago, provides a definition of international crimes:

> "*An internationally wrongful act which results from the breach by a State of an international obligation so essential for the protection of fundamental interests of the international community that its breach is recognized as crime by that community as a whole constitutes an international crime.*"

This definition contains two elements of all international crimes. First is that an internationally wrongful act must result from the breach by a State of an international obligation "essential for the protection of fundamental interests of the international community". However, only by this, an international crime would not be different from other norms of *jus cogens* within the meaning of Article 53 of the *1969 Vienna Convention on the Law of Treaties.* That provision will be quoted below. In addition, it was expressly provided for that the international obligation in question is so essential "*that its breach is recognized as a crime by that community as a whole*".

Paragraph 4 of that draft article provided a negative definition: "Any internationally wrongful act which is not an international crime in accordance with paragraph 2 constitutes an international delict."

Yet the final and the most authoritative text on the Responsibility of States, as adopted by the Commission on 9 August, 2001, turned all these things upside down. The former draft article 19 was suppressed altogether, and the adjective "criminal" was omitted throughout the newly adopted text. Rules providing rights of "injured States", and obligations for all other States in cases of commission of international crimes, were replaced with new provisions concerning "serious breaches of obligations under peremptory norms of general international law" (Articles 40-41).

That happened after a quarter of a century of existence of that essential definition of international crimes that was generally understood until that time as reflecting a customary rule of general international law.

That radical shifting of the position was a concession to representatives of a number of States in the Sixth Committee of the UN General Assembly. They vigorously argued that the responsibility of States is not of a criminal nature, and that these *Draft Articles* could not deal with international crimes at all.

However, in the Commission's comment, among the examples of these "serious breaches" (every breach of *jus cogens* is serious in itself), the following are quoted: prohibition of aggression, prohibition of slavery and slave trade, genocide, and racial discrimination and *apartheid*, torture, some basic rules of humanitarian law, and the right of peoples to self-determination. This means that even under that obsolete definition almost all these acts constitute proper "international crimes".

But shortly after the adoption of these final draft articles, tragic events occurred on 11 September,2001 on the soil of the United States: in New York, Washington, D. C. and Pennsylvania. The fact that the terrorist organization Al Q'aeda had its bases in Afghanistan under the Taliban regime was the pretext for the armed intervention in that State as an act of alleged "self-defence" by the United States (and the UK). If nothing else, it revealed the truth that active support by a State of some transnational terrorist organizations, acting abroad, could nevertheless have certain "criminal" features.

The suppression of the former draft article 19 introduced much of confusion in this subject-matter. Let us mention only one concerning terminology. On the basis of its jurisdiction under Article IX of the 1948 Genocide Convention, the International Court of Justice (ICJ) can be competent to establish the responsibility of a State which is a party to it for its violation. Article I of this Convention expressly states that genocide is a crime under international law. Acts provided in its Articles II and III mean that the responsible State committed that international crime on its own. Hence in the case brought to the Court by Bosnia-Herzegovina against Serbia and Montenegro, the Court considered exactly the commission of the international crime of genocide.

However, according to the new logic set up by the International Law Commission, this crime was in fact not committed in that case. What was committed was only a "serious breach of an obligation" under the norm of *jus cogens* prohibiting genocide. That is because of the fact that the responsibility of States is not criminal. The genuine crime of genocide can be committed, according to this logic, only by individuals for which the International Criminal Court (ICC) is competent, not the ICJ.

In spite of this curious logic, the matter is in both situations of the same internationally wrongful act. Even its qualification in Article Ⅱ of the *1948 Genocide Convention* and in Article 6 of the *1998 Rome Statute* is the same. This means that the ICJ and criminal tribunals apply the same legal rules, and that violations of the prohibited acts have the same heinous consequences for their victims. This was confirmed by the fact that the Court in its Judgment of 2007 relied exclusively on findings of the existence of criminal intent ("*dolus specialis*") in commission of this crime on Judgments rendered by the International Criminal Tribunal for the Former Yugoslavia (ICTY). ①

The shortcomings of the efforts to codify secondary rules specifically relating to *erga omnes* obligations seem to be a result of an equal neglect in studying different patterns of the primary rules giving rise to rights and obligations of this kind. These primary rules are not so plentiful in the positive international law to make such an effort impossible.

*

In a perfect legal order which, in an international community divided by sovereign States, can never fully realize, all rules of general international law should have some *erga omnes* effects. Nevertheless, since the *Barcelona Traction Judgment of 1970*, all determinations of *erga omnes* obligations have had in view the larger group of norms having the features of *jus cogens*.

The personal effort of this author consists in this field in identifying primary rules of *erga omnes* obligations, which the International Law Commission avoided. ② For the purposes of this book we can explain here only the main conclusions.

Our first conclusion is that all *erga omnes* obligations derive from general customary international law as being articulated by codification conventions, or by some declarations of the UN General Assembly, or even by some decisions of the ICJ (like its *1970 Judgment in Barcelona Traction Case*). This was already the topic

① Genocide is distinguished from crimes against humanity and war crimes in this that all acts prohibited by the *Convention* were "committed with intent to destroy, in whole or in part a national, ethnical, racial or religious group as such".

② We already made this attempt *cf.* Vladimir Djuro DEGAN: "The scope and patterns of *Erga Omnes* obligations in Internationd law", *Bancaja Eurpediterranean Courses of International Law*, Vol. x, Castellon (Spain) 2006, pp. 271-371.

of our explanation of documentary evidences of general customary law in Chapter Ⅱ above.

However by this, only the positive rules of this law, which are confirmed in the States' practice and "accepted as law" by States (*opinio juris sive necessitatis*), are understood. It is not therefore a matter of "judge made law", i. e. of the "customary law" created by judges or legal experts (which was advanced in some judgments of international criminal tribunals), unless they were confirmed in practice and by *opinio juris* of sovereign States.

Nevertheless, these obligations should not be searched in *jus cogens* only, but can also be found in some general customary rules with the effects of *jus dispositivum*.

The results of the International Law Commission on State responsibility were largely grounded on the text of the *1969 Vienna Convention on the Law of Treaties*, and especially on its provisions concerning *jus cogens* (see its Articles 53, 64 and 71). However, according to applicable rules from that *Convention* there are several classes of the rules of *jus cogens*, what makes them a rather diffused concept. We made an effort to distinguish between several patterns of these norms, as supposedly being sources of *erga omnes* obligations.

1. International crimes. Among these different patterns of *erga omnes* obligations, the most important, and the most frequently invoked in the judgments of the ICJ and other international instruments, are *the obligations prohibiting international crimes.* In comparison with all the other norms of *jus cogens* of which will be further discussion here, they are the best defined in international instruments. And unlike other peremptory norms, international crimes are, in principle, of absolute character. As such, they are forbidden even as acts of countermeasures or of reprisals in armed conflicts. If for instance a party to a conflict murders its prisoners of war or unarmed civilians, the other party shall not commit the same crimes as alleged acts of reprisals (see Chapter Ⅺ bellow).

With these features, international crimes normally generate in the customary process articulated by codification conventions or by some resolutions of the UN General Assembly (like for instance its *1974 Resolution on the Definition of Aggression*). If a sufficient number of States become parties to these conventions, and the important group of "specially interested States" do not oppose them, the international crimes codified in them obtain the feature of being recognized as such by the international community of States as a whole.

It is useless to deny the responsibility of States for international crimes (for which individuals bear criminal responsibility), only because State responsibility is not of a criminal nature. As has been said, it is a matter of the same internationally wrongful acts producing the same harmful consequences to their victims. Most of them are defined in multilateral conventions which provide obligations for their States parties, including their obligation to enact the necessary legislation for prosecuting individual perpetrators of these crimes by their domestic courts.

Without further developing this concept, it can be argued that the following internationally wrongful acts constitute international crimes in general international law of the present time: (i) piracy on high seas; (ii) slavery and slave trade; (iii) the crime of aggression; (iv) crimes against humanity; (v) the crime of genocide; and (vi) war crimes. To this list some authors add torture committed in all circumstances.

The first of such a "candidate" for a new international crime is that of *international terrorism*. The reason that this particular crime has not attained so far all the features of other international crimes is that the international community as a whole has not as yet agreed on its definition. All the forms of international terrorism should be defined in a general codification convention, like for instance the *1948 Genocide Convention*.

Even a better solution seems to be to include in the text of the *1998 Rome Statute*, at the next Review Conference, the definitions of the crime of international terrorism, as well as that of the crime of aggression. There are no more appropriate impartial instances than the ICC for combating this actual scourge of the international community.

It is nevertheless hardly possible to define the consequences for a State found responsible for commission of international crimes in general terms. One of the reasons is, that it is not possible to establish an international tribunal for prosecution of sovereign States for these crimes attributing to them criminal responsibility and imposing punitive sanctions against them.

On the other hand, political reactions by other States in the cases of the commission of these international crimes on a large scale, is disorganized. These reactions can be individual or collective.① The actions by the UN Security Council are imperfect, because this organ is unable to impose sanctions against its own permanent members, or against other States acting under their protection, if they commit international crimes themselves.

However, exactly in order to prevent abusive reactions by powerful States, it seems highly desirable now to define all the forms of international terrorism, as was explained above.

2. Some other norms of *jus cogens*. According to the generally adopted definition of *jus cogens* from Article 53 of the *1969 Vienna Convention*:

> *"... a peremptory norm of general international law is a norm accepted and recognized by the international community of States as a whole as a norm from which no derogation is permitted and which can be modified only by a subsequent norm of general international law having the same character."*

There are in fact norms of *jus cogens* which correspond with this definition, but the international community did not as yet recognized serious breaches of obligations from them as international crimes.

In the sphere of human rights can be mentioned here a norm of *jus cogens* prohibiting all the measures of discrimination of human beings, either in the execution of municipal laws in force by State organs, or by irresponsible individuals or their groups, or committed in a State through an unlawful practice. Although unlawful, the most widespread and sophisticated practices of discrimination in everyday life are not recognized as international crimes.

Nevertheless, there is no doubt that the principle of non-discrimination has become a peremptory norm of general international law as such. It has already been declared in the *UN Charter*, and was subsequently reinforced in the *1948 Universal Declaration of Human Rights*, and virtually in all the human rights conventions which followed.

---

① An example of collective reactions was a number of economic sanctions imposed against Serbia and Serbian parties in conflicts in Bosnia-Herzegovina and Croatia. These severe sanctions could not immediately stop the commission of crimes, but they affected innocent civilian population including Albanians and other ethnic groups which were victims of Serbian government of that time.

To this class of *jus cogens* belong, in addition, all the human rights that cannot be derogated in any circumstances such as war, public danger or other emergency. Among them are: the right to human treatment (including prohibition of torture); freedom from imprisonment for debt; freedom from *ex post facto* laws;① right to juridical personality; or freedom of thought, conscience and religion. Nevertheless, the strict observance of all these human rights constitutes *erga omnes* obligations for all States and other international persons.

3. Some other mandatory rules of general international law. There are, in addition, important classes of customary rules of general international law which are definitely not *jus dispositivum*, but neither do they strictly correspond to *jus cogens* within the above meaning of the *1969 Vienna Convention*. However, there is not the slightest doubt that all of them constitute *erga omnes* obligations.

Three different categories of these mandatory rules will be discussed, but not enumerated, here.

(i) There are first certain civil and political rights of individuals in respect of which the conventional provisions allow to their States parties a large choice of measures, or even considerable restrictions in their implementation, in order to ensure such loose objectives as "national security", "public order", "morality", etc. Hence, these human rights are not absolute, although their restrictions should not be subject to arbitrary measures by a State authority. They all should be provided by law in advance.

The question is here of the freedom of movement and residence, right to privacy, right of expression, freedom of association in trade unions, special rights of child, and right to participate in government.

(ii) In general customary international law there is a plenty of other mandatory norms which prohibit the conduct contrary to them but only for the future. However, unlike the definition of *jus cogens* provided in the *1969 Vienna Convention*, these norms do not make void — but respect — all the already acquired rights of States based on prescription, historic title or particular customary law in force.

Such norms can be found especially in the law of the sea, relating to the

① This means that nobody can be punished for an act which was not prohibited by law at the time of its commission.

delimitation of the territorial sea and to so-called "historic bays". ①

(iii) Among mandatory rules of this kind, politically the most important is the group of the so-called "general or fundamental principles of international law" or "principles of the United Nations". They are of an axiomatic character, accepted virtually by all the States as being prerequisite to the existence and functioning of the present world political order, and to the maintenance of international peace and security.

The originally naturalist idea of fundamental rights and duties of all existing sovereign States was displayed in the principles of the United Nations, as laid down in Article 2 and in Article 1 (2) of the *1945 UN Charter*. These principles were elaborated in the already mentioned *Declaration on Principles Concerning Friendly Relations*. That *Declaration* was approved in the General Assembly on 24 October, 1970 by consensus.

These "general principles of international law" should not be confused with the general principles of law, as being one of the main sources of international law. They are not common to municipal legal systems, but are entirely based on general customary law of a given time.

The said *Declaration* announces and elaborates the following seven principles: (i) The principle of the non-use of force, i. e. "that States shall refrain in their international relations from the threat or use of force against the territorial integrity or political independence of any State, or in any other manner inconsistent with the purposes of the United Nations"; (ii) The principle of peaceful settlement of disputes, i. e. "that States shall settle their international disputes by peaceful means in such a manner that international peace and security and justice are not endangered"; (iii) The principle concerning the duty of non-intervention in matters within the domestic jurisdiction of any State, in accordance with the *Charter*; (iv) The duty of States to co-operate with one another in accordance with the *Charter*; ②

① On the same ground these mandatory rules respect a persistent objector's special rights as described by the ICJ in *Anglo-Norwegian Fisheries* case of 1951. *Cf.*, *I. C. J. Reports 1951*, pp. 131, 139.

② Because its breach does not produce international responsibility, this "duty" is formulated in that *Declaration* rather as an aim than as a precise legal obligation. States are, for instance, not legally obliged to establish and maintain diplomatic and consular relations with one another. Their economic, social, cultural, technical and other co-operation depends on their mutual agreements, which they are not bound to conclude.

(v) The principle of equal rights and self-determination of peoples; (vi) The principle of sovereign equality of States; and (vii) The principle that States shall fulfill in good faith the obligations assumed by them in accordance with the *Charter*.

It must be stressed here that there are no other rules of general international law which restrain to such an extent the freedom of action of all sovereign States. As a result, they are probably the most often violated legal obligations in international practice. However, just because of their ultimate goal which is the maintenance of international peace and security, even frequent violations of these principles cannot substantially modify their content and their legal character.

The reason why this set of fundamental legal principles cannot be categorized as *jus cogens* within the meaning of the *1969 Vienna Convention* is not their frequent disrespect, but the derogatory character of most of them. The principle of the non-use of force has an important exception in the "inherent right" of all States to individual or collective self-defence, as confirmed by Article 51 of the *UN Charter*. The principle of self-determination of peoples should be applied in the light of the territorial *status quo* of existing States, which can constitute its negation, etc. Hence, unlike international crimes, these principles are not absolute in their actual application.

4. Some norms of *jus dispositivum* having *erga omnes* character. However, the *erga omnes* obligations should also be searched in the so-called norms of *jus dispositivum* of general international law. This general international law is in fact far richer with norms of this legal scope than with its peremptory norms, i. e. *jus cogens*.

Jus dispositivum has a quite different scope of validity in international law than any peremptory or mandatory norms as described above. General customary rules of dispositive character are applicable only in the absence of a contrary treaty or particular customary rule. Their application is therefore subject to the general principle of law: *lex specialis derogat legi generali*. This means that all States are in their mutual relations free to regulate a matter differently than such a general customary rule provides. They can do that at any time and for whatever period they decide, without violating by that their legal obligations arising from the general norms.

However, in absence of such a special legal relation, every State is entitled to require from other States the full respect of these general customary rules. In these circumstances they are obligatory like all other legal rules and their violation entails international responsibility of the wrongdoing State. As such, they have also an *erga omnes* effect, unless previously derogated by a particular rule.

We found as politically the most important in this respect the principle of *uti possidetis*, which is applicable especially in delimitations between the territories of new States. In absence of an agreement on new frontiers freely arrived at (which in practice is almost impossible to accomplish), "the former boundaries become frontiers protected by international law".

This principle is of the essential importance especially in cases of decolonization, or of the dissolution of federal States such as the former USSR, Yugoslavia (SFRY) and Czecho-Slovakia.

5. Conclusion. We tried to explain here different categories of *jus cogens*. However it must be admitted here that other authors could envisage even more or less categories. And for decision-makers in a State, because they generally do not have a feeling to strictly observe such legal niceties, these doctrinal classifications can be irrelevant altogether. This only proves that the basic concept of peremptory norms of general international law (*jus cogens*) is diffused. If this is so, it cannot be different with the "serious breaches" of these the same norms that what provide for Articles 40 and 41 of the *International Law Commission's Draft Articles on State Responsibility*.

For this very reason it cannot be asserted that there exists a strict hierarchy between various categories of primary rules on State Responsibility as explained above, concerning especially the principles of the United Nations. But all of them are generally understood as constituting *erga omnes* obligations.

Nevertheless, because of their evil consequences for the entire mankind, norms prohibiting international crimes should be distinguished from all the other internationally wrongful acts. As was said, they are the best defined in international instruments, and there is the least doubt in their content.

Chapter V
On International Crimes
and on International Criminal Justice

Bibliography: Y. DINSTEIN-M. TABORI: *War Crimes in International Law*, The Hague 1996, 469 pages; H. ASCENSIO, E. DECAUX, A. PELLET: *Droit international pénal*, Paris 2000, 1053 pages; V. D. DEGAN: "Responsibility of States and Individuals for International Crimes", *International Law in the Post-Cold War World*, Essays in memory of Li Haopei, Edited by Sienho Yee and Wang Tieya, London 2001, pp. 202-223; "On International Crimes and on International Criminal Justice", *Studi di diritto internazionale in onore di Gaetano Arangio-Ruiz*, Napoli 2004, II, pp. 703-728; "On the Sources of International Criminal Law", *Chinese Journal of International Law 2005*, No. 1, pp. 45-83; "Responsibility of States and Individuals for Genocide and Other International Crimes", *International Law Between Universalism and Fragmentation*, Festschrift in Honour of Gerhard Hafner, 2008, pp. 511-530; A. CASSESE, P. GAETA, J. R. W. D. JONES: *The Rome Statute of the International Criminal Court*, A Commentary, Oxford 2002, Volume I, pp. 1-1048; Volume II, pp. 1049-2018; Antonio CASSESE: *International Criminal Law*, Oxford 2003, 472 pages.

We shall deal in this chapter only with specific *erga omnes* obligations of all States towards the international community. The matter is of their duty not to commit themselves, or order, or solicit, or aid or abet the commission of *international crimes*. As was stressed, this obligation relates to all States, but its breaches can also involve personal criminal responsibility of individual perpetrators of these crimes and of their superiors. In present international law this obligation has thus two aspects. Let us first deal with the first one.

With respect of *legal duties of States* in general, in its *2007 Judgment on the Application of the Genocide Convention* (Bosnia-Herzegovina *v.* Serbia and

Montenegro), the ICJ recalled:

> "... *the fundamental distinction between the existence and binding force of obligations arising under international law and the existence of a court or tribunal with jurisdiction to resolve disputes about compliance with these obligations. The fact that there is not such a court or tribunal does not mean that the obligations do not exist. They retain their validity and legal force. States are required to fulfill their obligations under international law, including international humanitarian law, and they remain responsible for acts contrary to international law which are attributable to them*..."①

This lack of competent courts and tribunals on the world-wider level proves in fact the total disorganization of the present international community. But it was even worst in past times. Namely, sovereign States cannot be sued for their internationally wrongful acts unless they agreed on the jurisdiction of such a tribunal. Hence, although the ICJ is according to Article 92 of the *Charter* the principal judicial organ of the United Nations, it has no jurisdiction over disputes between its member States and others, without their approval of it. There is no need to go into further details of this situation here, which is well known to all scholars of international law.

However, because States strongly condemns the crime of genocide, most of them became parties to the *1948 Convention* on the prevention and suppression of this particular international crime. Its Article Ⅸ provides the following:

> "*Disputes between the Contracting Parties relating to the interpretation, application or fulfillment of the present Convention, including those relating to the responsibility of a State for genocide, or for any of the other acts enumerated in Article* Ⅲ, *shall be submitted to the International Court of Justice at the request of any of the parties to the dispute.*"

① *Cf.*, *I.C.J. Reports 2007*, p. 56, para. 148.

It is on this basis the only opportunity for unilateral applications by a State party against another State party to this *Convention* before the ICJ for its violations. However, outsiders, including many politicians, are ignorant of the fact that there has never been concluded a similar convention on the prevention, suppression and punishment of the crime of aggression, neither does this seem to be politically conceivable.

Also, the four *1949 Geneva Conventions*, defining their grave breaches as international crimes, do not include a provision on the obligatory settlement of disputes between the parties to them. Shortly, except for genocide, no other international crimes are within the obligatory jurisdiction of the ICJ enabling unilateral applications by an injured State or other. ①

In this situation it is hard to expect that a State suspect of commission of international crimes other than genocide will voluntarily agree with a State its alleged victim, on the jurisdiction of the ICJ or of inter-State arbitration for a final settlement of their dispute. No political organ, including the UN Security Council, can impose such a jurisdiction on sovereign States. And the establishment of a criminal tribunal for prosecution of States for their commission of international crimes, which would render punitive sanctions against them, seems in this situation still less realistic.

*

Now we shall turn from the aspect of State responsibility to that of *personal criminal responsibility of individual suspects* of international crimes. The matter is here of international criminal law. As being at the present time a part of international law, this law has some specific features, which are still neglected by many scholars of public international law.

The first aspect is that of the sources of international criminal law. The sources from Article 38(1) of the International Court of Justice (which are conventions, customary rules and general principles of law), function generally in the international legal order of sovereign States and other international persons. There was the word on them in Chapter I.

---

① Public opinion in Bosnia-Herzegovina and Croatia was strongly disappointed after the ICJ declared in its *Judgment of 2007* its incompetence to condemn acts of aggression, and these of ethnic cleansing and other inhumane acts attributed to Serbia, because they do not correspond with the definition of genocide in Article II of the *1948 Convention*.

In international criminal law relations between judges, the prosecutor, the accused and his counsel, and the victims of the crime, are not the same as the relations between sovereign States that enjoy legal equality and possess the autonomy of will. Here is the matter of trials of accused persons, which should not be substantially different from criminal trials before national courts. However, one essential difference is that the source of law in the proceedings before international criminal tribunals is not the national criminal law of any State, but the law emanating from the sources listed in Article 38(1).

The general principle of all criminal law: *nullum crimen, nulla poena, sine lege* is by many called the principle of legality (in its narrow sense). It means that no one shall be convicted of any act that did not constitute a criminal offence under the applicable law at the time of its commission. It seems, however, more appropriate to embrace, under the principle of legality, the sum of general principles of criminal law, which should be observed in any criminal proceedings whatever.

The said principle of *nullum crimen sine lege* is an achievement of the *1789 French Declaration of the Rights of Man and of the Citizen.* It is embodied in the constitutions of a great many States as being one of the guarantees of human rights of individuals. Even if, strictly speaking, this general principle is perhaps not a peremptory norm of general international law (*jus cogens*), it is better to observe it than to undermine its importance in any criminal proceedings.

Where we actually take this principle into account—and there are no convincing reasons to do the contrary—all sources of international law provided in Article 38(1) appear in a somewhat different light than in inter-State relations. From this principle proceed the following requirements of what is called a *fair criminal trial*:

— *Nullum crimen sine lege scripta*: the basis of a criminal charge should be either in the national law of a State, or in a statute of an international criminal court or tribunal. In both instances the matter should be subject to a rule of positive law in written form. This excludes incriminations based exclusively on (unwritten) customary law, especially if that would be law was the invention of judges.

—*Nullum crimen sine lege certa*: the elements of crimes must be precisely defined by a rule. This forbids criminal judges to resort to analogy with some similar but not identical crimes.

—*Nullum crimen sine lege praevia*: a crime must be forbidden by law at the time of its commission. Retrospective application of new criminal laws is forbidden unless they were more favourable to the accused (*lex mitius*).

—*Nulla poena sine lege*: the penalties for specific crimes should also be provided by a legal rule in advance in order that potential perpetrators know about the sanctions that will follow. This requirement is difficult strictly to observe in international criminal proceedings. The scale of prison sentences for the crimes within the competence of international criminal tribunals have so far not been provided in their Statutes.

Hence in criminal law, either municipal or international, written sources have primacy over the unwritten ones. This means that, in international criminal law, customary rules cannot have the same importance as in the international legal order of sovereign States in which a near totality of rules of general international law is of a customary character.

There is another substantial difference to be noticed here. When two or more States agree on the jurisdiction of the International Court of Justice, or on international arbitration, they expect to obtain in these costly procedures the final judgment of their case. To this end, in order to avoid *non liquet* (lack of competence in case of deficiency of positive legal rules), judges resort to all the sources of law provided in Article 38 (1). They must find applicable legal rules to any dispute which States can refer to them.

By contrast, international criminal judges do not have such a large power. As stated above, they are strictly forbidden to resort to analogy, or to apply new rules of positive criminal law on the accused retrospectively, or even to invent new rules of "customary law" in order to cure the possible imperfections in public international law.

In order to prosecute international crimes such as genocide, there can be competent, either national jurisdictions of States, or international criminal courts and tribunals on the basis of their statutes. We shall deal first with domestic criminal courts in a State.

(a) Domestic courts. The *erga omnes* obligation of all States to prevent and suppress international crimes on behalf of general international law has not the immediate effect on the prosecution of these crimes, either by national organs or by international criminal courts and tribunals. Customary rules, even peremptory, cannot have a straightforward impact on criminal proceedings.

For this very reason multilateral conventions defining international crimes and providing other obligations of their States parties for the prevention, suppression and punishment of these crimes, including various kinds of judicial assistance, cannot be substituted by any peremptory norms of general international law as such.

In order that a domestic court could establish its jurisdiction for the prosecution of the offenses that constitute crimes under international law, it is not even sufficient that the respective State became a party to the convention in question. Even in the States which recognize the supremacy of international law in municipal sphere, or whose constitutions provide primacy of treaties over national legislative acts, an independent judge can proclaim his lack of competence if such an offence is not also expressly provided in national criminal law of his State.

The courts shall strictly apply the general principle of law, which was confirmed in human rights conventions, that no one should be convicted of any act, or omission that did not constitute a criminal offence under the applicable law at the time of its commission. ①

In order to prevent such situations the respective conventions provide themselves the obligation of their States parties to adjust their criminal legislation to their provisions, or to this end enact new laws that are necessary for the prosecution of perpetrators of the offenses in question, or for their extradition to other States.

Hence the *1948 Genocide Convention* provides, in Article V:

> "*The Contracting Parties undertake to enact, in accordance with their respective Constitutions, the necessary legislation to give effect to the provisions of the present Convention, and, in particular, to provide effective penalties for persons guilty of genocide or any of the other acts enumerated in Article III.*"

The common Paragraph 1 in the respective provisions of all the four *1949 Geneva Conventions on Humanitarian Law* also states:

---

① Although constitutions and other national laws in modern times prescribe that an offence can be provided by international law as well, general international law and the conventions in force do not provide penalties for the crimes prohibited. It is otherwise not wise to leave it to the discretion of domestic judges to establish and interpret rules of international law, because that can produce contradictory judicial practice on this subject matter even within one State.

"*The High Contracting Parties undertake to enact any legislation necessary to provide effective penal sanctions for persons committing, or ordering to be committed, any of the grave breaches of the present Convention...*"

It actually happens that some States have never adopted legislation to implement the convention they ratified; or have not properly published it in their Official Gazettes; or that the definition of the crime in the national legislation is incomplete; or that the obligation of universal jurisdiction is missing; etc. ① Usually, other States parties to these conventions will not care enough so as to have each one of them correctly adjusted its legislation to the crime defined in the convention.

It can be different only with the stipulations in these conventions of a contractual character providing various kinds of mutual legal assistance, including extradition. If one State party refused to comply with a lawful request by another party in these domains, it can expect reciprocal practice. However, the conventions codifying universally recognized international crimes are as yet scarce of the obligations of this kind. ②

On the other hand, States are free to incriminate in their national laws whatever international and transnational crimes they wish, even beyond their obligations assumed by treaties. Usually these lists are in national criminal laws more abundant than the crimes which are in competence of international criminal courts and tribunals.

Nonetheless, in the actual application of the above provisions, there are very few cases in which domestic courts adequately punished for the commission of international crimes members of their national armed forces. Sometimes a genuine international crime is qualified as a minor disciplinary offence, and sometime not even that. It is curious that the same thing is observed in many cases of international

① See some concrete examples of this unlawful practice—A. CASSESE: *International Criminal Law*, Oxford 2003, pp. 305-306.

② By contrast, these obligations are abundantly provided in more recent conventions prohibiting transnational organized crimes, including sectorial conventions on some kinds of terrorism.

crimes committed by enemy forces, probably for the fear of reciprocity.

This scarcity of actual practice strongly indicates that in including international crimes in their penal laws, States in fact pay lip service to their international obligations assumed. National courts are perhaps ready to prosecute individuals for crimes that they commit in their personal interests, such as these of drug trafficking or crimes of rape, murder or robbery committed by their soldiers. However, if a criminal act might even indirectly involve international responsibility of the respective State, persons responsible remain most frequently unpunished or get symbolic penalties.

(b) **The experiments with the ICTY and the ICTR.** The international criminal justice, like the domestic one, is faced with many challenges in its proper functioning. The first aim of all criminal proceedings is that *the law must be the same for all, whether it protects or punishes.*

The justice on the international level is frequently confronted with the world diplomacy. Some diplomats make use of international criminal justice as their auxiliary instrument in order to assure a lasting peace in a region, such as the Balkans or Africa. With suspects of international crimes who are still leaders of their countries they bargain about their possible prosecution or pardon, in exchange for far-reaching political concessions by the suspects.

For instance, indictments against Serbian leaders in Bosnia-Herzegovina Radovan Karadžić and Ratko Mladić were confirmed by the Judge on 27 June, 1996, almost a year after the massacre committed at Srebrenica. But one of them is still at large. The indictment against the leader of Serbia Slobodan Milošević was confirmed as late as on 25 May, 1999, after his final refusal of the draft agreement on Kosovo from the Rambouillet Conference. The proposed settlement had to assure "substantial autonomy" of that province within Serbia, but under international control. Milošević could perhaps never be accused in case that he agreed on that arrangement and implemented it to the letter.

It seems, however, that the exercise of this kind of diplomacy whatever its short-term advantages, can hardly go together with the international criminal justice. This practice can in the long run be disastrous to the objectives of the latter.

By its resolutions under Chapter Ⅶ of the *UN Charter*, the UN Security Council established two *ad hoc* tribunals. These are the International Criminal Tribunal for the Former Yugoslavia (ICTY)① and the International Criminal Tribunal for Rwanda (ICTR).② By this, the Statutes of these Tribunals became legally obligatory on all the member States of the UN, including five permanent members of the Security Council with the United States itself. This actually includes all the sovereign States in the world, with the one exception of the State of Vatican.

We shall deal from now on with the ICTY. The text of its Statute was hastily prepared, mostly by experts in public international law. These persons are familiar with the procedural rules of the ICJ and international arbitration rather than with all the problems of criminal proceedings. These flaws become more manifest when compared with the *1998 Rome Statute of the ICC*, its Rules of Procedure and Evidence and Elements of Crimes. In many aspects these new instruments are aimed at preventing wrong practices by *ad hoc* Tribunals.

According to Article 1 of its Statute, the jurisdiction of the ICTY *ratione loci* encompasses the territory of the former Yugoslavia, and that *ratione temporis* since 1991. The Tribunal has however *erga omnes* jurisdiction *ratione personae* for the crimes within its competence committed in the territory of the former Yugoslavia. This means that whoever is suspect of the commission of such a crime, regardless his nationality should fall within the jurisdiction of its Prosecutor.

Articles 2 to 5 of its Statute conferred the jurisdiction to the ICTY *ratione materiae* for the four international crimes: (i) The matter is according to its Article 2, of Grave breaches of the *Geneva Conventions of 1949*, but not the same breaches of the *Protocol I of 1977* to this *Convention*. The reason is that important States have not acceded to this *Protocol* as yet. (ii) In the summary text of its Article 3 are listed Violations of the Laws or Customs of War from the *1907 Hague Regulations Respecting the Laws and Customs of War on Land*. (iii) Article 4 relating to genocide is drafted in the same text as in Articles Ⅱ and Ⅲ of the *1948 Genocide Convention*. (iv) Finally, in Article 5 are provided Crimes against humanity, almost the same as in Article 6 of the *Charter of the International Military Tribunal at Nuremberg of 1945*.

It is to be noted that the supreme crime of aggression is in this *Statute of the*

① *Cf.* Resolution 827 (1993) of 25 May, 1993.

② Security Council Resolution 955 (1994), of 8 November, 1994.

are Indonesia and the Philippines, while Japan, New Zealand and the United Kingdom have not exercised this right as yet.

(3) *Territorial sea* is a belt of the sea along the entire coast of every coastal State, measured from baselines (beyond the margin of its internal waters), up to 12 nautical miles.

According to general international law of the sea as being mainly codified in the *1982 UN Law of the Sea Convention*, the respective coastal State enjoys in above three areas its full sovereignty. However, only in some parts of its internal waters this sovereignty is enjoyed to the same extent as over its land territory.

In the so-called "newly enclosed" parts of internal waters by straight baselines, as well as in archipelagic waters and territorial sea, this sovereignty is restrained with the right of all foreign ships to *innocent passage*. In the archipelagic waters and in the air space over them exists in addition the right of *sea lanes passage and overflight* by all ships and aircraft. The latter régime is similar to that of the "transit passage" over straits used for international navigation.

However, in spite of these obligations imposed by the general customary international law in favour of all ships and aircraft regardless their nationality, the coastal States are in right to consider all these maritime areas as parts of their national territory.

II. To the second group fall parts of the sea, sea-bed and subsoil thereof, in which coastal States enjoy "*sovereign*" *or some other rights*, but not the full sovereignty. They are: (4) *contiguous zone*; (5) *continental shelf*; and (6) *exclusive economic zone* (*EEZ*). These legal régimes, which do not encompass the superjacent air space, in the same maritime spaces overlap.

All these maritime areas are not parts of coastal States' national territory. Rights of these States are especially restrained in favour of *the freedom of navigation and overflight* by all ships and aircraft, just as in the high seas.

(4) In the *contiguous zone* up to 24 miles from the baselines from which the breadth of the territorial sea is measured, the coastal State does not enjoy even the so-called "sovereign rights". It enjoys only limited rights of control in order to prevent and repress the infringements of its customs, fiscal, immigration and sanitary laws and regulations (but only within its territory or territorial sea). In addition, the coastal State has the right to protect archeological and historical objects situated at its seabed. A coastal State must proclaim this zone. Otherwise this area belongs to the

high seas, or to the EEZ if the respective coastal State has proclaimed it.

(5) The *continental shelf* of a coastal State comprises only the seabed and its subsoil beyond its territorial sea. Some geographically disadvantaged States with short coastline cannot have the continental shelf of their own. Other coastal States, which are in a better geographical position, have their continental shelves *ipso facto* and without proclamation. They have sovereign rights in mineral and other non-living resources of its seabed and subsoil, and the same rights on living organisms belonging to sedentary species. This continental shelf can comprise all the natural prolongation of the coastal State's territory up to the outer edge of the continental margin. In some circumstances it can even go beyond the distance of 200 miles.

Finally, (6) the *exclusive economic zone* (EEZ) must be proclaimed by the coastal State over its continental shelf, but only up to 200 miles from the baselines. A coastal State enjoys in its EEZ sovereign rights over living and non-living natural resources of the waters superjacent to the continental shelf. The most important among them are the fishing rights. It has also important jurisdiction in the three domains: (i) in the establishment and use of artificial islands, installations and structures; (ii) in the marine scientific research; and (iii) in the protection and preservation of the marine environment. The last jurisdiction can in some circumstances affect the freedom of navigation of merchant ships and tankers.

III. Into our last category fall parts of the sea, seabed and its subsoil, which are *beyond national jurisdiction* of any State. They constitute: (7) the *high seas*; and (8) the *Area*, which is also called the International Seabed Area, or the Area of Ocean Floors. In these maritime areas no State may exercise exclusive jurisdiction, except over ships flying their own flag, and in some very special circumstances such as the right to visit these foreign ships which are suspect of piracy, or of transport of slaves.

(7) The *high seas* is an old institute of the law of the sea. Its régime comprises six basic freedoms in favour of all States, coastal or land-locked: (a) freedom of navigation; (b) freedom of overflight; (c) freedom to lay submarine cables and pipelines; (d) freedom to construct artificial islands and other installations; (e) freedom of fishing, which is now restricted by many special rules; and (f) freedom of scientific research.

(8) By contrast, the *Area* is an outcome of the modern law of the sea, as well as of the technological progress that presumably enabled the exploitation of its mineral

resources. It will be the topic of next Chapter VII relating to the Common Heritage of Mankind.

*

The problems of delimitation of maritime areas between neighbouring coastal States appear practically only in respect of their territorial sea, their EEZ and continental shelves.

Two positions of their coasts are to be distinguished. These coasts can be adjacent on the same coastline, or can be opposite to each other. The example of the first is adjacent coasts belonging to North Korea, China and Vietnam respectively. The example of the second is the opposite coasts between China, South Korea and Japan. In tracing delimitation line the first situation can create more practical problems than the second.

The *1982 UN Law of the Sea Convention* stipulates three provisions on this subject matter: Article 15 on the delimitation of the territorial sea; and common texts of Articles 74(1) and 83(1) concerning the delimitation of the EEZ and continental shelf.

It can be proved only that Article 15 reflects a customary rule of general international law of the sea. This is because the same norm as this was already stipulated in Article 12(1) of the *1958 Geneva Convention*. This is the proof that the matter is of a rule accepted and recognized by the international community of States as a whole. For instance, the United States, which has so far refused to ratify the *1982 Convention*, is bound by that rule as being a party to the *1958 Convention on the Territorial Sea*. However this provision is coached in terms of *jus dispositivum* and not of *jus cogens*. It reads as follows:

> "*Where the coasts of two States are opposite or adjacent to each other, neither of the two States is entitled, failing agreement between them to the contrary, to extend its territorial sea beyond the median line every point of which is equidistant from the nearest points on the baselines from which the breadth of the territorial sea of each of the two States in measured. The above provision does not apply, however, where it is necessary by reason of historic title or other special circumstances to delimit the territorial sea of the two States in a way which is at variance therewith.*"

Hence, the general customary rule of dispositive character providing the median, i. e. equidistance line does not apply in case of a contrary agreement between respective coastal States, or if any of them validly claims historic title or invokes some other special circumstances in favour of a different delimitation. But whenever a bordering State does not invoke or cannot prove any one of these exceptions, each of them can delimit its territorial sea with another State by the median line, even by its unilateral enactment.

Unlike the above rule, the main problem of Articles 74(1) and 83(1) of the *1982 Convention* is that they both do not provide any criteria for the delimitation of the exclusive economic zone and of the continental shelf respectively. They read as follows:

> "*The delimitation of the exclusive economic zone (or of the continental shelf) between States with opposite or adjacent coasts shall be effected by agreement on the basis of international law, as referred to in Article* 38 *of the Statute of the International Court of Justice, in order to achieve an equitable solution.*"

The ICJ was right in asserting in its *Judgment of 1985 on the Continental Shelf* (Libya/Malta), that: "The *Convention* sets a goal to be achieved, but is silent as to the method to be followed to achieve it."①

However the *2006 Arbitral Award Between Barbados and Trinidad and Tobago* offers a larger explanation of this rule:

> "222. *This apparently simple and imprecise formula allows in fact for a broad consideration of the legal rules embodied in treaties and customary law as pertinent to the delimitation between the parties, and allows as well for the consideration of general principles of international law and the contributions that the decisions of international courts and tribunals and learned writers have made to the understanding and interpretation of this*

① *Cf., I. C. J. Reports 1985*, pp. 30-31, para. 28.

body of rules."①

The said decisions of international courts and tribunals proved to be of a decisive importance in identifying and developing legal rules on this subject matter. There are several important outcomes of this judicial practice.

(a) In its actual practice was imposed as a necessity tracing of a "*single maritime boundary*" through the territorial sea and in its prolongation through the continental shelf and EEZ, or if the territorial sea is already delimited, only in the overlapping areas of continental shelves and the EEZ (or exclusive fisheries zones) of disputing parties. The ICJ found the grounds to impose this solution even if one of the disputing parties opposed it.

(b) In tracing such a single maritime boundary, the Court applied in its *2001 Judgment on the Maritime Delimitation and Territorial Issues Between Qatar and Bahrain*, that what it called "customary law". The *Judgment* stressed:

> "*The Court... notes that the equidistance/special circumstances rule, which is applicable in particular to the delimitation of the territorial sea, and the equitable principles/relevant circumstances rule, as it has been developed since 1958 in case-law and State practice with regard to the delimitation of continental shelf and the exclusive economic zone, are closely interrelated.*" (*Para.* 231).

The application of both these "rules" should achieve an "equitable solution". Wherefrom precedes the two steps approach in the delimitation of all maritime areas. This approach was best described in the *2006 Arbitral Award Between Barbados and Trinidad and Tobago*:

> "*First, a provisional line of equidistance is posited as a hypothesis and a practical starting point. While (being) a convenient starting point, equidistance alone will in many circumstances not ensure an equitable result in the light of peculiarities of each specific case. The second step accordingly requires the examination of this provisional line in the light of*

① *Cf.*, *International Legal Materials 2006*, (ILM) No. 4, pp. 798-869.

relevant circumstances, which are specific, so as to determine whether it is necessary to adjust the provisional equidistance line in order to achieve an equitable result... Certainty is thus combined with the need for an equitable result."

This statement should be now considered as a legal rule of general application, which also relates to the delimitation of the territorial sea alone. However, in case that it is a genuine legal rule, it is as such obviously not a peremptory norm of general international law (*jus cogens*).

There are some even more fundamental rules and methods applicable on maritime delimitations, which, like the most of previous ones, have not found their place in very text of the codification conventions.

(i) The basic rule is that "the land dominates the sea". It was confirmed in many statements by the ICJ. We shall quote here its last *Judgment Rendered on 8 October, 2007 Concerning Maritime Dispute Between Nicaragua and Honduras in the Caribbean Sea*:

> *"On a number of occasions the Court has emphasized that 'the land dominates the sea' (North Sea Continental Shelf (Federal Republic of Germany/Denmark; Federal Republic of Germany/Netherlands, Judgment, I. C. J. Reports 1969, p. 51, para. 96; Aegean Sea Continental Shelf (Greece v. Turkey) Judgment I. C. J. Reports 1978, p. 36, para. 86; Maritime Delimitation and Territorial Questions Between Qatar and Bahrain (Qatar v. Bahrain), Merits, I. C. J. Reports 2001, p. 97, para. 185). Accordingly, it is:*
>
> *'the territorial situation that must be taken as starting point for the determination of the maritime rights of a coastal State... (Maritime Delimitation and Territorial Questions Between Qatar and Bahrain (Qatar v. Bahrain), Merits, I. C. J. Reports 2001, p. 97, para. 185.).'"*①

The same principle was already expressed in the *1951 Judgment on Fisheries*

① *Cf.*, *I. C. J. Reports 2007*, pp. 34-35, para. 113.

coasts of two neighbouring States even in Oceans (such as between Canada and the U. S. both in the Atlantic and Pacific Oceans), the rules that follow apply *mutatis mutandis* to these situations too.

(b) The "area of delimitation" between the disputing parties can never affect the legal interests of third States in a larger maritime area, as being measured by frontal seaward projections from their own coastal facades. There the delimitation line must stop. This is applicable *a fortiori* in case of already reached agreements on maritime delimitations, either by a disputing party with a third State, or between two or more third States in the same wider area. ①

(c) Now we come to the specific "*area of delimitation*" between the disputing parties alone. Even then this area does not encompass the seaward projections along their entire coastlines.

In the areas in which these projections from coasts of the disputing parties do not overlap at all, each of them is entitled to its territorial sea and perhaps the EEZ, up to the areas of a third State possessing either opposite or adjacent coast.

The "area of delimitation" between the disputing parties is only that in which their coastal projections overlap, or are at least in contact. They overlap in case of a *concave shape* of the general direction of their coasts (like these between Libya and Tunisia). They are only *in contact* in case of a straight direction of their coastlines, what is rather infrequent in practice. In absence of any islands, islets and rocks in the vicinity of their coasts, the respective States can reach an agreement on a perpendicular line of delimitation by themselves, and the dispute between them will not arise at all.

Only in such a specific "area of delimitation" are applicable the rules from Articles 15, 74(1) and 83(1) of the *1982 Convention*. On the basis of these rules is applicable the already explained two steps approach in the delimitation. Drawing of a provisional median line is the first step, and the second step consists in examination of relevant circumstances which could produce the adjustment of this provisional line in order to achieve an equitable result of the delimitation.

---

① Thus, by the *1975 Treaty of Osimo* was delimited the territorial sea in the North Adriatic between Italy and the former SFRY. Now Croatia and Slovenia, as being successor States of the SFRY, must delimit their territorial sea between themselves in the same region. However, their own "area of delimitation" must stop at the borderline with Italy.

Nevertheless, in the dispute between Nicaragua and Honduras appeared a third geographical situation. Their respective coastlines in the Caribbean Sea are of a sharply *convex shape* and form a right angle that juts out to the sea. The very unstable river Coco, and the Cape Gracias a Dios, form their frontier on the land.

In this particular case, the ICJ found special circumstances in order to abolish the median line even as a practical starting point of delimitation. ① Instead, on the basis of the Nicaraguan proposal, the Court constructed in their area of delimitation a bisector line. That is the line formed by bisecting the angle created by the linear approximation of their coastlines.

For the use of this bisector line it was decisive to determine "relevant mainland coasts" as forming two straight lines. On the basis of its discretionary power, the Court has drawn these lines between Punta Patuca Lighthouse in Honduras up to the Cape Gracias a Dios, and from it until Wouhnta in Nicaragua. These straight lines did not follow all the coastal features. They even crossed some land territories near the coast. In view of the Court, the front from these lines "provides a coastal facade of sufficient length to account properly for the coastal configuration in the disputed area". ②

*

From the above explanation two conclusions of general character can be depicted.

First, for a long time ago judicial delimitations of maritime areas have ceased to be a matter of arbitrariness or of political expediency, if it ever was. In performing this task judges use legal rules and precedents that lead to more or less predictable results in delimitations. ③ However, as the matter of judicial discretion in particular cases remain the determination of the relevant coasts and of the area of delimitation.

Second, which is even more important, is the conclusion by the ICJ in its *1969 Judgment in the North Sea Continental Shelf Cases*, as follows:

---

① *I. C. J. Reports 2007*, p. 77, para. 281.

② *Ibid.* p. 81, para. 298.

③ See more details in—V. D. DEGAN: "Consolidation of Legal Principles on Maritime Delimitation: Implications for the Dispute Between Slovenia and Croatia in the North Adriatic", *Chinese Journal of International Law 2007*, Vol. 6, No. 3, pp. 601-634.

> *"Equity does not necessarily imply equality. There can never be any question of completely refashioning nature, and equity does not require that a State without access to the sea should be allotted an area of continental shelf, any more than there could be a question of rendering the situation of a State with an extensive coastline similar to that of a State with a restrictive coastline. Equality is to be reckoned within the same plane, and it is not such natural inequalities as these that equity could remedy...* "①

Because only possession of a coast gives the entitlement to the adjacent areas of the sea, land-locked States like Mongolia, Nepal or Afghanistan, are deprived of any maritime areas. By contrast, some tinny islands, such as Nauru and Galapagos in the Southern Pacific, or the Falkland Islands in the Southern Atlantic, generate huge areas of their territorial sea, EEZ and continental shelf, incomparable with the size of their land territories. There is no justice in all of that.

① *I. C. J. Reports 1969*, pp. 49-50, para. 91.

Chapter VII The Common Heritage of Mankind in the Present Law of the Sea

Bibliography: A. C. KISS: "La notion du patrimoine de l'humanité. *RCADI 1982*, II, tome 175, pp. 99-256; V. D. DEGAN: "The Common Heritage of Mankind in the Present Law of the Sea"; *Liber Amicorum Judge Shigeru Oda*, Volume 2, *The Hague 2002*, pp. 1363-1376.

This author has been involved in studying various problems of International Law for about half a century. During this relatively long period in a human lifetime, he was witnessing the appearance and collapse of some issues that attracted huge interest especially among young generations of international lawyers. Among these topics could be mentioned here the following:

(1) The space law, after the launching of the first Soviet satellite "Sputnik" on 4 October, 1957.

(2) The New International Economic Order. The UN General Assembly adopted, all in 1974: a *Declaration*, a *Program of Action*, and finally a *Charter of Economic Rights and Duties of States.* The last text was however strongly opposed by the industrialized States. This initiative failed, especially after the imposition of globalization in economic and other relations, and by the creation of the World Trade Organization in 1994.

(3) After the fall of the Soviet bloc, there was a strong desire to prevent the impunity of perpetrators of the most heinous international crimes. Parallel with the creation of *ad hoc* tribunals and of the International Criminal Court (ICC), there is now a wish to impose on all States, through a new rule of *jus cogens*, the obligation for their national courts to exercise the "universal criminal jurisdiction" in respect of these international crimes. This ambition also proved futile. States do not honour even their treaty engagements in this respect. Their domestic jurisdictions simply do

not exercise this kind of criminal jurisdiction, or do it hardly ever.

*

We shall discuss now the idea of the Common Heritage of Mankind in the Law of the Sea. In modern times this concept is a reflection of the same idea from Roman law. According to Roman law the air, the water streams, the sea and the coast, were *res communis omnium*, hence not subject to appropriation by anybody (or *res extra commercium*). ①

Already in 1955 Georges Scelle, the famous French scholar of his time, upheld this idea in respect of the continental shelf. Because this shelf consisted at that time of the seabed and subsoil of the high seas, he pleaded for an international management in its exploitation. This implied an international mechanism very much similar to that provided later on by the *1982 Convention* for the International Seabed Area.

At that time this idea was strongly repulsed by the International Law Commission itself. The Commission stressed in its final report that: "In the present circumstances... such internationalization would meet with insurmountable practical difficulties, and would not ensure the effective exploitation of natural resources necessary to meet the needs of mankind."

What was then refused for the continental shelf was later on adopted as the basic principle of the entire Space Law. Hence, Article 1(1) of the *Treaty of 27 January, 1967* provides that:

> "*The exploration and use of outer space, including the Moon and other celestial bodies, shall be carried out for the benefit and in the interest of all countries, irrespective of their degree of economic and scientific development, and shall be the province of all mankind.*"

However, for the practical implementation of this principle no agency of the international community relating to the outer space is necessary yet, because the exploitation of its natural resources has never begun. It remained in the sphere of

---

① "*Et quidam naturali jure communia sunt omnium haec: aer et aqua profluens et mare et per hoc litora maris.*"

fantasy.

When various options of the future legal régime of the Deep Seabed Area under the high seas were discussed, it was the U. S. President Lyndon Johnson who declared in July 1966, "that the deep seabed and the ocean bottoms are, and remain, the legacy of all human beings."

Only a year after, the representative of Malta in the UN Arvid Pardo proposed that seabed and ocean floor beyond national jurisdiction be reserved exclusively for peaceful purposes and that their resources be declared "the common heritage of mankind".

On 17 December, 1970, the General Assembly adopted the *Declaration of Principles Governing the Sea-Bed and the Ocean Floor, and the Subsoil Thereof, Beyond the Limits of National Jurisdiction* (*Resolution 2749* (*XXV*), with 108 votes in favour, none against and 14 abstentions).

Among numerous other Member States, the United States voted in favour of this *Declaration*, the fact that is now hidden. The text of this *Declaration* contains some principles which, throughout the nineteen seventies of the last century, were believed to be *jus cogens*. In any case, they were couched in imperative language. Here are the essential provisions that reflected the core of the idea of the common heritage of mankind:

"1. The seabed and ocean floor, and the subsoil thereof, beyond the limits of national jurisdiction (hereinafter referred to as the area), as well as the resources of the area, are the common heritage of mankind.

2. The area shall not be subject to appropriation by any means by States or persons, natural or juridical, and no State shall claim or exercise sovereignty or sovereign rights of any part thereof.

3. No State or person, natural or juridical, shall claim, exercise or acquire rights with respect to the area or resources incompatible with the international régime to be established and (with) the principles of this *Declaration*.

4. All activities regarding the exploration and exploitation of the resources of the area and other related activities shall be governed by the international régime to be established.

5. The area shall be open to use exclusively for peaceful purposes by all States whether coastal or land-locked, without discrimination, in accordance with the international régime to be established ..."

*

Already before the *Convention* was adopted, the United States under the new administration of President Ronald Reagan, supported by other industrial countries, began to obstruct this system in the name of the supreme principle of free market economy. Through their domestic laws, and two agreements concluded *inter se*, they created a competing system of the exploration and exploitation of the Area, parallel with that as provided for in the *Convention* itself.

The first in this series was the *Deep Seabed Hard Mineral Resources Act* by the United States of 28 July, 1980, with some subsequent regulations. It was followed by *German Law* of 22 August, 1980, and by *British law* of 28 July, 1981. The United States representative explicitly announced at the Third Law of the Sea Conference that his country would not become the party to the *Convention* in its actual content.

Similar laws were adopted latter on by France in 1981, by the Soviet Union and Japan in 1982, by Italy in 1985, and by some other States. Nevertheless all these countries, except the United States, are now parties to the *1982 Convention.*

The most exhaustive and the most sophisticated is the *Act by the United States.* It inspired legislation of other States that, generally, is less detailed. All these laws were based on the regulations of respective States concerning mining on the Land, which were transposed to the marine environment.

These pieces of national legislations have some common features, but there are some subtle or even considerable differences on less important issues. We cannot go here into all these details. However, their most important common feature is that all these acts provide the issuing of a license for exploration and of a permit for commercial recovery of minerals from a location in the Area, by their own national agencies. As such this competing system, for which it was pretended to be transitional, pending the conclusion or entry into force of the *Law of the Sea Convention*, was at sharp variance with the basic principles set out in the above *1970 Declaration*, and with Part XI of the *1982 Convention* and its annexes.

This system was even in conflict with the legal régime as in force of the high seas. "Freedoms" of durable appropriations of some locations of the seabed, even for limited periods of time, but in exclusion of all other persons, have never existed as freedoms of the high seas.

In addition, never before in modern times did States venture to extend the effects of their national laws on exploitation of mineral resources—which are not renewable—beyond the limits of their territorial sea and continental shelf. Conventions having extra-territorial effects, such as these on the high seas, on conservation of living resources in the high seas, on the outer space, and on Antarctica, forbid such unilateral acts by any State. The matter was therefore initially of illegal acts done *ultra vires* (in excess of powers according to law).

*

Nevertheless, towards the close of the Third UN Law of the Sea Conference, concessions were granted to the claims of industrial States and to licenses issued by their domestic organs, but only subject to their signing of the *Convention*.

As an annex to the *Final Act of the Conference*, *Resolution II* was adopted: "Governing preparatory investment in pioneer activities relating to polymetallic nodules." On behalf of that resolution the Preparatory Commission was authorized to register "pioneer investors" and to grant them permits for their initial activities in exploration of polymetallic nodules in the Area. Its paragraphs 8 and 9 recognized priority to pioneer investors over all applicants other than the Enterprise, in the approval of plans of work and exploitation of the sites explored, after the entry into force of the *1982 Convention*.

The pioneer investors from the following States have registered their applications with the Preparatory Commission: Japan, the Soviet Union, France, China, India, Eastern Europe, and South Korea. Away from that procedure of authorization remained then entities that obtained permits by the national authorities of the U.S., Germany and the U.K., all States that did not sign the *Convention in 1982*. Three entities got licenses from the U.S. administration.

*

Twelve years after the signature of the *Convention*, the *1994 Agreement* was adopted, relating to the implementation of Part XI of the *UN Law of the Sea Convention of 1982*. The matter was of the resolution by the UN General Assembly 48/263 of 28 July, 1994, pending the entry into force of the *1982 Convention* set for 16 November of that year.

Article 4 of this *1994 Agreement* forbids accession of new States to the *1982 Convention* itself without their consenting to be bound by the *Agreement*. Hence Croatia notified to the UN Secretary-General its succession of the *1982 Convention* together with the *1994 Agreement* as forming a single instrument.

By that way the procedure for the amendments of the *1982 Convention* as provided in its text was bypassed. Section 4 of the *Annex to the 1994 Agreement* abrogated paragraphs 1, 3 and 4 of Article 155 of the *Convention*, concerning the Review Conference.

The *1994 Agreement* has deeply perturbed the entire Part XI of the *Convention*. According to its Article 1, the parties to this *Agreement* undertake to implement Part XI in accordance with this *Agreement*. On behalf of its Article 2 (1), in the event of any inconsistency between the *Agreement* and Part XI, the provisions of the *Agreement* shall prevail.

These States that have consented in the General Assembly to the adoption of the *1994 Agreement*, but have not acceded so far to the *1982 Convention* itself (the United States in the first place), got the privilege of its provisional application, but only until 16 November, 1998. It was expected that until that date they become parties to the *Convention*. In this provisional capacity these States become entitled to all rights provided, including the right to be members of all organs of the Authority.

The United States thus succeeded in obtaining a practically permanent seat in the Council of the Authority with much enlarged competencies then previously provided, as well as an effective right to veto all its decisions. ① It enjoys the right to veto any amendments to the text of the *1994 Agreement*. Finally, its Section 9 established a new Financial Committee with a strong influence on the management by the Authority.

Nevertheless, in spite of all these far-reaching concessions, the United States has to our knowledge still not become a party to the *1982 Convention*.

*

The law of the sea is an exemplary domain in which unilateral acts of some States, which were initially in contravention to positive law, at a later stage become

---

① In the Commentary of the *1982 Convention* and the *1984 Agreement* of 23 September, 1994, which was a part of a letter from the Secretary of State to the U. S. President, it was stressed that: "... this chambered voting arrangement will ensure that the United States and two other consumers, or three investors or producers acting in concert, can block substantive decisions in the Council... " *ILM 1995*, No. 5, p. 1433.

lawful by means of subsequent conventions on codification, or by deep formal amendments of existing ones as it occurred in this case. This is exactly what happened with regard to licenses and permits for activities in the Area issued by national administrations of some industrialized States.

The Council of the Authority is authorized to approve applications of plans of work for exploration on the basis of a recommendation of the Legal and Technical Commission. That procedure is expressly provided: (i) for the plans of work by pioneer investors approved by States non-parties to the *1982 Convention*; (ii) for the plans previously registered at the Preparatory Commission; and (iii) for the plans of new entities in accordance with the principle of non-discrimination.

Understandably, the Council of the Authority, in its new composition according to the *1994 Protocol*, approved the richest mine sites of polymetallic nodules to pioneer investors which have already been reserved under internal procedures of industrial States.

The *1994 Agreement* has profoundly modified Part XI of the *1982 Convention* in other important aspects. It was first of all with the elimination of the obligation of transfer of technology necessary in carrying out activities in the Area. Section 5 of the *Annex of the 1994 Agreement* provides that the Enterprise and developing States will obtain this technology "on fair and reasonable commercial terms and conditions on the open market, or through joint-venture arrangements".

The United States does not conceal its desire to eliminate the international Enterprise altogether. An intermediate solution was found that the Secretariat of the Authority performs the functions of the Enterprise until it begins to operate independently. However, Section 2, paragraph 3 suppressed the obligation of States parties to fund one mine site of the Enterprise. Under paragraph 5, a contractor which has attributed a particular area to the Authority under Kissinger's "parallel system", "shall be entitled to apply for a plan of work for that area provided it offers in good faith to include the Enterprise as a joint-venture partner".

But in case that the Enterprise becomes capable to operate independently sometimes in the future, States parties will not be allowed to subsidize its activities in the Area. The Enterprise will be bound to function according to sound commercial principles, like all other entities. But in spite of these concessions, the United States did not give up the idea to liquidate the Enterprise in the future. ①

The obligation of the Authority to render economic assistance to developing land-based producer States was also virtually abolished. According to Section 7 of the *Annex*, the Authority shall establish an "economic assistance fund" from a portion of its funds *exceeding its own administrative expenses.*

It is therefore obvious that the first concern in collecting the revenues from the activities in the Area will be to cover the expenses of a much reduced administration of the Authority. The *1994 Agreement* has no other necessities of the Mankind in view.

*

What can finally be concluded with regard to the principle of common heritage of mankind in the law of the sea? In the nineteen seventies there was a consensus among all States on the existence of a set of legal principles set out in the *1970 Declaration* of the UN General Assembly, as peremptory norms of general international law. The United States itself, as well as most other industrial States, participated in that *communis opinio juris.*

There is little doubt that the ICJ would at that time ascribe to the rules on legal régime of the International Area the character of *jus cogens.* On that basis it established later on, in its *1986 Judgment on Nicaragua*, the same feature of the principle of non-intervention. But in the nineteen seventies there was no UN organ or a State to request such a verdict from the ICJ.

The repetition in the preamble of the *1994 Agreement* of the wording that: "the seabed and ocean floor and subsoil thereof, beyond the limits of national jurisdiction... as well as the resources of the Area, are the common heritage of mankind," is a lip-service to this principle. Its operational clauses, together with its *Annex*, have destroyed its substance as was defined in the *1970 Declaration.*

Nobody worries now that the primary objective of the exploitation of hard mineral resources in the Area should or should not be carried out for the benefit of Mankind.

---

① In the above Commentary by the United States it was stated that: "... if a decision is ever made to make the Enterprise operational, it will only be on the basis that the United States would find acceptable... It is equally possible that, by the time commercial mining takes place, developing States as well as industrialized countries will recognize the Enterprise as a relic of the past and not seek to make it operational." *Cf.*, *ILM 1995*, No.5, p.1436.

Potential beneficiaries of the resources of the Area will be private enterprises,① and a much reduced bureaucracy of the Authority. It cannot be claimed that the international community, whatever the meaning of this term could be, has no other needs.

All this considered, nobody knows when, and whether at all, the commercial exploitation of hard mineral resources of the Area will commence. But the mine sites which are the richest in polymetallic nodules have been reserved forever.

This is the product of capitalism which is suicidal on itself, which in the name of profit destroys the concept of "Welfare State" even in the most developed countries. It is now in full crisis that must be urgently healed. Nevertheless, it does not seem realistic to expect radical changes in the regime of exploitation of the International Seabed Area.

On the other hand the atmosphere throughout the Third UN Law of the Sea Conference now seems to be surrealistic. Developing States impatiently expected revenues from the exploitation of the Area in the very near future, in order to settle all their urgent economic and social needs, and in order to fill the gap separating them from the industrial States in their economic development. These excessive expectations were in the roots of the deficiencies in solutions adopted already in Part XI of the *1982 Convention*.

*

If the principle of common heritage of mankind had constituted a peremptory norm of general international law (*jus cogens*) during the nineteen seventies, one can pose the question how it evolved later on. Some authors still doubt in accuracy of the qualification of *jus cogens* in Article 53 of the *1969 Vienna Convention on the Law of Treaties*. As is known, it provides that such a norm "is a norm from which no derogation is permitted and which can be modified only by a subsequent norm of general international law having the same character". There is in that provision a

---

① In respect of the principle of common heritage of mankind it was said in the above Commentary by the United States, that: "This principle reflects the fact that the Area and its resources are beyond the territorial jurisdiction of any nation and are open to use by all in accordance with commonly accepted principles ... It is worth noting that the *Agreement*, by restructuring the sea-bed mining regime along free market lines, endorses the consistent view of the United States that the common heritage principle fully comports with private economic activity in accordance with market principles." *Cf.*, *ILM 1995*, No. 5, p. 1429.

contradiction, because any new treaty which is in conflict with the existing *jus cogens* is, according to Article 53, void at the time of its conclusion and therefore cannot modify a norm of *jus cogens*.

The *1994 Agreement* has proved the fact that by a shift in *opinio juris* with the "States whose interests were specially affected", an actual rule of *jus cogens* can evaporate.

*

Finally, the most recent development has nearly closed the second stage in the evolution of the entire law of the seas and oceans. From *res communis omnium* in Roman law to appropriations by European States of entire oceans in the times of great geographic discoveries in the 16th and 17th centuries, and again from the *Mare Liberum* by Hugo Grotius in 1609 until the *1982 Convention* and the *1994 Agreement*, these are two phases of the same spiral which has lasted for two millennia.

Chapter VIII Creation, International Recognition and Disappearance of States

Bibliography: Krystyna MAREK: *Identity and Continuity of States in Public International Law*, Genève 1954, 613 pages; James CRAWFORD: *The Creation of States in International Law*, Oxford 1979, 498 pages; 2nd Edition, Oxford 2006, 948 pages; V. D. DEGAN: "Création et disparition de l'Etat (à la lumière du démembrement de trois fédérations multiethniques en Europe)", *RCADI 1999*, tome 279, pp. 197-375.

(I) Creation of States. The classical doctrine has distinguished between two kinds of creation of a State: "original" and "derived" types.

In case that a State is established on a territory which at that time is not under the sovereignty of any other State ("a no man's land", *terra nullius*), the matter is of *original formation* of a new State. In this event there is no situation of succession of States, because the predecessor State does not exist.

However, the last cases of this type of the formation of States happened in the 19th century. Liberia was created on the soil of western Africa in 1822 by freed slaves from the United States, with the help of an American philanthropic society. Equally, in 1836, Dutch settlers on the territories that now belong to the Republic of South Africa created two African republics of Transvaal and Orange.

Because there are practically not anymore no man's territories on our Planet except Antarctica, which is under a special international régime, and because the existing States are not keen to abandon their actual possessions, there are no more chances for original formation of new States.

All other cases of creation of States belong to the "*derived*" type. A "newly independent State" the territory of which was, immediately before its creation, a dependent territory under the rule of a colonial Power from Europe; or a new State created by uniting of two or more formerly independent States; or a State created by its separation from a larger State which continues to exist; or creation of several new States on the territory of a larger predecessor State which by this disintegrates and ceases to exist; these are all types of derived creation of States.

In all these cases it is to be distinguished between one "predecessor State" or more of them, "which has been replaced by another State on the occurrence of a succession of States", and one or more "successor States", which have replaced predecessor State (or predecessor States). These various situations of territorial changes will be more thoroughly discussed in next Chapter IX relating to State succession.

Some new States were established on the basis of legal acts, either of internal or of international character:

(i) India and Pakistan acquired their independence in 1947 on behalf of the *India Independence Act*, adopted by the British Parliament.

(ii) A newly independent State can be created by a treaty between the former colonial power and the respective national liberation movement which up to that time fought for its independence. This was the case of Algeria on the basis of the *Evian Agreement of 1962* entered between the Algerian National Liberation Front (FLN) and France. The same was with the former Portuguese colonies in Africa in 1974.

(iii) Some formerly trusteeship territories within the system of the United Nations got their independence as result of the resolutions of the General Assembly. Usually before the adoption of such resolutions, plebiscites were organized on independence among their local populations under international control.

(iv) Finally, there were very few cases of creation of new States by treaties between third States. One of them was Albania, which was established by the London Treaty of 1913, at the end of the First Balkan War. ①

There are therefore several modalities of creation of new States on the basis of legal acts or following some legal procedures. But this is not a legal precondition to this end.

The creation and disappearance of States are primarily questions of fact.

---

① Hence, although all intergovernmental organizations are created by treaties, there are few examples of creation of a State on this basis.

Nevertheless, international law prescribes certain criteria in order to ascertain whether a new State actually has appeared or not.

At the beginning of the Conference on Peace in Yugoslavia in 1991 in The Hague, the following question was put to its Arbitration Commission for a legal opinion in respect of actual events in that federation: whether the matter was of an illegal secession of some republics, members of the Yugoslav Federation; or in question was a disintegration or breaking-up of the Socialist Federal Republic of Yugoslavia (SFRY) as a whole. The Arbitration Commission under the presidency of Robert Badinter from France gave its answer to this important question in its Opinion No. 1 of 29 November, 1991.

The Commission first underlined: "a) that the answer to the question should be based on the principles of public international law which serve to define the conditions on which any entity constitutes a State, that in this respect, the existence or disappearance of the State is a question of facts, that the effects of recognition by other States are purely declaratory." Therefore, the creation of a new State is not a question of respect or disrespect of law or of legal procedures within the predecessor State, but simply a question of facts.

In this respect the Commission clearly adopted the dualistic approach to the relation between international law and municipal law: "c) that, for the purpose of applying these criteria, the form of internal political organization and the constitutional provisions are mere facts, although it is necessary to take them into consideration in order to determine the Government's sway (dominance) over the population and the territory."

Now follow specific criteria for effective creation of a new State, as well as for its very existence: "b) that the State is commonly defined as a community which consists of a territory and a population subject to an organized political authority; that such a State is characterized by sovereignty." ① Each of these three criteria needs a short explanation:

(i) **A State's territory**. Every State must have a territory in which its organs exercise their jurisdiction. At the same time, the territory constitutes the geographical limits of a State's power. For this reason nomadic tribes cannot create a State, at least

① *Cf.*, *International Legal Materials 1992*, (ILM), No. 6, pp. 1494-1497.

until they permanently settle on a determined land.

There have been States which at the time of proclamation of their independence had not all their frontiers defined and internationally recognized. That was for instance Belgium between 1830 and 1839. This is still the case with the State of Israel. Its unilateral annexations of Eastern Jerusalem and of some other Palestinian and Syrian territories that it keeps under occupation have never been internationally recognized. Nevertheless, this lack of fixed frontiers proved not to be the obstacle for the very existence of these States.

The loss of the entire territory should have as an outcome the disappearance of the State in question. However, even considerable reduction of the size of the territory of a State does not create the same consequences. Hence, a State can preserve its identity and international personality even on a reduced territory. Nevertheless, in case of a federation of States the situation can be different, as the situation of the SFRY has proved.

During the two World Wars in the 20th century, belligerent occupation by enemies of the entire territory of some States (Belgium, Serbia and Montenegro in World War I; Poland and Yugoslavia in World War II) did not produce their disappearance. That was because the governments and parts of their armed forces and navy continued to act and fight in exile.

(ii) A population. A State consists at the same time in a population. No State can exist without a permanent population on its territory. For this reason Antarctica cannot constitute a State.

A State's population consists of its own citizens and of foreigners (aliens). All its citizens do not need to speak the same language; neither need they be of the same ethnic origin. Today very few States are ethnically homogenous, without having a substantial number of national, linguistic or religious minorities. In China the most numerous is the Han people, but there are some fifty-six different minority groups, especially in its western part.

The absence of homogenous population in the ethnic sense is not an obstacle for existence of a State, provided that its minorities have their rights guaranteed and protected by an efficient legal system.

(iii) An organized political authority (sovereignty). Every State must exercise its powers through its own organs, the same as a juridical person under municipal law can act only through its organs.

In international law sovereignty is defined as the supreme power of a State within its territory, with the exclusion of the power of any foreign State. This power cannot be subdued to a higher power in the same State. In relations with other States, sovereignty is defined as independence.

There were many fruitless debates in legal doctrine on the substance of States' sovereignty. However, as being a test for appearance and existence of a new State, we agree with the pragmatic approach of the late British scholar Ian Brownlie. He was of the view that: "In the first place (the term of) independence may be used in close association with a requirement of effective government; if an entity has its own executive and other organs, conducts its foreign relations through its own organs, has its own system of courts and legal system and, particularly important, a nationality law of its own, then there is *prima facie* evidence of statehood."①

It should be added to this that sovereignty does not mean an absolute power. A State cannot arbitrarily enact its laws even for its territory alone. In the contemporary international community the sovereignty of States is a legal concept subject to international law. Most of peremptory norms of general international law (*jus cogens*) have as their objective to assure the respect of the sovereignty of all States by all other States members of the international community. These norms restrain the power and competencies of all the States in favour of the maintenance of sovereignty of each of them separately.

Hence, the *1970 Declaration on Principles Concerning Friendly Relations* prescribes, under the heading of sovereign equality, that "States are judicially equal" ("*Les Etats sont juridiquement égaux*").

(Ⅱ) *Recognition of States.* There are two rival doctrines on the effects of recognition of a new State: constitutive and declaratory.

According to the doctrine that is in minority, international recognition has *constitutive effects* and forms actually the fourth prerequisite for the very existence of a State. The partisans of this approach are of the view that only upon its recognition a new State becomes the full subject of international law and enters into the international community as its member equal in rights with others.

---

① *Cf.* Ian BROWNLIE: *Principles of Public International Law*, Fifth Edition, Oxford 1998, p. 72.

The advocates of this doctrine support the view that the recognition is not an arbitrary and political act belonging to the discretionary power of existing States. Due to the nonexistence of a central organ that could either grant or refuse recognition, the existing States function as representatives of the "international legal system". ① For this reason their decision to recognize a new State should be in accordance with legal principles. ②

Nevertheless, the majority of authors support the opposite view, which is also confirmed in some international instruments. ③ According to this doctrine recognition of a new State has purely *declaratory effects*, i. e. it is not more than declaratory of an existing fact. The existence of a new State, with all the legal effects that proceed, will not be jeopardized if one or a few States refuse to recognize it.

However only upon its recognition relations at all levels and on all issues between the recognizing State and that which has received the recognition, are normalized. A new State which was recognized by another can enter into agreements with it; it can send and receive diplomatic representatives, and can invoke the immunities in respect of its acts and property before the courts of the recognizing State.

Unlike this situation, the refusal to recognize a State that is endowed with an effective government, especially if it occurs for political reasons, leads to great anomalies. This is for instance the actual situation between the United States and North Korea, or of certain Arab States which still refuse to recognize the State of Israel. Hence, bilateral relations between States in question are faced with many problems of legal and factual nature.

In spite of this, the international community as a whole cannot ignore the existence of an unrecognized State. In this respect some aspects of declaratory doctrine prove their full accuracy.

---

① *Cf.*, Hans Kelsen: "Recognition in International Law, theoretical observations", *American Journal of International Law 1941*, pp. 605-617; Hersch LAUTERPACHT: *Recognition in International Law*, Cambridge 1947, pp. 55-58.

② *Cf.*, *Oppenheim's International Law*, Ninth Edition, Volume I, Peace, Introduction and Part 1; London 1992, p. 130.

③ That was for instance the regional *1933 Montevideo Convention on the Rights and Duties of States.*

The territory of an unrecognized State, which otherwise satisfies all the conditions of its statehood, cannot be considered as a no man's land (*terra nullius*), open for acquisition by its first occupant. Its territory cannot be over-flown without its permission. Ships navigating under the flag of an unrecognized State in the high seas cannot be treated as vessels without nationality, and still less as pirate ships. Besides, every coastal State is under the obligation to respect the right of innocent passage through its territorial sea by ships sailing under the flags of all States, be they recognized or unrecognized by it.

*

Recognition of a new State can be expressed in various forms. General international law does not impose any restrictions in this respect. It can be declared explicitly in a more or less solemn form with the clear intention to recognize.

But recognition can also be implied from various State acts or facts that are reserved for inter-State relations only. As a consequence the effects of these acts can sometimes be dubious. However, conclusion of a bilateral treaty with a new State, exchange of diplomatic representatives with it, or a message of congratulation to a new State when it gains independence, or sending an official delegation to the ceremony of its proclamation, all these acts are interpreted as the will to recognize.

The recognition can be granted either by one State in its individual capacity, or can be a collective act of several States. Individual recognitions are the most frequent in international practice and then they are not always devoid of reasons of political expediency.

But the recognition can also be a collective act at a diplomatic conference or within a regional organization. Then, sometimes some conditions for the recognition are imposed, which a new State must fulfill in advance or later on. In these events collective recognition can have some constitutive effects.

Comprehensive commitments were imposed in this respect by the *Declaration on the Guidelines on the Recognition of New States in Eastern Europe and in the Soviet Union* that the Council of the European Community (now Union) adopted on 16 December, 1991. The new States seeking to be collectively recognized by the Community and by all its member States were invited to adopt the following obligations unilaterally:

"— *respect for the provisions of the UN Charter and commitments*

Authors who disagree with this view consider under the loss of sovereignty transfer of the territory and population of the vanishing State to a new State or States. Hence, according to this hypothesis, the loss of territory and population is a part of the disappearance of a State's sovereignty. That was also the view of the (Badinter) Arbitration Commission when it came to the conclusion that the SFRY ceased to exist. In fact, both these hypotheses lead to the same result, namely that for disappearance of a State sufficient is loss of its sovereignty.

It should be however noted that other States do not interpret temporary disintegration of the central power in some States as their final dissolution. That happened in Lebanon, Cambodia, Albania, in some African States, etc. Foreign States continue to keep their diplomatic relations with the "legitimate government" which has lost control over its entire territory. These States preserve their seat in international organizations until they stabilize.

The *1970 Declaration on Principles Concerning Friendly Relations* states that, besides the establishment of a new sovereign and independent State, "the free association or integration with an independent State or the emergence into any other political status freely determined by a people constitute modes of implementing the right of self-determination by that people."

Hence, it is perfectly legitimate that in exercising of the right of self-determination of peoples a predecessor State ceases to exist. On this basis, in early 1990s three multinational federation in Europe—the Soviet Union, the Yugoslav Federation and Czecho-Slovakia—disappeared, and the German Democratic Republic freely united with the Federal Republic of Germany.

The consequence of disappearance of a predecessor State is that its entire territory with population is incorporated into one or more successor States. By this, its political power ceases to exist.

*

The (Badinter) Arbitration Commission of the Conference of Peace in Yugoslavia had the opportunity to examine and take its views on different questions of the disappearance of a State with a federal structure.

In its *Opinion No. 8 of 4 July, 1992* the Commission stressed that: "The dissolution of a state means that it no longer has legal personality, something which has major repercussions in international law. It therefore calls for the greatest caution."

Then follows a conclusion on the level of a principle: "The Commission finds that the existence of a federal state, which is made up of a number of separate entities, is seriously compromised when a majority of these entities, embracing a greater part of the territory and population, constitute themselves as sovereign states with the result that federal authority may no longer be effectively exercised."

The Commission reached the conclusion that the process of dissolution of the SFRY (whose beginning was established in its *Opinion No. 1 on 29 November, 1991*), "is now complete and that the SFRY no longer exists."

This conclusion was based on the fact that until 4 July, 1992 four successor States (all except Serbia and later on Montenegro), proclaimed their independence on the basis of the referendums held (hence in implementation of their right to self-determination). In addition, the Commission has stressed the fact of their recognition of each other's independence in mutual relations; of their recognition by all the Member States of the European Community and by numerous other States; as well as their admission to the membership of the United Nations on 22 May, 1992.

The Commission also took into consideration a new constitution of Serbia and Montenegro of 27 April, 1992, by which they have constituted a new State, under the name of the "Federal Republic of Yugoslavia". But probably the most important conclusion was that the authority of the former federal State no longer held sway (dominance) on the territories of the newly constituted states.

Of not lesser importance were acts concerning the status of the former Federation, adopted in international organizations. The UN Security Council *Resolutions Nos. 752 and 757 (1992)* contain a number of references to "the former SFRY". Furthermore, the *Resolution 757* concluded: "the claim by the Federal Republic of Yugoslavia (Serbia and Montenegro) to continue automatically (the membership) of the former Socialist Federal Republic of Yugoslavia (in the United Nations) has not been generally accepted." The declaration adopted by the Lisbon European Council (of the European Union) on 27 June makes also express reference to "the former Yugoslavia". ①

Hence, the Commission interpreted the above instruments as acts of withdrawal of recognition of the former State that no longer existed.

---

① *Cf.*, *ILM 1992*, No. 6, pp. 1521-1523.

(Ⅳ) *Recognition of Government.* Recognition of a new State and recognition of the new government in an existing State are two different issues. It is therefore necessary to say a few words about this second topic.

If in a State ensues a normal constitutional change of government, even comprising radical social reformations or replacement of a monarchy to a republic, other States have no right to intervene. The new government, which proceeded from these changes, is authorized to represent this State in its foreign relations. Other States can send messages of congratulation to the new Head of State, and their envoys will present new credentials to him.

However, if in a State occur unconstitutional changes of government, either by revolution or by counter-revolution, other States are not in legal obligation to continue their relations with its new authorities. Then the problem of recognition of the new government arises. Confusion can ensue in practice if two parallel governments pretend to exercise their power in one State, or if the replaced government continues to act in exile trying to overthrow the government in the country.

In the beginning of the 20th century there were numerous coups d'état, accompanied with more or less violence, especially in Latin America. The five Central American Republics embodied in their treaties of 1907 and 1923 the so-called *Tobar doctrine.* They obliged themselves not to grant recognition to any government coming into existence by revolutionary means, "so long as the freely elected representatives of people... have not constitutionally reorganized the country."

This doctrine met the strong opposition, especially after the U. S. President Woodrow Wilson refused to recognize, on the basis of this doctrine, the revolutionary government in Mexico in 1913. That government has previously overthrown the notorious dictator Porfirio Diaz. It was then claimed that the refusal to recognize is tantamount to the interference into domestic affairs of the State in question. This lead to the opposite *Estrada doctrine*, enunciated in 1930 by the Mexican Foreign Minister. It affirmed the duty of continuing international relations, so far as possible, without regard to revolutionary changes.

Today in international relations is dominant "the doctrine of effectiveness". According to it, the existence of a government in foreign State is a question of fact, where new facts are creative of law. There is in particular the question whether it is necessary at all to recognize an unconstitutional government, if the previous one disappeared, and there is no question of the choice between the two competing governments.

Hence recognition is usually granted to a government which stabilized and which assumed the effective control over the entire State's territory. It is in fact more difficult to ignore the new situation in neighbouring States, than in remote countries in which a State has no particular interests. For instance, the former Yugoslavia could not quit its diplomatic relations with neighbouring Greece after the coup d'état by the Colonels in 1967, but it could severe its relations with the new Pinochet Government in Chile since 1973.

However a premature recognition of a new government, when the old régime still functions, can complicate bilateral relations. It can raise accusations for unlawful interference in the domestic affairs of that State.

As with recognition of a new State, recognition or refusal to recognize a new government is not always an act intended simply to ascertain a new factual situation. They are frequently acts of political attitude towards the new régime in another State.

After 1949 occurred many absurd situations due to the refusal by the United States and most of its allies to recognize the new Government of the People's Republic of China in Beijing as the only Chinese government. As a result of this non-recognition, until 1971 China was represented in the UN Security Council and in other international organizations by the régime from Taiwan. During that long period of twenty-two years this generated the inefficiency of the entire collective security system of the UN. Hence, during equally long period of conflicts in Vietnam between 1946 and 1975, the Security Council was unable to adopt any resolutions on these issues.

It must be stressed here that a premature recognition of a new government when a foreign State has actively supported the overthrowing of the legitimate government (the United States in the Dominican Republic in 1965, and in Chile in 1973) is in function of unlawful intervention in internal affairs of these States. It can then be very close to aggression.

*

The recognition of a new government can be a formal act, expressed either in written form or orally, but can also be implied. An example of the first is the continuation of full diplomatic relations with the new government without revoking the head of the mission. Examples of the second can be the request of agreement for a new diplomatic envoy, or conclusion of a bilateral treaty with the new government.

A new government can be recognized either *de jure* or *de facto*. In practice the matter is again more of political decisions expressing the attitude towards the new régime, than of establishment of new factual situation in the respective State.

Recognition *de jure* is complete and final with retroactive effects, i. e. since the new government took the power and not from the time of recognition. Recognition *de facto* can be interpreted as partial, revocable, and can be granted before the new government stabilized and gained control over the entire State's territory. But no firm legal rules in this respect exist, because the recognizing State is free to interpret its own acts at will.

In recent times the United States, the United Kingdom and some other States decided not to recognize or refuse to recognize new governments in foreign States at all. They continue diplomatic relations with unconstitutional governments and assess whether these governments are able of themselves to exercise effective control of the territory of the State concerned, and seem likely to continue to do so.

Chapter IX
State Succession

Bibliography: D. P. O'CONNELL: *State Succession in Municipal and International Law*, Cambridge 1967, Vol. I-II, p. 430 and p. 595 ; V. D. DEGAN: "La succession d'Etats en matière de traités et les Etats nouveaux (issus de l'ex-Yougoslavie)", *Annuaire français de droit international* 1996, pp. 206-227. Mojmir MRAK (Ed.): *Succession of States*, The Hague 1999, 218 pages.

I. Introduction

Big territorial changes occurred during the 20th century three times. After World War I a number of new States appeared within their new frontiers, mostly on the territories of the former Russian, Austro-Hungarian and Ottoman Empires in Europe and Asia.

In the process of decolonization following World War II, a large number of "newly independent States" were created in Asia, Africa, the Caribbeans and Oceania. They were formerly dependent territories of Great Britain, France, the Netherlands, Belgium and Portugal.

Finally, near the end of the last century three socialist federations: the USSR, Yugoslavia (SFRY) and Czecho-Slovakia disintegrated into their former federal units within their existing frontiers. In addition, the German Democratic Republic was assimilated into the rest of Germany.

Because these territorial and political changes do not occur in everyday life, most of scholars of international law have no opportunity to apply rules on State succession in practice. This problem remains to some of them of purely academic interest, and to some others even not that.

It was not the case with this author. He had the bad luck of having to apply these rules in negotiations on State succession issues of the former SFRY for almost ten years. Previously, in 1991, he spent half a year studying this problem in all its aspects.

Although these problems are not of primary political importance for China, they are useful for training legal logic and legal reasoning of its students.

II. The codification conventions

On this subject-matter have been adopted and signed so far two codification conventions, previously prepared and drafted by the International Law Commission.

(i) The only one which formally entered into force but only between 17 or 18 parties so far is the *1978 Vienna Convention on Succession of States in respect of Treaties* (hereafter: "*the 1978 Convention*"). It must, however, be noted that from a technical point of view its text is an international instrument far inferior to the *1969 Vienna Convention on the Law of Treaties*, although both of them should constitute a whole.

The primary aim of this *Convention* was dealing with problems arising from decolonization. By and large the process of decolonization came to an end in 1974, when most of former Portuguese colonies finally obtained their independence. Hence, this happened before the adoption and signing of this *Convention*. It seems unlikely that its numerous, inadequately itemized and largely unnecessary provisions concerning "newly independent States" will ever find their application in practice. However, its provisions relating to other situations of territorial changes, which actually occurred in practice after 1990, are scanty and some of them are insufficient.

(ii) More important than the above is the *1983 Vienna Convention on Succession of States in Respect of State Property, Archives and Debts* (hereafter: "the *1983 Convention*"). It provides clear and straightforward principles, proposing reasonable solutions to most possible situations. Its obsolete provisions on newly independent States can be in its text easily dissociated from others.

(iii) In addition, within the Council of Europe in 2006 was adopted the regional *Convention on the Avoidance of Statelessness in Relation to State Succession*. It confirms important legal principles and provides for some practical solutions.

However, as with many other Council of Europe conventions, it is hard to expect that it will ever formally enter into force.

(iv) It should here be added that after negotiations of almost ten years, in 2001 was signed in Vienna the *Agreement on Succession Issues* by five successor States of the former Yugoslavia. That was possible only after the FRY (Serbia and Montenegro) abolished its claim for its identity and continuity with the former SFRY. That happened after Slobodan Milošević has lost his power in Belgrade.

(v) In the same 2001 the *Institute of International Law has* adopted at its Vancouver Session important resolution on "*State Succession in Matters of Property and Debts*". The matter is here of a non-conventional instrument.

*

Let us turn back to the two above codification conventions of universal character. Being of a very specialized nature, they have a very restrictive number of States which are eager to become parties to them. China has not signed any of them. Their main problem, especially of the one which has not formally entered into force, is how to distinguish the rules declaring the already existing law from their other provisions which are rather propositions *de lege ferenda*.

Rules of customary international law on State succession are for many other reasons scarce and insufficient. They cannot offer solutions to all possible situations that may occur in practice. However, the merit especially of the *1983 Convention* is that it actually provides a system of legal rules in respect of State property, archives and debts. Exactly for this reason even its statements *de lege ferenda* cannot be easily ignored. These rules are a useful basis for any meaningful negotiations, *inter alia* because most of them are couched in terms of *jus dispositivum*.

III. The notion of State succession

Both *Vienna Conventions*, that of 1978 and that of 1983, provide the definition of this legal phenomenon in the same terms. Article 2 (1b) of the first and Article 2 (1a) of the latter *Convention* provides that:

> "... '*succession of States*' *means the replacement of one State by another in the responsibility for the international relations of territory.*"

This definition seems to be hard to understand and too narrow at the same time. It seems more appropriate to understand the State succession as *a situation* (or rather a new situation) of consequences of territorial changes to which the rules of international law apply. However, as already stressed, the rules of positive international law applicable to these situations are scarce and insufficient.

Nevertheless, in all these situations of territorial changes it is to be distinguished between a "*predecessor State*" (or more than one), "which has been replaced by another State on the occurrence of a succession of States", and one or more "*successor States*", which have replaced predecessor State (or predecessor States) on the same occurrence. ①

The above means that the succession of States does not occur even if profound social or political changes are taking place in one State within its actual frontiers. Hence, China did not suffer territorial changes in 1949 after the new Socialist Government was established in Beijing. But the situation of State succession emerged when Hong-Kong was reunited with China on 1 July, 1997. The same happened with respect to Macao on 20 December, 1999.

On the same footing, Yugoslavia was one State between 1 December, 1918 and April 1992, when it finally dissolved; or Czecho-Slovakia since 1918 until the end of 1992. Many social and political changes occurred in these long periods there.

The main types of territorial changes resulting in application of the rules on State succession are as follows:

Cession. An existing predecessor State transfers a part of its territory to an existing successor State. This mostly occurs by treaties of peace as results of defeats in war. For instance, by the *Versailles Peace Treaty of 1919*, Alsace and Lorraine were reunited with France after their being a part of Germany since 1870.

Association or assimilation. The predecessor State wholly becomes a part of another already existing successor State and, as a consequence, it disappears. The recent example is the German Democratic Republic which in 1990 associated with the Federal Republic of Germany and ceased to exist as an international person. In such a situation it is the successor State which extends its territory and continues its

---

① *Cf.*, Article 2, 1(c) and (d) of the *1978 Convention*, and Article 2, 1(b) and (c) of the *1983 Convention*.

existence as the same legal person.

Uniting. Two or more formerly independent predecessor States unite and form quite a new and larger successor States. An example of this was the uniting of Tanganyika and Zanzibar in 1964 into the Federation of Tanzania. A more recent example was the uniting in 1990 of the Arab Republic of Yemen and the Democratic People's Republic of Yemen into the new State: the Republic of Yemen. In these cases all predecessor States cease to exist as international persons. But unlike an association, the uniting gives rise to quite a new successor State.

Separation, secession or emancipation. On a part of the territory of the predecessor State which continues to exist, although territorially reduced, appear one or more new successor States.

The process of decolonization in the wake of World War II led to the emancipation of a great number of formerly non-self-governing territories, which separated themselves from the United Kingdom, France, the Netherlands, Belgium and finally in 1964 from Portugal. Other examples of secession include: Singapore from Malaysia in 1965; and Bangladesh from Pakistan in 1971. The most recent example is the separation of Eritrea from Ethiopia in 1993.

Dissolution, demise, dismemberment. A larger predecessor State dissolves and ceases to exist. On parts of its former territory appear two or more new successor States. That happened with the Austro-Hungarian and the Ottoman Empires after World War I, and more recently with the demise of Yugoslavia, the Soviet Union and Czecho-Slovakia since 1991. Unlike separation, the predecessor State ceases to exist by its dissolution, and all its successor States are new States. The special position of the Russian Federation will be discussed at the end of this explanation.

Partition. Several successor States divide the territory of the predecessor State, which as a consequence ceases to exist. The most notorious historic example was the third and final partition of Poland by Prussia, Austria and Russia in 1795. This type of territorial changes is hardly imaginable today.

*

These quite diverse situations of territorial changes require different legal principles to deal with the ensuing problems. In some situations these rules are simple, and in others are more complicated, or non-existent at all.

For example, in cases of either association or uniting, the only possible legal solution is that all State property, archives and debts of the predecessor State (or

Arbitration in Canevaro case of 3 May, 1912 (*Italy/Peru*), a State cannot extend its diplomatic protection to its citizen in another State of which it is also citizen① In addition, in absence of agreements of respective States to the contrary, a dual citizen has the duty to serve the Army twice and to pay his taxes to both his countries.

*

Pensions. Everyone who acquired the right to pension in the predecessor State must preserve his right. The obligation of successor States is to conclude agreements on regular payment of pensions on the basis of pension funds of the predecessor State (in the Yugoslav case: the federal pension funds), or of pension rights acquired on the territory passed to another successor State.

Expecting such agreements, each of successor States has the duty to pay pension benefits to all its residents irrespective of citizenship or former domicile or residence of the beneficiary.

*

Protection of private property. The right to movable and immovable property, including the right to use such property, of all natural and juridical persons irrespective of citizenship, residence or domicile of the person, is a human right. As such it must be observed by all States taking part in the succession process.

On the same account, all contracts concluded by legal or natural persons, including those concluded by public authorities before the date of the succession of States, should be respected on a non-discriminatory basis.

Any purported transfers of rights to movable or immovable property which were concluded under duress must be treated as null and void.

Being one of human rights, the right to private property is not as such the matter of State succession and of apportionment among successor States.

A State victim of aggression is not bound to repair the property of alien citizens which was destroyed or plundered by the successor State which was engaged as aggressor in the conflict. However, if it extends help for repair of the property of its own citizens, it must do so to all, irrespective of their ethnic origin.

---

① *Cf.*, *Reports of International Arbitral Awards*, (RIAA), Vol. XI, pp. 405-410. The same principle found its place in Article 4. of the *Hague Convention of 12 April, 1930 on the Conflict of Nationality Laws.*

*

State property and debts. In the process of State succession State property and debts of the predecessor State, and their apportionment if any, should be considered in a correlation.

Article 8 of the *1983 Vienna Convention* defines the State property of the predecessor State in following terms:

> *"For the purposes of the articles in the present Part, 'State property of the predecessor State' means property, rights and interests which at the date of the succession of States were, according to the internal law of the predecessor State, owned by that State."*

The above "property, rights and interests", relate only to legal rights and interests, and not to some expectations which have no legal protection.

However, Article 33 of this *Convention* on State debts provides the following:

> *"For the purposes of the articles in the present Part, 'State debt' means any financial obligation of a predecessor State arising in conformity with international law towards another State, an international organization or any other subject of international law."*

Hence, while in the above definition of State property the terms "property, rights and interests" include the rights and interests of a predecessor State also in respect of foreign natural and juridical persons, Article 33 excludes the debts of a predecessor State to these persons from third States. For this very reason Western States refused to ratify this *Convention* as a whole. Nevertheless, in the succession process of the former Soviet Union, Yugoslavia and Czecho-Slovakia, no successor States did to our knowledge challenge this kind of debts, and did not prevail itself on the above restrictive definition.

This disequilibrium in legal rules was tried to be removed by the *2001 Resolution of the Institute of International Law on State Succession in Matters of Property and Debts.* The notion of State property is couched, in its Article 12, in more precise terms:

"1. In principle, the terms 'State property of the predecessor State' means all property, rights and interests which belong to the predecessor State at the date of the State succession pursuant to its domestic law and in conformity with international law.

2. The term 'State property' equally covers property of public institutions but does not include property of private legal persons, even if they have been created with public funds."

According to Article 22:

"The term 'State debt' covers:

a. any financial obligation of a predecessor State towards another State, an international organization or any other subject of international law, arising in conformity with international law;

b. any financial obligation of a predecessor State towards any natural or legal person under domestic law."

The above paragraph b. is new in respect of Article *33* of the *1983 Vienna Convention*, but it does not state that these financial obligations towards foreign private persons should be also in conformity with international law.

*

There are different categories of State property and debts. However in cases of either association or uniting, this classification is not of major practical importance because all State property and debts of the predecessor State (or States) pass to the successor State which is in these situations only one.

For other situations of State succession, **the State property** is divided into immovable and movable property. However, as will be seen, some of their categories are not the object of apportionment.

Here are the basic rules in this respect which apply in case that the States concerned do not agree otherwise (*jus dispositivum*):

(a) *Immovable State property* of the predecessor State shall pass to the successor State in the territory of which it is situated (Article 18 (1a) of the *1983 Convention*), in principle without compensations. This relates especially to public buildings, and premises of the Armed forces of the predecessor State which are situated in the territory of a successor State.

In case that it is very unequally distributed among successor States, its value can be assessed and equitable compensations paid (paragraph 2 of Article 18).

(b) *Movable State property* of the predecessor State connected with its activity in respect of the territory which later became the territory of a successor State shall pass to that State.

This principle, which is enshrined both in Article 17 (1b) and Article 18 (1c) of the *Vienna Convention of 1983*, is in some situations difficult to apply. It was in particular impossible to be applied after the aggressive armed conflicts in Croatia and Bosnia-Herzegovina occurred, in which a large part of arms and ammunition of the former Federal Army was used, abused and destroyed by Serbia (FRY) against these two successor States. The same happened in Kosovo since 1997.

(c) *All other immovable and movable property* of the predecessor State — including especially premises of diplomatic and consular missions and their accessories abroad — shall pass to successor States "in equitable proportions" (Article 18 (1b) and (1d) of the *1983 Convention*).

On the other hand, **State debts** of the predecessor State are divided into two main categories: allocated and unallocated or national debts.

All foreign debts incurred by former component States of a Federation, or by their other territorial entities or enterprises, or incurred (or guaranteed) by the Federation itself but entirely invested in the territory of one of successor States, should pass to that new State. Especially in case of dissolution and disappearance of the predecessor State, its former guarantees on foreign debts should be terminated by new agreements of successor States with foreign creditors.

On the other hand, the general unallocated debts (or "national debt") made by the predecessor State to the benefit of the whole State, such as these incurred for stability of national currency or for other common expenditures, should be divided among all successor States according to the key valid for the apportionment of the

State property of the predecessor State. ①

*

Some of the above provisions call for an *ad hoc* key of apportionment that can be reached either by agreement of all successor States, or by a decision of an impartial judicial body. ②

The *2001 resolution of the Institute of International Law* defined in its Article 8 some legitimate objectives in this respect: (1) the result of the apportionment of property and debts must be equitable; (2) if this apportionment does not produce an equitable result and cannot be otherwise corrected, the States concerned shall settle this matter by equitable compensations; (3) unjust enrichment shall be avoided; and (4) the apportionment of property and debts shall preserve the capacity of States concerned to survive as viable entities.

From the practical point of view even more useful is Article 11 of this resolution concerning principles of apportionment, put in a hierarchical order.

First, apportionment is to be carried out, according to the territoriality principle, and it shall furthermore be in conformity with the principle that any unjust enrichment is to be avoided. Hence, successor States having a larger size of the territory, and presumably a larger population in it will have a more considerable share in property and debts than smaller successor States.

Second, property and debts that cannot be apportioned on the above basis shall be apportioned equitably, bearing in mind the result of the apportionment of other property or debts on the basis of the territoriality principle.

Third, amongst the criteria that may be used for the determination of an equitable apportionment, States shall take into account: (a) any special connection existing between the areas affected by a State succession, on the one hand, and the activities to which the property and debts to be apportioned relate, on the other; (b) the connection between property, rights and interests that pass to successor States, on

① In this respect Article 41 of the *1983 Convention* is more restrictive. It reads: "... the State debts of the predecessor State shall pass to the successor States in equitable proportions, taking into account, in particular, the property, rights and interests which pass to the successor States in relation to that State debt."

② See details—V. D. DEGAN: "Equity in Matters of State Succession", *Essays in Honour of Wang Tieya*, "Martinus Nijhoff", 1993, pp. 201-210.

the one hand, and State debts, on the other; (c) the respective parts in the Gross National Product (GNP) of the States concerned at the time of the succession (or at the time of the decision or agreement on apportionment); and (d) the formula adopted by the International Monetary Fund (IMF) for the apportionment of quotas among the States concerned.

Finally, if the application of the above criteria does not lead to a satisfactory result, the States concerned may take into account, *inter alia*, the parts of revenues of each State concerned which are derived from the exportation, or the fact that certain amongst them have more than others contributed to the financing of or benefited from the exploitation of a specific project.

All the above criteria were taken into account in specific keys of apportionment of different categories of State property and debts that were adopted in the *Agreement on Succession Issues* by five successor States of the former Yugoslavia of 2001. It is thus seen how these negotiations were complicated.

*

State archives. Under a definition from Article 20 of the *1983 Vienna Convention*, "State archives of the predecessor State" means "all documents of whatever date and kind, produced or received by the predecessor State in the exercise of its functions which, at the date of the succession of States, belonged to the predecessor State according to its internal law and were preserved by it directly or under its control as archives for whatever purpose". Under the term "documents" are now understood *inter alia* film, audio and video tapes and other recordings, as well as any form of computerized records.

The above means that from State succession and apportionment between successor States are excluded State archives of component States of a Federation, archives of communes, cities and other territorial entities, as well as church, private or other similar archives. If parts of these archives happen to be among State archives of the predecessor State or at another place, they should be returned to where they were produced or received, or to their legitimate owner.

All State archives of the predecessor State within the above definition are divided into three categories:

(i) Parts of these archives "which should be in the territory of a successor State for normal administration of its territory" shall pass (in copies) to that successor State (Article 31 (1a) of the *1983 Convention*).

(ii) The part of these archives "that relates directly to the territory of a successor State" shall pass to that successor State (in originals) (Article 31 (1b)). These are, for instance, parts of State archives relating to the frontiers of a successor State with a third State, or to its unregulated issues with third States. These are also the archives of historical character directly related to the territory of one or several successor States. If more than one of these States is entitled to a group of archives, they must agree which of them will receive the original, while the others shall be entitled to make copies thereof.

(iii) When it comes to the dissolution and disappearance of the predecessor State, according to Article 31 (2) of the *1983 Convention*, all its other State archives "shall pass to the successor States in an equitable manner, taking into account all relevant circumstances".

In order to preserve the integrity of groups of State archives referred to in its Article 25, successor States can unanimously agree that this by far the largest category of State archives shall be kept in joint custody, usually in the capital of the predecessor State where they are actually situated.

There is a rule of international law which did not find its place in the text of the *1983 Vienna Convention*. According to that rule all successor States and other interested States are entitled to a free access, including copying of, all State archives of the predecessor State wherever they are actually situated. This rule applies *a fortiori* in respect of current State archives of the predecessor State which are necessary for establishing the volume and value of State property, debts, and of State archives themselves to which the succession of State applies, and which are subject to apportionment.

*

Treaties. There is a rule of positive international law, confirmed in Articles 11 and 12 of the *1978 Vienna Convention*, which stipulates that the succession of States does not affect as such the boundaries and boundary régimes, as well as other territorial régimes.

Hence, State succession does not affect existing frontiers of successor States with third States. Here is applied the principle of paramount importance of territorial *status quo*.

With regard to boundaries between former political subdivisions of a predecessor State which became new States, applicable is a similar rule of *uti possidetis*. As already explained in Chapter IV, section 4, this rule has an *erga omnes* character, but is a norm of *jus dispositivum*. Unless the States concerned agree on their new frontiers, their former boundaries become frontiers protected by international law. ①

For the purposes of the succession of States all other treaties, the party to which was the predecessor State, should be divided into three categories: (i) multilateral conventions in general; (ii) multilateral treaties of a restricted character; and (iii) bilateral treaties. ②

Before this division is being explained in details, it must be stressed that a predecessor State preserving its personality, or a successor State with its recognized continuity (such as the Russian Federation), remains a party to all treaties in force (and keeps its membership in all international organizations). What applies to its treaties is the "moving treaty-frontiers rule". This means that all treaties continue to apply within the new frontiers of such a State. Only if a specific treaty was formerly concluded in respect of the territory which was transferred by cession to another State, or on which a new State appeared, that treaty terminates in respect of the predecessor State. ③

A more complex problem is that of new successor States arising from territorial changes which either do not claim continuity, or whose claim to this end was refused. The *1978 Vienna Convention* divides these new successor States into two quite separate categories: (a) newly independent States, "the territory of which immediately before the date of the succession of States was a dependent territory for the international relations of which the predecessor State was responsible"; ④ and (b) all other new States arisen from their separation, or from dissolution of the

---

① This important rule was confirmed in *Opinion No. 3 of the (Badinter) Arbitration Commission of 11 January, 1992*. *Cf.*, *ILM 1992*, No. 6, pp. 1499-1500.

② Although the International Law Commission has invoked this division as its own (*cf.*, *Yearbook of the International Law Commission 1974*, Vol. II, Part One, p, 172, para. 72), its draft articles and the provisions of the *1978 Vienna Convention*, do not follow it consistently. This relates especially to provisions which *do not refer* to "newly independent States". That is one of shortcomings of that *Convention*.

③ This principle is contained in somewhat complicated terms in Article 15 of the *1978 Vienna Convention*.

④ *Cf.*, Article 2 (1f) of the *1978 Vienna Convention*.

predecessor State.

The rules applying in respect of these new States are as follows:

(i) *Multilateral conventions in general* should, according to Article 34(1) (and Article 38(1)) of the *1978 Convention*, automatically bind new successor States without any notification of succession to their depositaries. These conventions should be valid on the territory of these new States without interruption and legal vacuum in their application, irrespective of the date of their international recognition or of their admission to the UN and other international organizations. ①

In this respect Article 17(1) of the *1978 Convention* provides an exception privileging newly independent States only. Unlike other new States, they may notify to depositaries the succession of only these multilateral treaties to which they wish to be parties. Thus they may reject some conventions concluded for them by the former colonial power, by simply failing to notify their succession.

The practice of the UN Secretary-General in his capacity of depositary of many multilateral conventions has neglected the above distinction. Subsequent to all territorial changes that happened since 1990, the Secretary General did not make any distinction between newly independent States and other new States. He invariably waited for the admission of these new States into the membership of the UN, and then asked them to notify their succession of the conventions according to their choice. Thus, he extended the privilege provided to "newly independent States" to all new States.

By this unfortunate practice the UN Organization has precluded the transformation of the principle enshrined in Article 34(1) of the *1978 Convention* into a new customary rule of general international law. It has thus created the problem of retroactive validity of multilateral conventions between the date of

---

① All new States arisen from the dissolution of the Soviet Union, Yugoslavia and Czecho-Slovakia have considered this principle from Article 34(1) as a rule of positive international law. At the time of their proclamation of independence they all assumed the obligations from almost all treaties of their predecessor State, even including here bilateral treaties and multilateral treaties of a restricted character. Exception to this are only three Baltic States (Estonia, Latvia and Lithuania) which claim to continue their statehood between 1940 (when they were incorporated into the Soviet Union by force) and 1991. As such, they do not consider themselves as successor States of the former USSR.

proclamation of independence of a new State, and the date of its notification of succession upon its admission to the UN.

The most serious problems appeared in respect of human rights conventions. The UN Human Rights Committee stated since 1994 that all new States were automatically bound by obligations under international human rights instruments as of the respective date of independence.

This view on special régime of human rights conventions is nowadays prevailing in doctrine. But there is no rational explanation why the same should not apply to the conventions of the International Labour Organizations which are also human rights conventions in a larger sense, or to any other codification conventions such as those on the law of the sea, the law of treaties, diplomatic and consular relations, etc.

(ii) *Multilateral treaties of a restricted character*. New States cannot automatically become parties to this category of treaties. This means that these treaties are in fact excluded from the process of State succession.

If the text of a treaty of this kind provides procedural rules for accession to it by third States, a new successor States must submit itself to this procedure if it wishes to become its party. Otherwise, it must negotiate on its accession with all its actual States parties.

The problem of participation of new States in the *Danube Convention* concluded in 1948 in Belgrade was solved by conclusion of the *Additional Protocol* to it of 26 March, 1998. Upon its signature the contracting parties of the *Danube Convention* are considered to be: Austria, Bulgaria, Croatia, Germany, Hungary, Moldova, Rumania, the Russian Federation, Slovakia, Ukrainia and the Federal Republic of Yugoslavia (now Serbia). All of them are riparian States of this international river except the Russian Federation which thus has succeeded this status from the former Soviet Union.

(iii) *Bilateral treaties*. There are no satisfactory provisions on this topic in the *1978 Convention*. A customary practice has appeared since World War II that in absence of a refusal by either interested party (i. e. by the original State party and by the successor State at stake); these treaties continue to apply on a temporary basis until an agreement is reached on their future. These States can then agree that some of these bilateral treaties remain in force on a bilateral basis with a new successor State. Others can be replaced by new treaties, and some of them can be terminated but only for the future (*ex nunc*).

These agreements regulate only the bilateral relations between the original State party and each of new successor States. New successor States themselves, and the predecessor State if it continues its existence, must negotiate and conclude a network of fresh bilateral treaties *inter se* for their mutual relations. For this very reason the succession of States in respect of bilateral treaties is not a matter of primary importance for regulation of relations between successor States themselves.

*

Succession of States in membership of international organizations. Article 4 of the *1978 Vienna Convention* provides that this *Convention* applies in respect of:

> "(*a*) *any treaty which is the constituent instrument of an international organization without prejudice to the rules concerning acquisition of membership and without prejudice to any other relevant rules of the organization*; [...]"

The above to some extent obscure provision proves the fact that no pre-established rules of general international law in this domain exist. Except for the State which has preserved its identity, in all other situations of territorial changes the final decision on this issue depends on the political will of a majority of member States as represented in the political organs of the organization competent *to decide on the admission of new members.*

By virtue of such a political decision a successor State can preserve the seat of the predecessor State in an organization without having to subject itself to the admission procedure. But the claims of other successor States to this effect can be refused.

There were two different situations in this respect which appeared in the process of dissolutions of the former Yugoslav Federation and of the former Soviet Union.

The UN and the international community in general, refused the claim by the Federal Republic of Yugoslavia (Serbia and Montenegro) since 1992, to its continuity with the Yugoslav Federation (SFRY). Ultimately, this State abolished that claim, and near the end of 2001 it was admitted to the membership of the UN as a new State, equal in rights and duties with other successor States of the former SFRY.

It was not the case with the Russian Federation. In December 1991 Russia recognized itself that the Soviet Union ceased to exist as an international person and political reality. But all other members of the newly created Commonwealth of Independent States, as well as all third States, recognized the continuity of the Russian Federation with respect to its membership in all international organizations, including the permanent seat in the UN Security Council. They also recognized its quality of the party to all treaties (including those on the reduction of armaments), the party of which was the former USSR. By this, the formal and complicated procedure of amendments of the text of the *UN Charter* under its Articles 108 and 109 was avoided.

Chapter X
State Responsibility for Internationally Wrongful Acts

Bibliography: Ian BROWNLIE: *System of the Law of Nations: State Responsibility* (Part I), Oxford 1983; James CRAWFORD: *The International Law Commission's Articles on State Responsibility*, Cambridge Univ. Press 2002, 387 pages. See other bibliographical references, pp. 368-380.

I. Introduction

In our first lecture we have noted that the matters of sources of international law and of States' responsibility for internationally wrongful acts form the core of the entire discipline of international law.

We have already discussed some aspects of State responsibility, especially that following from the breaches of *erga omnes* obligations of all the States in the world. We also criticized the abolishment of the concept of international crimes in the final text of *Draft Articles* adopted by the International Law Commission on 9 August, 2001. Our conclusion was that the concept of *jus cogens*, as provided in its Articles 40 and 41, which replaced that of international crimes, is much confused, although the commission of these crimes by States does not involve criminal responsibility on their part in the legal sense.

Yet in the absence of obligatory judicial procedures for the settlement of all inter-State disputes, the very concept of State responsibility for internationally wrongful acts can seem somewhat utopian. Sovereign States cannot be sued for their acts of such a nature unless they agree to the jurisdiction of the ICJ or of arbitral tribunals.

The only exception to this relates to States parties to the *1948 Genocide*

Convention. Each of them can submit a unilateral application to the ICJ against another State party, for its violations. Besides that, it is illusory to expect that an alleged aggressor State would voluntarily agree with a State which is its presumed victim, on the jurisdiction of the ICJ for a final settlement of their dispute on that subject matter. No political organ, including the UN Security Council, can impose such a jurisdiction on sovereign States.

It happens most often in practice that a State suspect of aggression, or of other "serious breaches of peremptory norms of general international law", will simply deny its involvement in such an unlawful act, or will try to justify its conduct as an alleged act of self-defence. On this ground it will refuse to apply all the rules of general international law on State responsibility.

Nevertheless, the codification of these rules was not a useless job. It is a paradox of international relations that most States wishing to maintain their normal relations and cooperation with all other States in political, economic, cultural and other fields will voluntarily submit themselves to these rules and procedures. ① They will even not easily avoid their duty to make reparation for the injuries they caused to the injured State, or to persons or entities entitled to reparation. Even the most powerful States cannot behave in the long run irresponsibly if they do not wish to be isolated from the rest of the world. Their isolation can harm their long term political, commercial and other interests.

As already stated, the International Law Commission adopted the final text of its *Draft Articles on State Responsibility* in 2001. But States themselves have never approved this legal text of the utmost importance in the form of a codification convention. This situation has certain advantages.

In case of convocation of a diplomatic conference on this subject-matter, much discussion will arise among the participating States again on some issues already determined in this text. Just like with the *1982 UN Law of the Sea Convention*, some States could extort concessions for their particular claims. They can finally refuse to become parties to the future convention, even if it is adopted and signed at

① It can be said that this group of States includes China with the declarations of its leadership on achievement of a Harmonious World. See some details—Sienho Yee: "Towards a Harmonious World: The Role of International Law of Co-progressiveness and Leader States", *Chinese Journal of International Law*, Volume 7, No. 1, March 2008, pp. 99-105.

the conference by necessary majority. In face of such a risk, it is much better that the actual Draft Articles find their confirmation in the practice of States and of international courts and tribunals as an instrument reflecting customary rules in force. Therefore, from now on, we shall call these *Draft Articles*, for reasons of convenience, the *Rules on State Responsibility*, as did the ICJ.

We made some remarks on the solutions adopted, but we still consider the text of almost all of these Rules as reflecting the precepts of positive international law on State responsibility. As such, this text will be the basis of our explanation here with occasional critical comments. ①

*

The core of all international legal relations is in fact based on the respect of two general principles of law: that of *pacta sunt servanda*, and that according to which a breach of any international obligation, regardless it source, entails international responsibility of the respective State and its duty to make reparation for the injury caused.

There has, however, for a longtime been a rule of positive international law that reduced responsibility of the wrongdoing State to rendering its duty to make reparation only for an injury already inflicted by it. Hence, an unlawful act did not involve itself the responsibility of the State until an actual damage was caused. In this respect the International Law Commission has enlarged the concept of State responsibility. It is today generally agreed that the obligation to make reparation is a *consequence* of an unlawful act, and not a restrictive element in the very definition of State responsibility.

Nevertheless, the existence of injury cannot be neglected altogether. On the nature of the injury caused depends the form and extent of reparation. To this end these Rules differentiate, with good reason, between an "injured State" and "States other than an injured State", because they are entitled to different claims.

*

① The comment by J. CRAWFORD: *The International Law Commission's Articles on State Responsibility*, Cambridge Univ. Press 2002, contains indications of abundant jurisprudence of international courts and tribunals under each of the proposed rules. Here will be added some new cases, especially the *Advisory Opinion by the ICJ of 2004 on the Israeli Wall.* This author himself has largely used that book in his explanation here.

The entire text of these Rules is divided into four parts: Part I: The internationally wrongful act of a State; Part II: Content of the international responsibility of a State; Part III: The implementation of the international responsibility of a State; and Part IV: General provisions. Our treatment here will not strictly follow this order.

II. Restrictions on the scope of the adopted Rules

We shall first deal with the last Part that provides essential restrictions on the application of the entire text of *Rules on State Responsibility*.

(*i*) *Article* 55: *Lex specialis*

> "*These Articles do not apply where and to the extent that the conditions for the existence of an internationally wrongful act or the content or implementation of the international responsibility of a State are governed by special rules of international law.*"

As its title indicates, this Article reflects the rule *lex specialis derogat legi generali*. Hence, the provisions of these Rules have a "residual character". When some matter otherwise dealt with in these Articles is governed by a special rule of international law, the latter will prevail to the extent of any inconsistency. The matter can be of States' primary obligations.

For the application of this principle it does not suffice that the same subject matter is dealt with by two provisions. There must be some actual inconsistency between them, or else a discernable intention that one provision is to exclude the other. Thus the question is essentially the one of interpretation. ① This, however, does not affect peremptory norms of general international law (*jus cogens*).

(*ii*) *Article* 56: *Questions of State responsibility not regulated by these articles*

> "*The applicable rules of international law continue to govern*

① *Cf.*, J. CRAWFORD: *op. cit.* pp. 306-308.

questions concerning the responsibility of a State for an internationally wrongful act to the extent that they are not regulated by these Articles."

The present Article relates to secondary rules of State responsibility and it complements the previous one. It has two aspects. First, it preserves the application of the rules of customary international law concerning State responsibility on matters not covered by these Rules. ① In addition, it preserves other rules concerning the effects of a breach of an international obligation, which do not only involve issues of State responsibility, but stem from the law of treaties or other areas of international law. ②

(*iii*) *Article 57*: *Responsibility of an international organisation*

"*These Articles are without prejudice to any question of the responsibility under international law of an international organisation, or of any State for the conduct of an international organisation.*"

The matter is here of a saving clause that reserves two related issues from the scope of these Rules. The first issue is responsibility of an intergovernmental organization for its unlawful conduct when it acts as a separate international person. The second is the more complex question concerning the responsibility of any State for the conduct of an organization of which it is a member.

By contrast, where a number of States act together through their own organs as being distinct from those of an international organization, their conduct is attributable

① Its equivalent is found in the preamble of the *1969 Vienna Convention on the Law of Treaties*, which provides that "the rules of customary international law will continue to govern questions not regulated by the provisions of the present *Convention*". Similar provisions figure in most other codification conventions.

② Examples include the invalidity of a treaty procured by an unlawful use of force (Article 52 of the *1969 Vienna Convention*); or the termination of the international obligation in case of a material breach of a bilateral treaty (Article 60(1)); or impossibility to invoke fundamental change of circumstances by the State party which caused this change by its own breach of its obligation under the treaty, "or of any other international obligation owed to any other party to the treaty" (Article 62-(2)-(b)). See CRAWFORD, *op. cit.* p. 309.

to each of them and falls under these Rules (Chapter II of Part I, and Article 47).①

(iv) *Article 58: Individual responsibility*

> "*These Articles are without prejudice to any question of the individual responsibility under international law of any person acting on behalf of a State.*"

In Chapters IV and V above we largely dealt with the relationship between international responsibility of States for international crimes and criminal responsibility of individuals for the commission of the same acts. This saving clause should be understood so that these Rules do not address any question of individual responsibility of any physical or legal person under international law, but only State responsibility. As such, it does not exempt from responsibility a person acting as a State organ, neither does it exempt States from their responsibility for such acts if committed under their control.

(v) *Article 59: Charter of the United Nations*

> "*These Articles are without prejudice to the Charter of the United Nations.*"

This last saving clause corresponds to Article 103 of the *UN Charter*, which provides: "*In the event of a conflict between the obligations of the Members of the United Nations under the present Charter and their obligations under any other international agreement, their obligations under the present Charter shall prevail*". Hence, although the focus of Article 103 is on treaty obligations, Article 59 can have a larger scope of application in practice. It is, for instance, not excluded that the Security Council orders a responsible State on behalf of Chapter VII of the *UN Charter* to repair damages inflicted by it in a particular case.

In addition, the sum of these *Rules on State Responsibility* is to be interpreted in conformity with the *Charter* itself, which is the international instrument, above all others. This is because practically all the sovereign States in the world are today UN

① CRAWFORD, *op. cit.* pp. 310-311.

omission occurs which, taken with the other actions or omissions, is sufficient to constitute the wrongful act. [...] 2. In such a case, the breach extends over the entire period starting with the first of the actions or omissions of the series and lasts for as long as these actions or omissions are repeated and remain not in conformity with the international obligation."

Ⅳ. The question of objective responsibility for risk

As already said, secondary rules on State responsibility do not require for its appearance any fault or wrongful intent of perpetrators of an internationally wrongful act. The principle set out in Article 2 of the Rules only requires the attribution of such an act to a particular State and the breach by that State of its international obligation. In addition, Articles 40 and 41 distinguish among other unlawful acts "serious breaches of obligations under peremptory norms of general international law". The latter was an unhappy substitute for the concept of international crimes.

Because actions and omissions by wrongdoing States have the same relevance for State responsibility, the matter is here still not of an "objective responsibility" in all the circumstances and for all consequences that can proceed from a wrongful conduct.

However, as the comment of these Rules indicates: "If the States parties (to a treaty) wished to provide for specific intent, for the measure of culpability or for a specific level of harm or damages as a prerequisite for responsibility, they were free to do so". ① But it is then a matter of primary rules of international law that operate as *lex specialis* under the above cited Article 55.

The question is what kinds of primary rules can be provided as additional conditions of State responsibility for some particular acts. Here are some examples:

(i) The crime of genocide is distinguished from other international crimes in the so-called *dolus specialis*. The acts forbidden must be committed "*with the intent to destroy, in whole or in part, a national, ethnical, racial or religious group, as such*". Without that specific subjective intent of perpetrators, it is not a matter of genocide but possibly of a crime against humanity or of a war crime. Nevertheless, the act in question remains in all circumstances an international crime.

---

① CRAWFORD, *op. cit.* p. 12.

(ii) On the other hand, responsibility of a State for *omission* very often proceeds from its failure of *due diligence*, because it did not do enough to prevent the injury. Although not precisely defined as yet, this criterion is becoming more and more a standard rule in international law. Every State has the duty to prevent and repress any actions on the territory under its jurisdiction or control that could be harmful to other States or foreigners. This general rule finds its application especially in respect of the protection of the environment.

An example of the determination of the content of this obligation can be found in Article 194 (1) of the *1982 UN Law of the Sea Convention*. According to it, States shall take measures "that are necessary to prevent, reduce and control pollution of the marine environment from any source, using for this purpose the best practical means at their disposal and in accordance with their capabilities". In case that a State can prove such a conduct, and taking into account other circumstances of the pollution ensued, it can decline its responsibility for the damage that actually occurred.

Because of the broad scope of application of this criterion, it is now presumed to exist in related domains, unless otherwise provided. Then the exceptions to this obligations fall under the rules of *lex specialis*, as provided in Article 55 of the Rules. This must be taken into account despite its qualification as a primary rule, and thus not of relevance for the general definition of internationally wrongful acts as set out in Article 2 of the Rules.

(iii) By contrast, "objective responsibility" of a State in its narrow sense, for all the consequences of its unlawful act (i. e. responsibility for risk), is sometimes provided in special rules, especially in the domains of launching of the objects in outer space, of peaceful uses of nuclear energy, and of the pollution of the marine environment by oil or dumping. It is, therefore, a matter of some hazardous activities, which are otherwise not forbidden by law.

This extreme kind of responsibility does not exist unless provided by special rules. However, in case that it is actually provided, the responsible State, or its natural and juridical persons, is obliged to make full reparation for the injury caused regardless of any guilt or wrongful intent on their part.

V. Legal consequences of internationally wrongful acts

"*Every internationally wrongful act entails the international responsibility of the wrongdoing State*" (Articles 1 and 28 of the Rules). General international law provides the scope of international obligations of a responsible State on a very large basis.

"*These obligations may be owed to another State, to several States, or to the international community as a whole, depending in particular of the character and content of the international obligation and on the circumstances of the breach*" (Article 33 (1)). It is in addition provided that the respective provisions are "... *without prejudice to any right, arising from the international responsibility of a State, which may accrue directly to any person or entity other than a State*" (Article 33(2)).

The commission of an internationally wrongful act creates in fact a new set of legal relationship between the responsible State and the State or States to whom the international obligation is owed. This relationship is encompassed by the concept of "international responsibility". It lasts until the responsible State repairs the injury, or until the injured State has validly waived (relinquished from) its claim or its claim has gone into oblivion (prescription).

There is a hard rule of international law according to which: "*The responsible State may not rely on the provisions of its internal law as justification for failure to comply with its obligations*" (Article 32).

There is another hard rule, which is based on the respect of the general principle of law of good faith. A responsible State cannot enjoy any advantage from the breach of its international obligation. Especially, it cannot claim that its obligation by such a fact has terminated.

Unlike the wrongdoing State, injured States have several options in their reaction. In case of material breach of a bilateral treaty the other party can unilaterally terminate it. When the matter is of a breach of a multilateral treaty by one of the parties, other parties can suspend its operation (Article 60 of the *1969 Vienna Convention on the Law of Treaties*). But instead of its termination, the injured parties can choose to insist on the continuing duty of the responsible State to fulfill the obligations breached. In any case, this does not affect the duty of the responsible

State to make reparation for its breach.

This general principle of law is confirmed in Article 29 of the Rules, which affirms that: "*The legal consequences of an internationally wrongful act under this Part do not affect the continued duty of the responsible State to perform the obligation breached.*"

According to Article 30, "*The State responsible for the internationally wrongful act is under an obligation: (a) to cease that act, if it is continuing; and (b) to offer appropriate assurances and guarantees of non-repetition, if circumstances so require.*" These are today obligations under general international law. Nevertheless, the latter obligation applies in absence of special rules, according to the above Article 55.

The forms of reparation of injury will be elaborated on in our next Chapter.

VI. Attribution of internationally wrongful acts

Attribution of a breach of an international obligation to a particular State is the essential condition of its international responsibility. Without attribution to a particular State, its responsibility under international law does not exist. But, as Article 2 of the Rules provides, the conduct of a State can consist both in actions and omission.

It was explained in Chapter VIII of these Lectures, above, that the sovereignty of a State is defined as its supreme power within its territory, with the exclusion of the power of any foreign State. But as a corollary to this sovereignty there are some duties of every State on its territory.

In the *Tellini* case of 1923 it was the matter of the assassination on Greek territory of the Chairman and several members of an international commission entrusted with the task of delimiting the Greek-Albanian border. A Committee of Jurists set up in respect of that incident by the Council of the League of Nations, issued the following statement:

> "*The responsibility of a State is only involved by the commission in its territory of a political crime against the persons of foreigners if the State has neglected to take all reasonable measures for the prevention of the crime and the pursuit, arrest and bringing to justice of the criminal*".

Hence, a State can be responsible for acts committed on its territory by individuals or insurrectional movements that are not its organs. It is then responsible for the failure of its duty of due diligence that consists in the prevention and repression of unlawful acts committed by such individuals or movements.

The *Rules on State Responsibility* provide three sets of provisions relating to the attribution of conduct to a State. Articles 4 and 7 in its Chapter II relate to the conduct of organs of a State. Articles 5, 6 and 8 to 12, regulate the conduct of organs that are not State organs but which, under certain conditions, can be attributed to the State. Finally, Articles 16 to 19 of Chapter IV regulate the questions of responsibility of a State in connection with the acts of another State.

*

(a) Among all these rules the most important are in practice those from the first group, which regulate the conduct of organs proper to a State. Its Article 4 has a very large scope of application:

> "*1. The conduct of any State organ shall be considered an act of that State under international law, whether the organ exercises legislative, executive, judicial or any other functions, whatever position it holds in the organisation of the State, and whatever its character as an organ of the central government or of a territorial unit of the State.*
>
> *2. An organ includes any person or entity which has that status in accordance with the internal law of the State.*"

However, the above means that if a person which otherwise exercises governmental functions acts in his or her personal capacity and for his or her own interests, acts of this nature cannot be attributed in that particular case to its State. Nevertheless, this difference is sometimes not easy to discern, especially in States with corrupt government.

On the other hand, according to Article 7:

> "*The conduct of an organ of a State or of a person or entity empowered to exercise elements of the governmental authority shall be considered an act of the State under international law if the organ, person*

or entity acts in that capacity, even if it exceeds its authority or contravenes instructions."

There is an old legal rule that unauthorized or *ultra vires* acts engage the responsibility of the State, provided that the respective organs have acted in their official capacity. The State is responsible here again for the failure of its duty to prevent such acts that are in excess of authority, or in contravention of instructions.

Here is a short explanation of other parts of Article 4.

(i) Organs exercising *legislative functions* can engage international responsibility of their State if they fail to enact laws and other regulations necessary for the implementation of the State's international obligations. It happens even more often that acts adopted by the legislative organ are not fully in conformity with these obligations and that the application of these deficient laws results in internationally wrongful acts.

(ii) State organs exercising *executive functions*, such as administrative organs, these of the police, or of armed forces, can engage international responsibility of their State mostly by their unlawful conduct against foreigners or stateless persons. It is, however, no different if these organs violate international obligations of their State against their own citizens in the domain of human rights.

It can be a matter of unlawful imprisonment of these persons, or their torture, or of their unlawful expulsion from the State's territory, or of preventing them from enjoying their acquired rights, or of the conduct of their armed forces both in peace and in an armed conflict.

The position of these persons in governmental hierarchy is not of relevance, provided they act in official capacity.

(iii) *Domestic courts* can commit internationally wrongful acts by their *denial of justice to* certain persons. There is now a general legal rule that all persons, regardless of their nationality, have the right to appear before courts of any State and request justice from them. In this respect there is one of the fundamental human rights that everyone and everywhere has the right to be recognized as a person before the law (Article 6 of the *1948 Universal Declaration of Human Rights*). Hence, courts must not deny justice to any individual, be they their nationals, foreigners, or stateless person.

The above Article 4 provides in addition that a State is also responsible for the attributable to the United States, unless there was evidence of its instructions to this end, or if these acts were committed under its direction or "effective control". ①

The *1999 Appeals Judgment of the ICTY in the Tadić Case* dismissed this statement by ICJ and insisted on the so-called test of "overall control" exercised by the Federal Republic of Yugoslavia over the Bosnian Serb forces. Hence, in the Tribunal's view there was no need to prove that each operation in which international crimes were committed was carried out on FRY's instructions or under its effective control.

The test of "overall control" was strongly criticize and repudiated by the ICJ in its *2007 Judgment on Genocide Convention*. Apart from the acts carried out by a State's official organs, or those that can be equated with them, a State's responsibility can be incurred for the acts committed by persons or groups of persons ... only assuming those acts are attributable to it under the rule of customary international law reflected in Article 8 of the *Rules on State Responsibility*. The Court added:

> "*This is so where an organ of the State gave the instructions or provided the direction pursuant to which the perpetrators of the wrongful act acted or where it exercised effective control over the action during which the wrong was committed. In this regard the 'overall control' test is unsuitable, for it stretches too far, almost to breaking point, the connection which must exist between the conduct of a State's organ and its international responsibility.*" ②

(iv) *Conduct carried out in the absence or default of the official authorities.* Article 9 states that:

> "*The conduct of a person or group of persons shall be considered an act of a State under international law if the person or group of persons is in fact exercising elements of the governmental authority in the absence or default of the official authorities and in circumstances such as to call for the exercise of*

① *I. C. J. Reports 1986*, p. 51, para. 86: pp. 62 and 65-66, paras. 109 and 112.

② *I. C. J. Reports 2007*, pp. 144-145, para. 406.

those elements of authority."

In revolutions or other internal armed conflicts, or during foreign occupation, regular authorities of a State can disintegrate. This can also happen if State authorities become helpless to control activities of large and powerful criminal groups. Classical international law admits in addition *levée en masse*, which in fact consists of self-defence of citizens against foreign assault in situations of necessity, in absence of regular armed forces.

In these unusual situations unauthorized persons or groups can in fact exercise some government authority. But three cumulative conditions must be fulfilled under Article 9: first, the conduct must effectively relate to the exercise of elements of the governmental authorities; secondly, the conduct must have been carried out in the absence or default of the official authorities; and thirdly, the circumstances must have been such as to call for the exercise of those elements of authority. ①

(v) *Conduct of an insurrectional or other movement.* Article 10 consists in three following paragraphs:

> "*1. The conduct of an insurrectional movement which becomes the new government of a State shall be considered as an act of that State under international law.*
>
> *2. The conduct of a movement, insurrectional or other, which succeeds in establishing a new State in part of the territory of a pre-existing State or in a territory under its administration shall be considered an act of the new State under international law.*
>
> *3. This Article is without prejudice to the attribution to a State of any conduct, however related to that of the movement concerned, which is to be considered an act of that State by virtue of Articles 4 to 9.*"

---

① *Cf.*, CRAWFORD, *op. cit.* p. 114.

be used for unlawful purposes, there is no responsibility on its part. The common objective element is that the act would be internationally wrongful if committed by that other State. In all situations both these conditions must be satisfied.

(i) *Aid or assistance in the commission of an internationally wrongful act.* Article 16 of the Rules provides:

> "*A State which aids or assists another State in the commission of an internationally wrongful act by the latter is internationally responsible for doing so if: (a) that State does so with knowledge of the circumstances of the internationally wrongful act; and (b) the act would be internationally wrongful if committed by that State.*"

As already said, both of the above requirements must be fulfilled. However, even in these situations the assisting State is not obliged to make full reparation for the wrong committed to the injured State. It is responsible only for the damage proportionate to its aid or assistance.

(ii) *Direction and control exercised over the commission of an internationally wrongful act.* Article 17 reads in this respect as follows:

> "*A State which directs and controls another State in the commission of an internationally wrongful act by the latter is internationally responsible for that act if: (a) that State does so with knowledge of the circumstances of the internationally wrongful act; and (b) the act would be internationally wrongful if committed by that State.*"

After the process of decolonization has ended, this rule is of a rather historical importance. It is hard to apply it to the States that are now placed under some kind of temporary protectorate of the UN, like Bosnia-Herzegovina or Kosovo. This is so because representatives of the international community do not exercise direction and control over acts of these States in the name of a single State. There is in fact a flaw in international law in this respect because international organizations have been known to escape their international responsibility for the acts or omissions of their appointed agents.

The rule from Article 17 does not relate to component States of a Federation. This is because for all unlawful acts of these entities the international responsibility lies with the Federation as the only subject of international law.

In case that in an occupied territory the occupying power puts the local police under its control, this power is responsible for all the acts of the police. This does not, however, exclude personal criminal responsibility of policemen as perpetrators of offenses.

(iii) *Coercion of another State.* Finally, Article 18 reads as follows:

" *A State which coerces another State to commit an act is internationally responsible for that act if: (a) the act would, but for the coercion, be an internationally wrongful act of the coerced State; and (b) the coercing State does so with knowledge of the circumstances of the act.*"

Coercion over the State perpetrator of the act must have the features from Article 23 bellow relating to *force majeure*. It must therefore consist in "an irresistible force" over the perpetrator. If not, it can be a matter of situations provided either in Article 17 or 16 above. However, in case that this condition is met, the perpetrator acts as a mere instrument of the dominating State which bears the main responsibility for the act committed.

However, Article 2(4) of the *UN Charter* forbids any threat or use of force, which now constitutes a peremptory norm of general international law. Therefore, coercion itself constitutes an internationally wrongful act.

(iv) *Effect of this Chapter.* Article 19 provides in addition that:

" *This Chapter is without prejudice to the international responsibility, under other provisions of these Articles, of the State which commits the act in question, or of any other State.* "

It is here a matter of a saving clause with the aim of preserving international *cogens*. In addition, it can be vitiated by the same acts that invalidate a treaty, such as error, fraud, corruption or coercion. Accordingly, Article 20 speaks of "valid consent" that must be freely given and clearly established. In cases of doubt it is not presumed.

Consent can be given in advance, or even at the time of the occurrence of the otherwise wrongful act by another State. When it is given *ex post facto*, after the conduct has taken place, it is not anymore the matter of consent, but of waiver or acquiescence leading to the loss of the right of the consenting State to invoke responsibility under Article 45.

(ii) *Self-defence*. The succinct provision of Article 21 reads as follows:

> "*The wrongfulness of an act of a State is precluded if the act constitutes a lawful measure of self-defence taken in conformity with the Charter of the United Nations.*"

At stake is Article 51 of the *UN Charter* which relates to "the inherent rights" of States, both of their individual and collective self-defence. The above Article 21 of the Rules does not go into details of this "primary rule" on which a rich literature was published.

To this end, conclusions adopted by the Institute of International Law in Santiago de Chile in October 2007 can be of some guidance. It was stated in that resolution *inter alia* that necessity and proportionality are essential components of the normative framework of self-defence. This right arises only in case of an actual or manifestly imminent armed attack and until the Security Council takes effective measures necessary to maintain international peace and security. The State exercising this right is under the obligation immediately to report to the Security Council actions taken in self-defence. In addition, an armed attack triggering the rights of self-defence must be of a certain degree of gravity. Collective self-defence may be exercises only at the request of the target State.

It was also stressed that there is no basis in international law for the doctrines of "preventive" self-defence (in the absence of an actual or manifestly imminent armed attack).

However, a State victim of an armed aggression is also obliged to respect its obligations from humanitarian law and on human rights. These conventional obligations, which are now customary rules of general international law, apply equally to all parties to an armed conflict.

(iii) *Countermeasures in respect of an internationally wrongful act.* Article 22 provides in this respect the following:

> "*The wrongfulness of an act of a State not in conformity with an international obligation towards another State is precluded if and to the extent that the act constitutes a countermeasure taken against the latter State in accordance with Chapter II of Part Three.*"

Unlike the right to self-defence, restrictive rules on this kind of self-help are set out in Articles 49 to 51 of these Rules. We shall explain them in the next Chapter.

*

Before explaining the details about *force majeure*, distress and necessity, it seems useful to clarify their differences. These terms are sometimes misunderstood not only in municipal law, but in some arbitral awards as well. Besides, necessity is sometimes confused with self-defence and with countermeasures or reprisals in armed conflicts.

Force majeure is a situation of irresistible force which is beyond the control of the State concerned, not allowing it a free choice and which makes it materially impossible to perform its international obligation.

Distress is a situation of peril mainly caused by a natural disaster. The State agent is not acting involuntarily, but his choice of action is in these situations radically nullified. The immediate interest is not compliance with the obligation of his State, but saving his life and the lives of persons under his care, irrespectively of their nationality.

Finally, the state of necessity offers a choice of conduct. However, unlike consent, self-defence or countermeasures, it is not dependent on the prior conduct of the injured State. Unlike *force majeure* it does not involve conduct which is involuntary or coerced. Unlike distress, necessity consists not in a danger to the lives of individuals, but in a grave danger either to the essential interests of the State or of the international community as a whole. The disrespect of the international obligation "rendered necessary by *force majeure* or distress or for the purpose of rendering assistance to persons, ships or aircraft in danger or distress".

*

(vi) *Necessity.* In order to prevent abuses Article 25 is couched restrictively and entirely in negative language:

> "*1. Necessity may not be invoked by a State as a ground for precluding the wrongfulness of an act not in conformity with an international obligation of that State unless the act*
>
> *(a) is the only way for the State to safeguard an essential interest against a grave and imminent peril; and*
>
> *(b) does not seriously impair an essential interest of the State or States towards which the obligation exists, or of the international community as a whole.*
>
> *2. In any case, necessity may not be invoked by a State as a ground for precluding wrongfulness if:*
>
> *(a) the international obligation in question excludes the possibility of invoking necessity; or*
>
> *(b) the State has contributed to the situation of necessity.*"

In respect of the condition under Paragraph 1 above, "the interest relied on must outweigh all other considerations, not merely from the point of view of the acting State but on a reasonable assessment of the competing interests, whether these are individual or collective". ①

In respect of the condition under Paragraph 2 (a), certain humanitarian conventions applicable to armed conflicts expressly exclude reliance on "military

① CRAWFORD, *ibid.* p. 184.

necessity".

One of the rare cases in which all the above restrictive conditions were met was the accident of the Liberian oil tanker *Torrey Canyon* in 1967. The ship being situated on the high seas and abandoned by its crew spilled a large amount of oil threatening British and French coastlines. The British Government bombed the ship to burn the remaining oil. No international protest to its unilateral action ensued. ①

One of the cases in which the plea of necessity was dismissed was the ICJ's advisory opinion of 2004 on the *Legal Consequences of the Construction of a Wall in the Occupied Palestinian Territory*. The Court cited its previous *Judgment of 1997 on the Gabčikovo-Nagyimaros Project Between Hungary and Slovakia*, according to which: "the state of necessity is a ground recognized by customary international law" that "can only be accepted on an exceptional basis"; it "can only be invoked under certain strictly defined conditions which must be cumulatively satisfied; and the State concerned is not the sole judge of whether those conditions have been met". ②

In its *2004 Advisory opinion* the Court asserted that one of those conditions in terms of Article 25 of the Rules adopted by the International Law Commission, was that the act being challenged was "the only way for the State to safeguard an essential interest against a grave and imminent peril". "In the light of the material before it, the Court is not convinced that the construction of the wall along the route chosen was the only means to safeguard the interests of Israel against the peril which it has invoked as justification for that construction". ③

---

① After this event, the *International Convention Relating to Intervention on the High Seas in Cases of Oil Pollution* was signed in 1969. Article 221 of the *1982 Law of the Sea Convention* also permits similar measures to avoid pollution arising from maritime casualties beyond territorial sea.

② See, *I. C. J. Reports 1997*, p. 40, para. 51.

③ *I. C. J. Reports 2004*, pp. 56-57, para. 140.

Chapter XI
Injury and Modes of Its Redress

Bibliography: Brigitte BOLLECKER-STERN: Le préjudice dans la théorie de la responsabilité internationale, Paris 1973, 382 pages; Theodor MERON: "The Insurer and the Insured under International Claims Law", *AJIL 1974*, pp. 628-647.

I. The injured State and other States

As stressed in the previous Chapter, according to Article 1 of the Rules, every internationally wrongful act attributable to a State entails its international responsibility. Injury or damage caused by such a State is not the essential element of that act as such. ① In order to be an element of a State's responsibility it depends on the content of the primary rule that was breached. Therefore, the injury suffered remains an important problem of State responsibility which cannot be neglected in any circumstances.

This problem must be viewed in relationship between a State responsible for an internationally wrongful act and an "injured State". The State actor engages its international responsibility by breaching its primary obligation, even before the damage ensued and regardless of it. Unlike it, the injured State can claim reparation only after its suffering of the damage caused. It can be either a matter of material or of moral damage. ②

The statement of the ICJ in its *Barcelona Traction Judgment of 1970* that was

---

① These Rules use the broad term of "injury" and "*préjudice*" in French, although the word "damage" is also employed in Articles 31, 36, and 47.

② It can be imagined that a State claims revocation of a law of another State before a damage resulted from its application. But in actual practice it will rarely be so, if ever.

quoted in Chapter IV of these Lectures, above, and which had a substantial impact on further development of the rules of international law, related to two situations only: obligations of a State vis-à-vis another State in the field of diplomatic protection, and *erga omnes* obligations of all States towards the international community as a whole.

When it is a matter of a right to claim reparation for an internationally wrongful act, the existence of three situations is proved in practice. They are as such implied in Articles 33(1) and 42 of the *Rules on State Responsibility*.

(i) First are the obligations vis-à-vis another State in the field of diplomatic protection, which are not the concern of third States. They are for other States *res inter alios acta*. Obligations of this nature can arise from a bilateral treaty, or can be assumed towards natural or juridical persons to which another State is entitled to render its diplomatic protection. Most of the rules on State responsibility relate to legal consequences of violations of this kind of obligations.

(ii) Next to the above are the so-called obligations *erga omnes partes* that can result from the violation of a multilateral treaty by one of its party. If the treaty provides or so implies, each of its other parties can require the breaching State to abide by its obligations, even if the claiming State or its natural or juridical persons have not suffered any loss or damage. When it is a matter, for instance, of obligations from a human rights convention, or of that concerning humanitarian law applicable in armed conflicts, any of its parties is entitled to consider that the obligations are due to it, even if the victims are citizens of the State in breach, or any other persons. ①

(iii) Last but not least are the obligations *erga omnes* proper, in respect of all

① Article 1(b) of the resolution on: "Obligations *erga omnes* in International Law", adopted by the Institute of International Law in 2005, defines an obligation *erga omnes partes* as: "(b) an obligation under a multilateral treaty that a State party to the treaty owes in any given case to all the other States parties to the same treaty, in view of their common values and concern for compliance, so that a breach of that obligation enables all these States to take action."

States. Their basis lies in some customary rules of general international law. ①

This kind of obligations can emerge not only from peremptory norms of general international law under Article 40 of the Rules, nor from international crimes committed alone. Articles 42 and 48, which will be commented bellow, relate also to obligations from the rules of general international law of dispositive character, whenever interested States have not established a legal relationship *inter se* in derogation of these norms. ②

Hence, under the Rules on State Responsibility an "injured State" is a State entitled to invoke the responsibility of another State in the situations described under (i) above and also if a breach of *erga omnes* obligations under (ii) and (iii) has specially affected that State. In all these situations the injured State endured a material or moral damage.

All other States envisaged under (ii) and (iii), that did not suffer a loss from the breach of *erga omnes* obligations, are entitled only to claim cessation of the wrongful act and reparation of damage caused by the breaching State, but only in the interest of the injured State or of the beneficiaries of the obligation in question.

In the operative part of the *Advisory Opinion of the ICJ of 2004 on Legal Consequences of the Construction of a Wall in the Occupied Palestinian Territory*, it was stated in para. 163 under (D), that all States are under an obligation not to recognize the illegal situation resulting from the construction of the wall and not to render aid or assistance in maintaining the situation created by such a construction. The matter is here of their obligation *erga omnes* proper. Furthermore, all States parties to the *Fourth Geneva Convention* relative to the Protection of Civil Persons in Time of War of 1949 have also the obligation "to ensure compliance by Israel with international humanitarian law as embodied in that *Convention*". The latter is their obligation *erga omnes partes.*

The above situations are regulated by two provisions of the *Rules on State*

---

① The said resolution by the Institute of International Law defines such an obligation as: "(a) an obligation under general international law that a State owes in a given case to the international community, in view of its common values and its concern for compliance, so that a breach of that obligation enables all States to take action ..." The above statement from the *Barcelona Traction Judgment* relates exactly to these obligations.

② See the explanation of *erga omnes* obligations operating as *jus dispositivum*, *supra*, Chapter IV, under 4.

Responsibility. Article 42, entitled "Invocation of the responsibility by an injured State", provides:

> "*A State is entitled as an injured State to invoke the responsibility of another State if the obligation breached is owed to*:
>
> (*a*) *that State individually*; *or*
>
> (*b*) *a group of States including that State*, *or the international community as a whole*, *and the breach of the obligation*:
>
> (*i*) *specially affect that State*; *or*
>
> (*ii*) *is of such a character as radically to change the position of all the other States to which the obligation is owed with respect to the further performance of the obligation.*"

The alternative condition under (b)-(ii) is inspired by Article 60-(2)-(c) of the *1969 Vienna Convention on the Law of Treaties*. The said Article 60 provides that a material breach of a multilateral treaty by one of the parties entitles any other party to invoke the breach as a ground for its suspension, "if the treaty is of such a character that a material breach of its provisions by one party radically changes the position of every party with respect to the further performance of its obligations under the treaty." In both cases it is a matter of violations of obligations from treaties on disarmament or on denuclearized zones, where any other State party is directly affected by such a breach.

On the other hand, Article 48 entitled "Invocation of responsibility by a State other than an injured State", provides the following:

> "*1. Any State other than an injured State is entitled to invoke the responsibility of another State in accordance with paragraph 2 if*:
>
> (*a*) *the obligation breached is owed to a group of States including that State*, *and is established for the protection of a collective interest of*

between the two States.

Unlike a sovereign State, an *international organization* can only render "functional protection" to its agent or to other persons in its employment who suffered injury in its service. Because these persons have also the nationality of a State, that State can render diplomatic protection to it too. In its *Advisory Opinion of 1949*, on the *Reparation for Injury suffered in the UN Service*, the ICJ stated that: "In such a case, there is no rule of law which assigns priority to the one or to the other, or which compels either the State or the Organization to refrain from bringing an international claim." ①

On the basis of its personal sovereignty a State can provide its diplomatic protection only to its own citizens, and not to foreigners or stateless persons. For a valid citizenship to be opposable to other States there must be an effective bond or relationship between a person and its State. A change of citizenship is not opposable to another State if the new citizenship is not effective. ②

In case of a dual or multiple citizenship, it was already said in Chapter IX under 4 above, that a State cannot extend its diplomatic protection to its citizen in another State, of which it is also a citizen.

There is, however, no legal obligation of a State to render its diplomatic protection to its citizens, unless such a duty was provided either in its laws or constitution.

The International Court of Justice stated in its *1970 Judgment in Barcelona Traction*: "The State must be viewed as the sole judge to decide whether its protection will be granted, to what extent it is granted, and when it will cease. It retains in this respect a discretionary power the exercise of which may be determined by considerations of a political or other nature, unrelated to the particular case." ③

In practice, it is most difficult to establish nationality of a juridical person. Because every State determines its bond of citizenship itself, there appeared three criteria in practice: (i) the criterion of the seat (*siege social*) of the company; (ii) the criterion of its incorporation, i. e. of the place where a company or its branch was

① *I. C. J. Reports 1949*, p. 185.

② See in this respect *Judgment of the ICJ of 1955 in Nottebohm Case Between Guatemala and Liechtenstein*, *I. C. J. Reports 1955*, especially p. 26.

③ *I. C. J. Reports 1970*, p. 45, para. 79.

registered; and (iii) the criterion of control either by a majority of its shareholders or by persons who actually manage the company.

In its above quoted *Judgment of 1970*, the Court confirmed that "in the particular field of the diplomatic protection of corporate entities, no absolute test of the 'genuine connection' has found general acceptance. Such tests as have been applied are of a relative nature, and sometimes links with one State have had to be weighed against those with another". ①

In that concrete case of *Barcelona Traction Ltd.*, the Court dismissed the claim by the State of the majority of shareholders (Belgium), after the State of incorporation (Canada) had ceased to render its diplomatic protection to the Company in respect of Spain, which liquidated it.

The *Rules on State Responsibility* do not provide detailed regulations on this important subject matter as explained above. Article 44, entitled "Admissibility of the claim", simply states:

> "*The responsibility of a State may not be invoked if*:
>
> (*a*) *the claim is not brought in accordance with any applicable rule relating to the nationality of claims*;
>
> (*b*) *the claim is one to which the rule of exhaustion of local remedies applies and any available and effective local remedy has not been exhausted.*"

This other important problem will be discussed in our next section.

Ⅲ. Exhaustion of local remedies

In its *Judgment in Mavrommatis Case* the ICJ also stressed that a State is entitled to protect its citizens in respect of the acts of another State "from which they have been unable to obtain satisfaction through the ordinary channels". These

---

① *Ibid.*, p. 43, para. 70.

"ordinary channels" can be judicial or consist in a procedure before administrative organs of a foreign State, or combined.

It is a matter of an old customary rule according to which a State can render its diplomatic protection to its national only after he or she has exhausted all the judicial or other remedies in the allegedly wrongdoing State. Hence, before diplomatic protection takes place, national organs should have another chance to redress the injury to the foreigner.

This principle has its reasons in States' sovereignty. Without it, foreign persons would be in a privileged position compared to the citizens of a country. As plaintiffs, they would enjoy direct protection of their State in a foreign territory, whereas other persons could not sue them for their own unlawful acts in the territorial State.

The principle of exhaustion of local remedies does not relate to States, unless their commercial transactions are involved. Sovereign States settle their claims in direct negotiations, or bringing them to international arbitral or judicial procedures if both disputing parties agree so.

Nevertheless, this principle has important limitations in its application. Foreign natural and juridical persons are not obliged to use local remedies which offer no possibility of redressing the situation. Hence an appeal to the constitutional court of a State is only justified if that jurisdiction can adjudicate pecuniary compensation when necessary. Article 44(2) of the Rules speaks in this sense of "available and effective local remedies". ①

The *1989 Judgment of the ICJ in Elettronica Sicula Case Between the United States and Italy* stated that:

"*for an international claim to be admissible, it is sufficient if the*

---

① Article 22 of the previous *Draft Articles on State Responsibility*, which the International Law Commission adopted in the first reading in 1996, provided the following: "When the conduct of a State has created a situation not in conformity with the result required of it by an international obligation concerning the treatment to be accorded to aliens, whether natural or juridical persons, but the obligation allows that this or an equivalent result may nevertheless be achieved by subsequent conduct of the State, there is a breach of obligation only if the aliens concerned have exhausted the effective local remedies available to them without obtaining the treatment called for by the obligation or, where that is not possible, an equivalent treatment."

essence of the claim has been brought before the competent tribunals and pursued as far as permitted by local law and procedures, and without success. "①

The question is: did a foreign natural or juridical person lose the possibility of diplomatic protection of its State if it missed, without reason, the time limits in domestic procedure for its application or appeals. There has not been so far a clear answer to it.

On the other hand, the silence of justice, i. e. the failure of a local court or administrative organ to decide a case in a reasonable time, is interpreted as the denial of justice. In case that it actually occurred, the person has satisfied its obligation of the exhaustion of local remedies.

In this context the so-called *Calvo* clause should also be discussed, whose author was a famous scholar and diplomat from Argentina (1824-1906). Some contracts concluded between private persons or with a State contain a clause by which foreigners relinquished at the outset the diplomatic protection of their State, and restrained themselves only to available local remedies in the territorial State.

Opinions on the effect of such a clause are divided. According to one view, to these acts of self-abnegation should be given full effect whenever they are clearly expressed. According to the opposite view, a private person is not entitled in its own right to renounce diplomatic protection; that is a sovereign right of his or her State.

The problem of exhaustion of local remedies is very complex in its practical application. This is because States are engaged more and more in commercial transactions in respect of which they do not enjoy immunity. Then they have the same rights and duties as natural or juridical persons, including the obligation of the exhaustion of local remedies in another State. Hence, in particular cases that occur, abundant literature on this subject matter must be consulted. ②

---

① *I. C. J. Reports 1989*, p. 46, para. 59.

② See among others — A. A. CANÇADO TRINIDADE: *The Application of the Rule of Exhaustion of Local Remedies in International Law: Its Rationale in the International Protection of Individual Rights*, Cambridge Univ. Press 1983; C. F. AMERASINGHE: *Local Remedies in International Law*, Cambridge Univ. Press 1990; E. WYLER: *L' illicite et la condition des personnes privées*, Paris 1995.

IV. Rights of the injured State and obligations of the responsible State

(a) *Introduction.* The matter is here again of the application of certain general principles of law that were first formulated in some judgments of the Permanent Court of International Justice. They were later on invoked and confirmed many times in the practice of international courts and tribunals. These principles were also the basis of the codification of the *Rules on State Responsibility* by the International Law Commission. It is worth quoting them as such.

In its *Judgment of 1928 concerning the Factory at Chorzów on Merits* (*Germany v. Poland*), the Court stated that: "it is a principle of international law, and even a general conception of law, that any breach of an engagement involves an obligation to make reparation."①

It was further explained: "The essential principle contained in the actual notion of an illegal act—a principle which seems to be established by international practice and in particular by the decisions of arbitral tribunals—is that reparation must, as far as possible, wipe out all the consequences of the illegal act and reestablish the situation which would, in all probability, have existed if that act had not been committed. Restitution in kind, or, if this is not possible, payment of a sum corresponding to the value which a restitution in kind would bear; the award, if need be, of damages for loss sustained which would not be covered by restitution in kind or payment in place of it—such are principles which should serve to determine the amount of compensation due for an act contrary to international law." These principles were provided in this same content in the Rules on State Responsibility.

Sometimes a State declines to recognize its responsibility for its act, but nevertheless agrees to pay an *ex gratia* compensation to the injured State or a persons from it. In case the injured State agrees to this arrangement, the responsible State

① P.C.I.J., *Series A.* — *No.* 17, p. 29.

has thereby fulfilled its obligation of reparation. ①

(b) *The duty of cessation and non-repetition.* Article 30 of the Rules, the same as the above quoted Article 48-(2)-(a), provides the obligation of cessation and non-repetition of an internationally wrongful act, but this time in terms of a general obligation. It reads:

> "*The State responsible for the internationally wrongful act is under an obligation:*
>
> *(a) to cease that act, if it is continuing;*
>
> *(b) to offer appropriate assurances and guarantees of non-repetition, if circumstances so require.*"

According to Article 2 of the Rules, cessation of a continuing act covers both action and omission. As already stated in the previous Chapter, on behalf of the principle confirmed in Article 29 of the Rules, cessation of an unlawful act does not affect the continuing duty of the responsible State to perform the obligation breached.

The duty of cessation can be imposed in a concrete situation by the UN Security Council, when acting under Chapter VII of the *Charter* in cases of threat to the peace, breaches of the peace, or acts of aggression.

In the *2004 Advisory Opinion of the ICJ on Legal Consequences of the Construction of a Wall in the Occupies Palestinian Territory*, this duty was confirmed in the following terms: "The Court observes that Israel ... has an obligation to put an end to the violation of its international obligation flowing from the construction of the wall in the Occupied Palestinian Territory." It was added that this obligation is well established in general international law, and the Court confirmed its existence on a number of occasions. ②

---

① One of the recent examples was an agreement between the United States and China on *ex gratia* compensation by the U. S. of the lump sum of 4.5 millions of US dollars to the families of the persons killed or wounded during the bombing of the Chinese Embassy in Belgrade on 7 May, 1999. See the details, *American Journal of International Law 2000*, (AJIL), No. 1, pp. 127-131.

② *I. C. J. Reports 2004*, p. 197, para. 150.

According to the Court, this obligation entails dismantling forthwith of the parts of this structure situated within the Occupied Palestinian Territory, including in and around East Jerusalem. In addition, all the legislative and regulatory acts adopted with a view to its construction must be repealed or rendered ineffective, "except in so far as such acts, by providing compensation or other form of reparation for the Palestinian population, may continue to be relevant" for compliance by Israel with its obligations to repair these acts. ①

Offering appropriate assurances and guarantees of non-repetition is aimed to restore the confidence in continuing relations between the respective States.

Assurances are normally given verbally, while guarantees of non-repetition can involve something more. However, a claim of guarantees by an injured State might not be appropriate in all circumstances. Sometimes, they are of abusive or excessive character. Therefore the wording: " if circumstances so require." These circumstances depend on the nature of the obligations, as well as of their breach. ②

(c) *The duty of reparation.* The main legal consequence of the commission of an internationally wrongful act is the duty of the wrongdoing State to make *reparation* of the injury caused. In this respect Article 31 provides:

> "*1. The responsible State is under an obligation to make full reparation for the injury caused by the internationally wrongful act.*
>
> *2. Injury includes any damage, whether material or moral, caused by the internationally wrongful act of a State.*"

The above provision confirms the statement of the Permanent Court of International *Justice in its Judgment of 1927 in the Factory at Chorzów Case* (*Jurisdiction*), that:

> "*It is a principle of international law that the breach of an engagement involves an obligation to make reparation in an adequate form. Reparation*

① *Ibíd.*, pp. 197-198, para. 151.

② See more details, CRAWFORD, *op. cit.* pp. 198-200.

therefore is the indispensable complement of a failure to apply a convention and there is no necessity for this to be stated in the convention itself. Differences relating to reparations, which may be due by reason of failure to apply a convention, are consequently differences relating to its application." ①

However, under the principle set out in Article 12 of the Rules, the duty of reparation relates to breaches of any international obligation of a State, whatever the nature of the primary obligation in question is. As such, it is not confined to breaches of conventional obligations alone.

A general obligation of "full reparation" ("*réparation intégrale*" in French) in the sense of Articles 31 and 34 applies both to material and moral damages. As already stated in the above cited part of the *1928 Judgment on the Factory at Chorzów Case*: "reparation must, as far as possible, wipe out all the consequences of the illegal act and reestablish the situation which would, in all probability, have existed if that act had not been committed."

Yet this far-reaching obligation has two important limits. First, as already said, it does not relate to "indirect damage" in case that the causal link between it and direct damage is too remote. Besides, this duty has nothing of the punitive character in the legal relations between sovereign States. Its objective is not to punish or humiliate the wrongdoing State, but only to ensure "full reparation" of the injury caused. ②

The forms of reparation are provided in Article 34, which in this respect is of a limitative character:

"*Full reparation for the injury caused by the internationally wrongful act shall take the form of restitution, compensation and satisfaction, either singly or in combination, in accordance with the provisions of this Chapter.*"

---

① P. C. I. J., *Series A. — No. 9*, p. 21.

② Only perpetrators of international crimes in the competence of the ICC can bear criminal responsibility for their acts in their personal capacity.

Besides restitution, compensation and satisfaction, or a combination of them, general international law does not recognize any other form of reparation. Here are short comments on each of these forms.

(i) *Restitution.* Article 35 provides:

> "*A State responsible for an internationally wrongful act is under an obligation to make restitution, that is, to re-establish the situation which existed before the wrongful act was committed, provided and to the extent that restitution*
>
> *(a) is materially impossible;*
>
> *(b) does not involve a burden out of all proportion to the benefit deriving from restitution instead of compensation.*"

Invoking the statement from the *1928 Judgment in the Factory at Chorzów Case*, the ICJ, in its *2004 Advisory Opinion on Israeli Wall*, concluded the following: "Israel is accordingly under an obligation to return the land, orchards, olive groves and other immovable property seized from any natural or legal person for purposes of construction of the wall in the Occupied Palestinian Territory."①

If an internationally wrongful act consists in a law or a decision of administrative organs, the responsible State is under obligation to repeal such acts. The obligation falls to the wrongdoing State itself, because no international agency can replace it in this capacity. However, in case that the executive power in a State cannot revoke a final decision of its independent judiciary, compensation will take place under Article 36, because restitution remains impossible.

In the *2004 Advisory Opinion*, the Court stressed the obligation of Israel to repeal its legislative and regulatory acts, "except in so far as such acts, by providing compensation or other form of reparation for the Palestinian population, may continue to be relevant" for compliance by Israel with its obligations to repair these acts.

In some situations of material damage its full reparation is possible simply by

① *I.C.J. Reports 2004*, p. 198, para. 153.

returning unlawfully seized property to its legal owners, or in building or repairing objects that were destroyed or damaged.

However, as provided in Article 35, in some other situations restitution becomes materially impossible, if an unlawful State act or judicial decision produced irreparable consequences, or if restitution should involve "a burden out of all proportion to the benefit deriving from restitution instead of compensation".

In this second case it is a matter of balance of the competing interests, which should normally be in favour of the injured State or persons. However, restitution could jeopardize political or economic stability of the wrongdoing State, too, and that should also be taken into account. ①

(ii) *Compensation.* Although restitution has priority on the level of principle, because of frequent cases of its impracticability, pecuniary compensation is the most frequent form of reparations in practice. ②

Sometimes, an injured State can find its own interest in compensation instead of restitution. Or an arbitral compromise can authorize the arbitrator to decide on the most adequate form of reparation, which he can find in compensation.

Article 36 of the Rules states:

"1. The State responsible for an internationally wrongful act is under an obligation to compensate for the damage caused thereby, insofar as such damage is not made good by restitution.

2. The compensation shall cover any financially assessable damage

---

① See CRAWFORD, *op. cit.* pp. 216-217. For the rest, Paragraph (c) of Article 43 of the former *Draft Articles* that the International Law Commission adopted in the first reading in 1996, expressly provided an exception from the rule of "restitution in kind". Restitution was not applicable if it would "seriously jeopardize the political independence or economic stability of the State which has committed the internationally wrongful act, whereas the injured State would not be similarly affected if it did not obtain restitution in kind". It was, nevertheless, provided that this exception should not apply to a State responsible for an international crime (Article 52(a)).

② Only exceptionally is compensation not of pecuniary character. For instance, in case of some objects of art destroyed or lost, the responsible State can compensate them with similar artifacts of comparable value.

The first Paragraph above applies to both material and moral damage. Satisfaction can be provided for a material damage that is not financially assessable, or in combination with restitution or compensation. Nevertheless, satisfaction is mostly used as a form of reparation of moral, i. e. non-pecuniary damage.

The modalities of satisfaction in Paragraph 2 are not limitative. Assurances or guarantees of non-repetition may also be a form of satisfaction.

Other possibilities can be: establishment of a trust fund to manage compensation payment in the interest of beneficiaries; disciplinary or penal action against persons who committed an act for which the State bears responsibility; or the award of a symbolic sum for non-pecuniary injury (formerly one French franc). ①

Whatever the modality at stake, it is subject to the requirements from Paragraph 3 of Article 37. In particular, these forms of satisfaction cannot be of a humiliating character, as was the practice of the European Powers throughout the 19th century.

*

Finally, in some situations the wrongdoing State is not solely responsible for an internationally wrongful act. That should be taken into account in the determination of reparation. Hence, Article 39 entitled "Contribution to the injury" provides that:

> "*In the determination of reparation, account shall be taken of the contribution to the injury by willful or neglected action or commission of the injured State or any person or entity in relation to whom reparation is sought.*"

The injured State, as well as other victims of a wrongful act can contribute to it either by their acts or passivity in situations that call for action. All these elements should be taken into account in determining the mode of reparation, including the amount of compensation, if any.

*

(d) *Serious breaches of obligations under peremptory norms of general international law.* A lot was already said in Chapters IV and V above about the concept of international crimes committed by States, as well as about its replacement

---

① See CRAWFORD, *op. cit.* pp. 232-233.

in the final text of the *Rules on State Responsibility* by "serious breaches" of obligations under *jus cogens*.

Although this new concept has many disadvantages, it must be admitted that the International Law Commission was unable to ascertain itself particular legal consequences for a State committing such acts in both sets of rules it proposed. What was possible to do was only to provide specific *erga omnes* obligations of third States in respect of these acts of the responsible State.

In this respect Article 41 of the *2001 Rules provides* "Particular consequences of a serious breach of an obligation under this Chapter":

> "*1. States shall co-operate to bring to an end through lawful means any serious breach within the meaning of Article 40.*
>
> *2. No State shall recognize as lawful a situation created by a serious breach within the meaning of Article 40, nor render aid or assistance in maintaining that situation.*
>
> *3. This Article is without prejudice to the other consequences referred to in this Part and to such further consequences that a breach to which this Chapter applies may entail under international law.*"

The duty of co-operation referred to in Paragraph 1 above, seems to be an aim, rather than a precise *erga omnes* obligation of legal character. States which are friendly to the perpetrating State will rather passively watch such an act and its consequences, than endeavor to bring it to an end.

It seems to be different with the duty of non-recognition as referred to in Paragraph 2 above. There is a lot of proof that all or most States did never recognize an unlawful situation, such as the unilateral annexation of East Jerusalem by Israel, or the creation of the "Turkish Republic of Northern Cyprus" resulting from the Turkish occupation of that part of the Cypriot territory. [1]

Finally, Paragraph 3 of Article 41 is a saving clause from which follow that

---

[1] Hence, the *2004 Advisory Opinion of the ICJ on Israeli Wall* orders that: "All States are under an obligation not to recognize the illegal situation resulting from the construction of the wall and not to render aid or assistance in maintaining the situation created by such a construction." *Cf, I. C. J. Reports* 2004, p. 202, para. 163-(3)-(D).

serious breaches of obligations of *jus cogens* entail consequences of commission of all other internationally wrongful acts. Among others, they are the duty of cessation and non-repetition, assurances and guarantees, and the duty of the responsible State of full reparation for such an act. Further consequences can be established by a future legal regime applicable to these situations.

(e) *Procedure.* There is a provision in Chapter I of Part III of the Rules that strictly speaking does not consist in a legal obligation, but is nevertheless useful in practice. Article 43 concerning "Notice of claim by an injured State" provides:

> "*1. An injured State which invokes the responsibility of another States shall give notice of its claim to that State.*
>
> *2. The injured State may specify in particular:*
>
> *(a) the conduct that the responsible State should take in order to cease the wrongful act, if it is continuing;*
>
> *(b) what form of reparation should take in accordance with the provisions of Part Two.*"

Such a notice in written is in the interest of the protection of the rights of the supposedly injured State. The content of Paragraph 2 is also important, at least as a basis of future negotiations. The form of reparation claimed can consist, as already explained, either in restitution, or compensation, or satisfaction.

However, it must be stressed that the alleged injured State does not acquire any right on the basis of its unilateral notice. The other State at stake can deny the very existence of the internationally wrongful act in question, or can decline its responsibility in case it admits its existence.

Nevertheless, the content of that notice can be useful as a basis for direct negotiations between the respective States on all the issues alleged, and perhaps for their agreement on the solution, or for their joint decision to bring their dispute before an impartial body for the final settlement.

*

Article 45 of the Rules relates to "Loss of the right to invoke responsibility":

> "*The responsibility of a State may not be invoked if:*
>
> *(a) the injured State has validly waived the claim;*

(b) the injured State is to be considered as having, by reason of its conduct, validly acquiesced in the lapse of the claim."

There was a short explanation of these two situations in Chapter Ⅲ above.

Waiver, i.e. renunciation of the claim, can be part of an agreement with other interested State, but can also consist in a unilateral act. Its written form is not necessary, but it must be explicit and reach the other interested party in order to produce legal effects.

For the rest, a waiver can be invalidated for the same reasons as a treaty. This is in case of error in it, fraud by its other party, corruption of a representative of the State to waive the claim, or coercion. For this reason the injured State must "validly" waive its claim. ①

On the other hand, acquiescence takes place in the absence of raising the claim by the injured State. Hence, its silence in a longer lapse of time, in situation that calls for an action on its side, can be implied as its tacit waiver of its legitimate claim by acquiescence. ②

V. Countermeasures

The wrongfulness of an act that is otherwise not in conformity with a legal obligation towards another State, is precluded "if and to the extent that the act constitutes a countermeasure taken against the latter State in accordance with Chapter Ⅱ of Part Three" (Article 22 of the Rules). Hence, a wrongful act of another State can be a circumstance legalizing countermeasures against that State, which would in other circumstances constitute an internationally wrongful act.

Countermeasures, or formerly "reprisals in time of peace", served throughout the 19th century as the pretext for acts of forcible intervention by the European powers against weaker States. That was in pursuit of their imperialist policy. However, the *Arbitral Award of 1928 in Naulilaa Case* (*Germany/Portugal*),

① See a more comprehensive explanation of waiver — V. D. DEGAN: *Sources of International Law*, The Hague 1997, pp. 316-325.

② *Ibid.* pp. 348-354.

established a definition of legitimate reprisals and prescribed restrictive conditions for their lawful use. ① Since then, the doctrine has almost unanimously adopted these statements as reflecting customary rules of general international law. That did not, however, prevent many international crimes committed as alleged "reprisals" during World War Ⅱ, and in the conflicts that occurred after it.

To countermeasures as a mode of self-help is attributed an important place in the *Rules on State Responsibility*. This is not without reason. Because sovereign States cannot be sued by or before any international courts or tribunals without their agreement, an injured State would otherwise be deprived even of the opportunity to react against the infringements of its rights.

The *Draft Articles* as proposed in 1996 provided rules on the settlement of disputes between the parties to the future convention, to be concluded on this subject-matter in a diplomatic conference. They included rules on obligatory negotiations, and in case of their failure, of mediation. Arbitration was provided only if all disputing parties agreed to it. However, a State against which countermeasures were taken would have the right unilaterally to set the arbitral procedure in motion in respect of the legality of these measures directed against it.

After the International Law Commission renounced from its goal to prepare a basic draft for a future diplomatic conference, it provided the rules on countermeasures that are better formulated than in its previous text.

However, when any type of measures of self-help is at stake, including legitimate self-defence in case of an armed aggression, one should never overlook the warning by the International Court of Justice in its *1949 Judgment in the Corfu Channel Case between the United Kingdom and Albania*:

---

① It was there stated: "Reprisals are an act of self-help of the injured State, in retaliation of an unredressed act of the offending State contrary to international law... They are limited by the rules of humanity and good faith... They would be illegal unless a previous act in violation of international law has furnished the justification. They tend to impose on the offending State reparation for the offence or the return to legality and avoidance of new offenses." *Cf.*, *Reports of International Arbitral Awards*, vol. II, p. 1026. Furthermore: "Reprisals are not licit except when they have been preceded by a request for redress which has been unavailing." Finally, "one must certainly consider as excessive, and consequently illicit, reprisals out of all proportions to the act which has motivated them." *Ibid.* pp,1027-1028.

"The Court can only regard the alleged right of intervention as the manifestation of a policy of force, such as has in the past, given rise to most serious abuses and such as cannot, whatever be the present defects in international organization, find a place in international law. Intervention is perhaps still less admissible in the particular form it would take here; for, from the nature of things, it would be reserved for the most powerful States, and might easily lead to perverting the administration of international justice itself." ①

All provisions on countermeasures as set out in Articles 49 to 54 of the Rules prescribe conditions or restrictions to a State when undertaking these unilateral measures. In addition, they prohibit specific acts in their exercise. This is done with a view to avoiding grave abuses of countermeasures themselves, or of their unlawful and inhumane consequences.

These provisions embody restrictions from the *Naulilaa* case. They develop them further on in light of Article 2(4) of the *UN Charter* prohibiting any threat or use of force and of conventions on the protection of human rights and of humanitarian law applicable in armed conflicts. It is now generally understood that the essential provisions from these general conventions reflect customary rules of international law.

As usual, it is the best way to quote these provisions as set out, and add short comments on each of them.

(i) *Object and limits of countermeasures.* Article 49 provides:

"1. An injured State may only take countermeasures against a State which is responsible for an internationally wrongful act in order to induce that State to comply with its obligations under Part II.

2. Countermeasures are limited to the non performance for the time

① *I. C. J. Reports 1949*, p. 35. In that particular case the British intervention in form of self-help consisted only in a minesweeping operation and collection of evidence. According to the Court it constituted a violation of the sovereignty of Albania in its territorial waters. That intervention occurred after the deaths of 44 and personal injuries to 42 British officers and men during the innocent passage of two British warships through that Channel in October 1946.

being of international obligations of the State taking the measures towards the responsible State.

3. Countermeasures shall, as far as possible, be taken in such a way as to permit the resumption of performance of the obligations in question."

This provision embodies the limits set in the *Naulilaa* case. By their nature, countermeasures are strictly of temporary or provisional character. Their aim is to restore conditions of legality between the injured State and the responsible State, and to insure the reparation of the injury caused. If they have some other goals, they do not constitute legitimate countermeasures. In any case they must not involve measures of punishment of the wrongdoing State.

Paragraph 3 has special importance. If the injured State has a choice between equally lawful and efficient measures, it should adopt the one which permits the resumption of performance of the obligations suspended by countermeasures.

(ii) *Obligations not affected by countermeasures.* Article 50 is of a complex nature. Its Paragraph 1 deals with certain obligations which, being norms of *jus cogens*, are above the right to countermeasures. Paragraph 2 deals with the obligations relating in particular to the maintenance of channels of communications between the interested States. This entire Article reads as follows:

"*1. Countermeasures shall not affect*:

(*a*) *the obligation to refrain from the threat or use of force as embodied in the Charter of the United Nations*;

(*b*) *obligations for the protection of fundamental human rights*;

(*c*) *obligations of a humanitarian character prohibiting reprisals*;

(*d*) *other obligations under peremptory norms of general international law.*

2. A State taking countermeasures is not relieved from fulfilling its obligations:

(*a*) *under any dispute settlement procedure applicable between it and the responsible State*;

(*b*) *to respect the inviolability of diplomatic and consular agents, premises, archives and documents.*"

First, let us deal with the far-reaching restrictions from Paragraph 1.

(a) According to Paragraph 1(a), any countermeasures i. e. reprisals consisting in the use of armed force have been outlawed on behalf of Article 2(4) of the *UN Charter*. As provided in Article 49(2) above, legitimate countermeasures in time of peace are limited to the non-performance, for the time being, of international obligations of the State taking them towards the responsible State, and nothing more.

(b) Average citizens in a wrongdoing State usually bear no responsibility for the unlawful acts of their government. Therefore, even in extending political and economic pressure, the target of these measures should be the government élite, to impel them to conform to international law, rather than to punish other citizens as their collateral victims. Gross violations of human rights could result in international crimes which, as retaliatory measures, are prohibited even in armed conflicts.

(c) The four *Geneva Conventions* of 1949, as well as the *1977 Protocol I* to them, provide many explicit rules prohibiting reprisals in armed conflicts against "protected persons", i. e. civilian population, wounded, sick and shipwrecked persons, as well as against medical personnel, buildings, installations and ships.

To these rules explicitly prohibiting reprisals should be added all the provisions concerning "grave breaches" of these conventions. These acts constitute international crimes either in international or in internal armed conflicts. Hence, all these deeds must also not be undertaken as acts of legitimate countermeasures, even in retaliation to the same crimes committed by the hostile party.

Most of the States are today parties to the *Geneva Conventions* and their *Protocol* and they are bound to respect them as their treaty obligations. However, their essential rules are also applicable to non-parties to these conventions, having already been transformed into customary rules of general international law.

(d) The above far-reaching legal obligations are not of a limitative character. Other obligations of *jus cogens* are of the *erga omnes* effect and as such they are binding on all States as well. Hence, if under Article 53 of the *1969 Vienna Convention* States are precluded from entering into treaties that are not in conformity with the peremptory norms of general international law, these norms of *jus cogens* cannot be unilaterally derogated by a State in the form of its countermeasures.

However, the countermeasures can be excluded altogether on behalf of *lex specialis*, as confirmed in Article 55 of the Rules. That is the case when a treaty provides as a replacement its own system of enforcement. This is the case with the Treaties on European Union, and with the dispute settlement procedure within the World Trade Organization.

Paragraph 2(a) of Article 50, which is of a different scope, does not allow a State to take its act of countermeasures as a pretext for refusing dispute settlement procedures with the alleged responsible State. Hence, if the respective States have previously agreed on the procedures of mediation, arbitration or judicial settlement, all these procedures should be used in order to settle the dispute, and to put countermeasures to their end. Nevertheless, these procedures are obligatory only in this context, in respect of the dispute in question, and not of other unrelated issues between the States concerned.

Furthermore, Paragraph 2(b) forbids countermeasures against diplomatic and consular agents, premises, archives and documents. Unlawful acts of this kind are prohibited by the rules of *jus cogens*. Depending on the circumstances, other measures are not prohibited, including the termination or suspension of diplomatic relations, recall of ambassador, or measures temporarily affecting diplomatic or consular privileges, if all other requirements of legitimate countermeasures were met.

(iii) *Proportionality*. The short text of Article 51 reads as follows:

> "*Countermeasures must be commensurate with the injury suffered, taking into account the gravity of the internationally wrongful act and the rights in question.*"

The requirement of proportionality is a safeguard against abuses, not only of countermeasures but also of self-defence or of any other measures of self-help. ① It prevents that incidents of minor importance serve as a pretext for unilateral measures

① In this respect see a critical review of the *2004 Advisory Opinion of the ICJ* by late British scholar Sir Arthur Watts: "Physical Barriers to Armed Infiltration: Self-defence and Israel's Wall in the Occupied Palestinian Territory", in V. CRNIĆ-GROTIĆ, M. MATULOVIĆ(Ed): *International Law and the Use of Force at the Turn of Centuries*, Essays in honour of V. D. Degan, Rijeka 2005, pp. 239-253. In the view of this author, the construction of that wall was not in accordance with the requirement of necessity (and, it would seem, proportionality), "which is required for a lawful exercise of the right is 'strict and objective' and allows the State concerned 'no room for any 'measure of discretion'. This is a salutary reminder to States that their relations are based upon an objectively applied legal order rather than upon their own, possibly self-serving, assessment of their rights and obligations".

by a powerful "injured State", out of all proportions to the act which has motivated them. Such kinds of measures are excessive, and consequently unlawful.

In reality, the assessment of proportionality is not an easy task in concrete situations. This requirement also excludes punitive character of countermeasures.

(iv) *Conditions relating to resort to countermeasures.* In addition Article 52 provides precise procedural conditions in taking lawful countermeasures. Some of them were already embodied in the *Arbitral Award on Naulilaa Case.* This complex provision reads as follows:

> "*1. Before taking countermeasures, an injured State shall:*
>
> *(a) call on the responsible State, in accordance with Article 43, to fulfil its obligations under Part II;*
>
> *(b) notify the responsible State of any decision to take countermeasures and offer to negotiate with that State.*
>
> *2. Notwithstanding paragraph 1(b), the injured State may take such urgent countermeasures as are necessary to preserve its rights.*
>
> *3. Countermeasures may not be taken, and if already taken must be suspended without undue delay if:*
>
> *(a) the internationally wrongful act has ceased, and*
>
> *(b) the dispute is pending before a court or tribunal which has the authority to make decisions binding on the parties.*
>
> *4. Paragraph 3 does not apply if the responsible State fails to implement the dispute settlement procedure in good faith.*"

In respect of the requirement under Paragraph 1 above, having in mind harsh consequences that countermeasures could have for the targeted State, there is a legal duty to previously call on the responsible State to conform to its obligations under international law. Unlike the notice of claim in other situations as referred in Article 43 above, there is a legal duty of the injured State taking countermeasures to notify the responsible State of its decision, which must be accompanied with an offer of fresh negotiations with it.

This, however, does not exclude urgent countermeasures under Paragraph 2 in order to preserve the rights of the injured State. One of the legitimate countermeasures is freezing the assets of the responsible State in the banks of the injured State. In case of a prior notification, the responsible State would have enough time to withdraw these assets, and the countermeasures would lose their purpose.

According to Paragraph 3 countermeasures may not be taken, and if already taken they must be suspended without undue delay, if the internationally wrongful act has ceased and the dispute is pending before a court or tribunal.

Paragraphs 3 and 4 should be read together. An alleged responsible State that submits itself to an arbitral or judicial procedure which comprises a final obligatory judgment, exempts itself from the countermeasures altogether. That is because it may request from such an organ to order provisional measures pending final decision. In such a situation countermeasures lose their purpose. This requirement does not include referring the case to a political organ such as the UN Security Council, nor to a tribunal with the jurisdiction between a private person and the responsible State.

On the other hand, the right to forestall countermeasures is not enjoyed by a responsible State that frustrates the arbitral or judicial procedure in any of its phases, as provided in Paragraph 4. This can involve its non-appearance before the tribunal, or its non-compliance with the order on provisional measures, or its refusal to accept or to carry out the final judgment.

(v) *Termination of countermeasures.* Article 53 orders:

> "*Countermeasures shall be terminated as soon as the responsible State has complied with its obligations under Part II in relation to the internationally wrongful act.*"

This not only embraces cessation of the unlawful act, but also the reparation of its consequences. In such a case, countermeasures lose their purpose.

(vi) *Measures taken by States other than an injured State.* It is a matter here of a saving clause that does however not relate to institutional reactions against some unlawful acts, such as under Chapter VII of the *UN Charter.* Article 54 reads:

> "*This Chapter does not prejudice the right of any State, entitled under Article 48, paragraph 1 to invoke the responsibility of another State, to take lawful measures against that State to ensure cessation of the breach and reparation in the interest of the injured State or of the beneficiaries of*

the obligation breached."

It is to be noticed that Article 54 speaks of "lawful measures" and not of countermeasures in the context of other Articles referred to above. It was a hard rule in classical international law that the rights to take countermeasures belonged only to the injured State, victim of infringements of its own rights. Unlike the right to collective self-defence, there was then nothing similar to the right of "collective countermeasures".

The situation developed by the affirmation of the concept of *erga omnes* obligations of all States towards the international community as a whole. Article 54 does not offer a clear answer to these situations.

Nevertheless, the resolution adopted by the Institute of International Law in 2005 on "Obligations *erga omnes* in international law", in its Article 5 (c) provides: "Should a widely acknowledged grave breach of an *erga omnes* obligation occur, all the States to which the obligation is owed:... (c) are entitled to take non-forcible counter-measures under conditions analogous to those applying to a State specially affected by the breach."

This problem is still unclear in positive international law.

Selected Documents

Ⅰ. *Charter of the United Nations (As Amended) (1945)*

We, the Peoples of the United Nations, Determined

to save succeeding generations from the scourge of war, which twice in our lifetime has brought untold sorrow to mankind, and

to reaffirm faith in fundamental human rights, in the dignity and worth of the human person, in the equal rights of men and women and of nations large and small, and

to establish conditions under which justice and respect for the obligations arising from treaties and other sources of international law can be maintained, and

to promote social progress and better standards of life in larger freedom,

And For These Ends

to practice tolerance and live together in peace with one another as good neighbours, and

to unite our strength to maintain international peace and security, and

to ensure, by the acceptance of principles and the institution of methods, that armed force shall not be used, save in the common interest, and

to employ international machinery for the promotion of the economic and social advancement of all peoples,

Have Resolved to Combine Our Efforts to Accomplish These Aims

Accordingly, our respective Governments, through representatives assembled in the city of San Francisco, who have exhibited their full powers found to be in good and due form, have agreed to the present *Charter of the United Nations* and do hereby establish an international organization to be known as the United Nations.

Chapter I Purposes and Principles

Article 1

The Purposes of the United Nations are:

1. to maintain international peace and security, and to that end: to take effective collective measures for the prevention and removal of threats to the peace, and for the suppression of acts of aggression or other breaches of the peace, and to bring about by peaceful means, and in conformity with the principles of justice and international law, adjustment or settlement of international disputes or situations which might lead to a breach of the peace;

2. to develop friendly relations among nations based on respect for the principle of equal rights and selfdetermination of peoples, and to take other appropriate measures to strengthen universal peace;

3. to achieve international co-operation in solving international problems of an economic, social, cultural, or humanitarian character, and in promoting and encouraging respect for human rights and for fundamental freedoms for all without distinction as to race, sex, language, or religion; and

4. to be a centre for harmonizing the actions of nations in the attainment of these common ends.

Article 2

The Organization and its Members, in pursuit of the Purposes stated in Article 1, shall act in accordance with the following Principles:

1. The Organization is based on the principle of the sovereign equality of all its Members.

2. All Members, in order to ensure to all of them the rights and benefits resulting from membership, shall fulfill in good faith the obligations assumed by them in accordance with the present *Charter*.

3. All Members shall settle their international disputes by peaceful means in such a manner that international peace and security, and justice, are not endangered.

4. All Members shall refrain in their international relations from the threat or use of force against the territorial integrity or political independence of any State, or in any other manner inconsistent with the Purposes of the United Nations.

Article 11

1. The General Assembly may consider the general principles of co-operation in the maintenance of international peace and security, including the principles governing disarmament and the regulation of armaments, and may make recommendations with regard to such principles to the Members or to the Security Council or to both.

2. The General Assembly may discuss any questions relating to the maintenance of international peace and security brought before it by any Member of the United Nations, or by the Security Council, or by a State which is not a Member of the United Nations in accordance with Article 35, paragraph 2, and, except as provided in Article 12, may make recommendations with regard to any such questions to the State or States concerned or to the Security Council or to both. Any such question on which action is necessary shall be referred to the Security Council by the General Assembly either before or after discussion.

3. The General Assembly may call the attention of the Security Council to situations which are likely to endanger international peace and security.

4. The powers of the General Assembly set forth in this Article shall not limit the general scope of Article 10.

Article 12

1. While the Security Council is exercising in respect of any dispute or situation the functions assigned to it in the present *Charter*, the General Assembly shall not make any recommendation with regard to that dispute or situation unless the Security Council so requests.

2. The Secretary-General, with the consent of the Security Council, shall notify the General Assembly at each session of any matters relative to the maintenance of international peace and security which are being dealt with by the Security Council and shall similarly notify the General Assembly, or the Members of the United Nations if the General Assembly is not in session, immediately the Security Council ceases to deal with such matters.

Article 13

1. The General Assembly shall initiate studies and make recommendations for

the purpose of:

(a) promoting international co-operation in the political field and encouraging the progressive development of international law and its codification;

(b) promoting international co-operation in the economic, social, cultural, educational, and health fields, and assisting in the realization of human rights and fundamental freedoms for all without distinction as to race, sex, language, or religion.

2. The further responsibilities, functions and powers of the General Assembly with respect to matters mentioned in Paragraph 1 (b) above are set forth in Chapters IX and X.

Article 14

Subject to the provisions of Article 12, the General Assembly may recommend measures for the peaceful adjustment of any situation, regardless of origin, which it deems likely to impair the general welfare or friendly relations among nations, including situations resulting from a violation of the provisions of the present *Charter* setting forth the Purposes and Principles of the United Nations.

Article 15

1. The General Assembly shall receive and consider annual and special reports from the Security Council; these reports shall include an account of the measures that the Security Council has decided upon or taken to maintain international peace and security.

2. The General Assembly shall receive and consider reports from the other organs of the United Nations.

Article 16

The General Assembly shall perform such functions with respect to the international trusteeship system as are assigned to it under Chapters XII and XIII, including the approval of the trusteeship agreements for areas not designated as strategic.

3. Each member of the Security Council shall have one representative.

Functions and Powers

Article 24

1. In order to ensure prompt and effective action by the United Nations, its Members confer on the Security Council primary responsibility for the maintenance of international peace and security, and agree that in carrying out its duties under this responsibility the Security Council acts on their behalf.

2. In discharging these duties the Security Council shall act in accordance with the Purposes and Principles of the United Nations. The specific powers granted to the Security Council for the discharge of these duties are laid down in Chapters VI, VII, VIII, and XII.

3. The Security Council shall submit annual and, when necessary, special reports to the General Assembly for its consideration.

Article 25

The Members of the United Nations agree to accept and carry out the decisions of the Security Council in accordance with the present *Charter*.

Article 26

In order to promote the establishment and maintenance of international peace and security with the least diversion for armaments of the world's human and economic resources, the Security Council shall be responsible for formulating, with the assistance of the Military Staff Committee referred to in Article 47, plans to be submitted to the Members of the United Nations for the establishment of a system for the regulation of armaments.

Voting

Article 27

1. Each member of the Security Council shall have one vote.

2. Decisions of the Security Council on procedural matters shall be made by an affirmative vote of nine members.

3. Decisions of the Security Council on all other matters shall be made by an affirmative vote of nine members including the concurring votes of the permanent

members; provided that, in decisions under Chapter VI, and under Paragraph 3 of Article 52, a party to a dispute shall abstain from voting.

Procedure

Article 28

1. The Security Council shall be so organized as to be able to function continuously. Each member of the Security Council shall for this purpose be represented at all times at the seat of the Organization.

2. The Security Council shall hold periodic meetings at which each of its members may, if it so desires, be represented by a member of the government or by some other specially designated representative.

3. The Security Council may hold meetings at such places other than the seat of the Organization as in its judgment will best facilitate its work.

Article 29

The Security Council may establish such subsidiary organs as it deems necessary for the performance of its functions.

Article 30

The Security Council shall adopt its own rules of procedure, including the method of selecting its President.

Article 31

Any Member of the United Nations which is not a member of the Security Council may participate, without vote, in the discussion of any question brought before the Security Council whenever the latter considers that the interests of that Member are specially affected.

Article 32

Any Member of the United Nations which is not a member of the Security Council or any State which is not a Member of the United Nations, if it is a party to a dispute under consideration by the Security Council, shall be invited to participate, without vote, in the discussion relating to the dispute. The Security Council shall lay down such conditions as it deems just for the participation of a State which is not a

Article 41

The Security Council may decide what measures not involving the use of armed force are to be employed to give effect to its decisions, and it may call upon the Members of the United Nations to apply such measures. These may include complete or partial interruption of economic relations and of rail, sea, air, postal, telegraphic, radio, and other means of communication, and the severance of diplomatic relations.

Article 42

Should the Security Council consider that measures provided for in Article 41 would be inadequate or have proved to be inadequate, it may take such action by air, sea, or land forces as may be necessary to maintain or restore international peace and security. Such action may include demonstrations, blockade, and other operations by air, sea, or land forces of Members of the United Nations.

Article 43

1. All Members of the United Nations, in order to contribute to the maintenance of international peace and security, undertake to make available to the Security Council, on its call and in accordance with a special agreement or agreements, armed forces, assistance, and facilities, including rights of passage, necessary for the purpose of maintaining international peace and security.

2. Such agreement or agreements shall govern the numbers and types of forces, their degree of readiness and general location, and the nature of the facilities and assistance to be provided.

3. The agreement or agreements shall be negotiated as soon as possible on the initiative of the Security Council. They shall be concluded between the Security Council and Members or between the Security Council and groups of Members and shall be subject to ratification by the signatory States in accordance with their respective constitutional processes.

Article 44

When the Security Council has decided to use force it shall, before calling upon a Member not represented on it to provide armed forces in fulfilment of the obligations assumed under Article 43, invite that Member, if the Member so desires, to participate in the decisions of the Security Council concerning the employment of contingents of that Member's armed forces.

Article 45

In order to enable the United Nations to take urgent military measures, Members shall hold immediately available national air-force contingents for combined international enforcement action. The strength and degree of readiness of these contingents and plans for their combined action shall be determined within the limits laid down in the special agreement or agreements referred to in Article 43, by the Security Council with the assistance of the Military Staff Committee.

Article 46

Plans for the application of armed force shall be made by the Security Council with the assistance of the Military Staff Committee.

Article 47

1. There shall be established a Military Staff Committee to advise and assist the Security Council on all questions relating to the Security Council's military requirements for the maintenance of international peace and security, the employment and command of forces placed at its disposal, the regulation of armaments, and possible disarmament.

2. The Military Staff Committee shall consist of the Chiefs of Staff of the permanent members of the Security Council or their representatives. Any Member of the United Nations not permanently represented on the Committee shall be invited by the Committee to be associated with it when the efficient discharge of the Committee's responsibilities requires the participation of that Member in its work.

3. The Military Staff Committee shall be responsible under the Security Council for the strategic direction of any armed forces placed at the disposal of the Security Council. Questions relating to the command of such forces shall be worked out subsequently.

4. The Military Staff Committee, with the authorization of the Security Council and after consultation with appropriate regional agencies, may establish regional sub-committees.

principle of equal rights and self-determination of peoples, the United Nations shall promote:

a. higher standards of living, full employment, and conditions of economic and social progress and development;

b. solutions of international economic, social, health, and related problems; and international cultural and educational cooperation; and

c. universal respect for, and observance of, human rights and fundamental freedoms for all without distinction as to race, sex, language, or religion.

Article 56

All Members pledge themselves to take joint and separate action in co-operation with the Organization for the achievement of the purposes set forth in Article 55.

Article 57

1. The various specialized agencies, established by intergovernmental agreement and having wide international responsibilities, as defined in their basic instruments, in economic, social, cultural, educational, health, and related fields, shall be brought into relationship with the United Nations in accordance with the provisions of Article 63.

2. Such agencies thus brought into relationship with the United Nations are hereinafter referred to as specialized agencies.

Article 58

The Organization shall make recommendations for the co-ordination of the policies and activities of the specialized agencies.

Article 59

The Organization shall, where appropriate, initiate negotiations among the States concerned for the creation of any new specialized agencies required for the accomplishment of the purposes set forth in Article 55.

Article 60

Responsibility for the discharge of the functions of the Organization set forth in this Chapter shall be vested in the General Assembly and, under the authority of the

General Assembly, in the Economic and Social Council, which shall have for this purpose the powers set forth in Chapter X.

Chapter X The Economic and Social Council

Composition

Article 61

1. The Economic and Social Council shall consist of fifty-four Members of the United Nations elected by the General Assembly.

2. Subject to the provisions of paragraph 3, eighteen members of the Economic and Social Council shall be elected each year for a term of three years. A retiring member shall be eligible for immediate re-election.

3. At the first election after the increase in the membership of the Economic and Social Council from twenty-seven to fifty-four members, in addition to the members elected in place of the nine members whose term of office expires at the end of that year, twenty-seven additional members shall be elected. Of these twenty-seven additional members, the term of office of nine members so elected shall expire at the end of one year, and of nine other members at the end of two years, in accordance with arrangements made by the General Assembly.

4. Each member of the Economic and Social Council shall have one representative.

Functions and Powers

Article 62

1. The Economic and Social Council may make or initiate studies and reports with respect to international economic, social, cultural, educational, health, and related matters and may make recommendations with respect to any such matters to the General Assembly to the Members of the United Nations, and to the specialized agencies concerned.

2. It may make recommendations for the purpose of promoting respect for, and observance of, human rights and fundamental freedoms for all.

3. It may prepare draft conventions for submission to the General Assembly, with respect to matters falling within its competence.

4. It may call, in accordance with the rules prescribed by the United Nations, international conferences on matters falling within its competence.

Article 63

1. The Economic and Social Council may enter into agreements with any of the agencies referred to in Article 57, defining the terms on which the agency concerned shall be brought into relationship with the United Nations. Such agreements shall be subject to approval by the General Assembly.

2. It may co-ordinate the activities of the specialized agencies through consultation with and recommendations to such agencies and through recommendations to the General Assembly and to the Members of the United Nations.

Article 64

1. The Economic and Social Council may take appropriate steps to obtain regular reports from the specialized agencies. It may make arrangements with the Members of the United Nations and with the specialized agencies to obtain reports on the steps taken to give effect to its own recommendations and to recommendations on matters falling within its competence made by the General Assembly.

2. It may communicate its observations on these reports to the General Assembly.

Article 65

The Economic and Social Council may furnish information to the Security Council and shall assist the Security Council upon its request.

Article 66

1. The Economic and Social Council shall perform such functions as fall within its competence in connexion with the carrying out of the recommendations of the General Assembly.

2. It may, with the approval of the General Assembly, perform services at the request of Members of the United Nations and at the request of specialized agencies.

3. It shall perform such other functions as are specified elsewhere in the present *Charter* or as may be assigned to it by the General Assembly.

Voting

Article 67

1. Each member of the Economic and Social Council shall have one vote.

2. Decisions of the Economic and Social Council shall be made by a majority of the members present and voting.

Procedure

Article 68

The Economic and Social Council shall set up commissions in economic and social fields and for the promotion of human rights, and such other commissions as may be required for the performance of its functions.

Article 69

The Economic and Social Council shall invite any Member of the United Nations to participate, without vote, in its deliberations on any matter of particular concern to that Member.

Article 70

The Economic and Social Council may make arrangements for representatives of the specialized agencies to participate, without vote, in its deliberations and in those of the commissions established by it, and for its representatives to participate in the deliberations of the specialized agencies.

Article 71

The Economic and Social Council may make suitable arrangements for consultation with non-governmental organizations which are concerned with matters within its competence. Such arrangements may be made with international organizations and, where appropriate, with national organizations after consultation with the Member of the United Nations concerned.

Article 72

1. The Economic and Social Council shall adopt its own rules of procedure, including the method of selecting its President.

2. The Economic and Social Council shall meet as required in accordance with its rules, which shall include provision for the convening of meetings on the request of a majority of its members.

Chapter XI Declaration Regarding Non-Self-Governing Territories

Article 73

Members of the United Nations which have or assume responsibilities for the administration of territories whose peoples have not yet attained a full measure of self-government recognize the principle that the interests of the inhabitants of these territories are paramount, and accept as a sacred trust the obligation to promote to the utmost, within the system of international peace and security established by the present *Charter*, the well-being of the inhabitants of these territories, and, to this end:

a. to ensure, with due respect for the culture of the peoples concerned, their political, economic, social, and educational advancement, their just treatment, and their protection against abuses;

b. to develop self-government, to take due account of the political aspirations of the peoples, and to assist them in the progressive development of their free political institutions, according to the particular circumstances of each territory and its peoples and their varying stages of advancement;

c. to further international peace and security;

d. to promote constructive measures of development, to encourage research, and to co-operate with one another and, when and where appropriate, with specialized international bodies with a view to the practical achievement of the social, economic, and scientific purposes set forth in this Article; and

e. to transmit regularly to the Secretary-General for information purposes, subject to such limitation as security and constitutional considerations may require, statistical and other information of a technical nature relating to economic, social, and educational conditions in the territories for which they are respectively responsible other than those territories to which Chapters XII and XIII apply.

Article 74

Members of the United Nations also agree that their policy in respect of the territories to which this Chapter applies, no less than in respect of their metropolitan areas, must be based on the general principle of good-neighbourliness, due account being taken of the interests and well-being of the rest of the world, in social, economic, and commercial matters.

Chapter XII International Trusteeship System

Article 75

The United Nations shall establish under its authority an international trusteeship system for the administration and supervision of such territories as may be placed thereunder by subsequent individual agreements. These territories are hereinafter referred to as trust territories.

Article 76

The basic objectives of the trusteeship system, in accordance with the Purposes of the United Nations laid down in Article 1 of the present *Charter*, shall be:

a. to further international peace and security;

b. to promote the political, economic, social, and educational advancement of the inhabitants of the trust territories, and their progressive development towards self-government or independence as may be appropriate to the particular circumstances of each territory and its peoples and the freely expressed wishes of the peoples concerned, and as may be provided by the terms of each trusteeship agreement;

c. to encourage respect for human rights and for fundamental freedoms for all without distinction as to race, sex, language, or religion, and to encourage recognition of the interdependence of the peoples of the world; and

d. to ensure equal treatment in social, economic, and commercial matters for all Members of the United Nations and their nationals, and also equal treatment for the latter in the administration of justice, without prejudice to the attainment of the foregoing objectives and subject to the provisions of Article 80.

Article 77

1. The trusteeship system shall apply to such territories in the following categories as may be placed thereunder by means of trusteeship agreements:

a. territories now held under mandate;

b. territories which may be detached from enemy States as a result of the Second World War; and

c. territories voluntarily placed under the system by States responsiblefor their administration.

2. It will be a matter for subsequent agreement as to which territories in the foregoing categories will be brought under the trusteeship system and upon what terms.

Article 78

The trusteeship system shall not apply to territories which have become Members of the United Nations, relationship among which shall be based on respect for the principle of sovereign equality.

Article 79

The terms of trusteeship for each territory to be placed under the trusteeship system, including any alteration or amendment, shall be agreed upon by the States directly concerned, including the mandatory power in the case of territories held under mandate by a Member of the United Nations, and shall be approved as provided for in Articles 83 and 85.

Article 80

1. Except as may be agreed upon in individual trusteeship agreements, made under Articles 77, 79, and 81, placing each territory under the trusteeship system, and until such agreements have been concluded, nothing in this Chapter shall be construed in or of itself to alter in any manner the rights whatsoever of any States or any peoples or the terms of existing international instruments to which Members of the United Nations may respectively be parties.

2. Paragraph 1 of this Article shall not be interpreted as giving grounds for delay or postponement of the negotiation and conclusion of agreements for placing mandated and other territories under the trusteeship system as provided for in Article 77.

Article 81

The trusteeship agreement shall in each case include the terms under which the trust territory will be administered and designate the authority which will exercise the administration of the trust territory. Such authority, hereinafter called the administering authority, may be one or more States or the Organization itself.

Article 82

There may be designated, in any trusteeship agreement, a strategic area or areas which may include part or all of the trust territory to which the agreement applies, without prejudice to any special agreement or agreements made under Article 43.

Article 83

1. All functions of the United Nations relating to strategic areas, including the approval of the terms of the trusteeship agreements and of their alteration or amendment shall be exercised by the Security Council.

2. The basic objectives set forth in Article 76 shall be applicable to the people of each strategic area.

3. The Security Council shall, subject to the provisions of the trusteeship agreements and without prejudice to security considerations, avail itself of the assistance of the Trusteeship Council to perform those functions of the United Nations under the trusteeship system relating to political, economic, social, and educational matters in the strategic areas.

Article 84

It shall be the duty of the administering authority to ensure that the trust territory shall play its part in the maintenance of international peace and security. To this end the administering authority may make use of volunteer forces, facilities, and assistance from the trust territory in carrying out the obligations towards the Security Council undertaken in this regard by the administering authority, as well as for local defence and the maintenance of law and order within the trust territory.

Article 85

1. The functions of the United Nations with regard to trusteeship agreements for all areas not designated as strategic, including the approval of the terms of the trusteeship agreements and of their alteration or amendment, shall be exercised by the General Assembly.

2. The Trusteeship Council, operating under the authority of the General Assembly shall assist the General Assembly in carrying out these functions.

Chapter XIII The Trusteeship Council

Composition

Article 86

1. The Trusteeship Council shall consist of the following Members of the United Nations:

a. those Members administering trust territories;

b. such of those Members mentioned by name in Article 23 as are not administering trust territories; and

c. as many other Members elected for three-year terms by the General Assembly as may be necessary to ensure that the total number of members of the Trusteeship Council is equally divided between those Members of the United Nations which administer trust territories and those which do not.

2. Each member of the Trusteeship Council shall designate one specially qualified person to represent it therein.

Functions and Powers

Article 87

The General Assembly and, under its authority, the Trusteeship Council, in carrying out their functions, may:

a. consider reports submitted by the administering authority;

b. accept petitions and examine them in consultation with the administering authority;

c. provide for periodic visits to the respective trust territories at times agreed upon with the administering authority; and

d. take these and other actions in conformity with the terms of the trusteeship agreements.

Article 88

The Trusteeship Council shall formulate a questionnaire on the political, economic, social, and educational advancement of the inhabitants of each trust territory, and the administering authority for each trust territory within the competence of the General Assembly shall make an annual report to the General Assembly upon the basis of such questionnaire.

Voting

Article 89

1. Each member of the Trusteeship Council shall have one vote.

2. Decisions of the Trusteeship Council shall be made by a majority of the members present and voting.

Procedure

Article 90

1. The Trusteeship Council shall adopt its own rules of procedure, including the method of selecting its President.

2. The Trusteeship Council shall meet as required in accordance with its rules, which shall include provision for the convening of meetings on the request of a majority of its members.

Article 91

The Trusteeship Council shall, when appropriate, avail itself of the assistance of the Economic and Social Council and of the specialized agencies in regard to matters with which they are respectively concerned.

Chapter XIV The International Court of Justice

Article 92

The International Court of Justice shall be the principal judicial organ of the United Nations. It shall function in accordance with the annexed Statute, which is based upon the Statute of the Permanent Court of International Justice and forms an integral part of the present *Charter*.

Article 93

1. All Members of the United Nations are *ipso facto* parties to the Statute of the International Court of Justice.

2. A State which is not a Member of the United Nations may become a party to the Statute of the International Court of Justice on conditions to be determined in each case by the General Assembly upon the recommendation of the Security Council.

Article 94

1. Each Member of the United Nations undertakes to comply with the decision of the International Court of Justice in any case to which it is a party.

2. If any party to a case fails to perform the obligations incumbent upon it under a judgment rendered by the Court, the other party may have recourse to the Security Council, which may, if it deems necessary, make recommendations or decide upon measures to be taken to give effect to the judgment.

Article 95

Nothing in the present *Charter* shall prevent Members of the United Nations from entrusting the solution of their differences to other tribunals by virtue of agreements already in existence or which may be concluded in the future.

Article 96

1. The General Assembly or the Security Council may request the International Court of Justice to give an advisory opinion on any legal question.

2. Other organs of the United Nations and specialized agencies, which may at any time be so authorized by the General Assembly, may also request advisory opinions of the Court on legal questions arising within the scope of their activities.

Chapter XV The Secretariat

Article 97

The Secretariat shall comprise a Secretary-General and such staff as the Organization may require. The Secretary-General shall be appointed by the General Assembly upon the recommendation of the Security Council. He shall be the chief administrative officer of the Organization.

Article 98

The Secretary-General shall act in that capacity in all meetings of the General Assembly, of the Security Council, of the Economic and Social Council, and of the Trusteeship Council, and shall perform such other functions as are entrusted to him by these organs. The Secretary-General shall make an annual report to the General Assembly on the work of the Organization.

Article 99

The Secretary-General may bring to the attention of the Security Council any matter which in his opinion may threaten the maintenance of international peace and security.

Article 100

1. In the performance of their duties the Secretary-General and the staff shall not seek or receive instructions from any government or from any other authority external to the Organization. They shall refrain from any action which might reflect on their position as international officials responsible only to the Organization.

2. Each Member of the United Nations undertakes to respect the exclusively international character of the responsibilities of the Secretary-General and the staff and not to seek to influence them in the discharge of their responsibilities.

Article 101

1. The staff shall be appointed by the Secretary-General under regulations established by the General Assembly.

2. Appropriate staffs shall be permanently assigned to the Economic and Social Council, the Trusteeship Council, and, as required, to other organs of the United Nations. These staffs shall form a part of the Secretariat.

3. The paramount consideration in the employment of the staff and in the determination of the conditions of service shall be the necessity of securing the highest standards of efficiency, competence, and integrity. Due regard shall be paid to the importance of recruiting the staff on as wide a geographical basis as possible.

Chapter XVI Miscellaneous Provisions

Article 102

1. Every treaty and every international agreement entered into by any Member of the United Nations after the present *Charter* comes into force shall as soon as possible be registered with the Secretariat and published by it.

2. No party to any such treaty or international agreement which has not been registered in accordance with the provisions of paragraph 1 of this Article may invoke that treaty or agreement before any organ of the United Nations.

Article 103

In the event of a conflict between the obligations of the Members of the United Nations under the present *Charter* and their obligations under any other international agreement, their obligations under the present *Charter* shall prevail.

Article 104

The Organization shall enjoy in the territory of each of its Members such legal capacity as may be necessary for the exercise of its functions and the fulfilment of its purposes.

Article 105

1. The Organization shall enjoy in the territory of each of its Members such privileges and immunities as are necessary for the fulfilment of its purposes.

2. Representatives of the Members of the United Nations and officials of the Organization shall similarly enjoy such privileges and immunities as are necessary for the independent exercise of their functions in connexion with the Organization.

3. The General Assembly may make recommendations with a view to determining the details of the application of paragraphs 1 and 2 of this Article or may propose conventions to the Members of the United Nations for this purpose.

Chapter XVII Transitional Security Arrangements

Article 106

Pending the coming into force of such special agreements referred to in Article 43 as in the opinion of the Security Council enable it to begin the exercise of its responsibilities under Article 42, the parties to the *Four-Nation Declaration*, signed at Moscow, 30 October,1943, and France, shall, in accordance with the provisions of paragraph 5 of that *Declaration*, consult with one another and as occasion requires with other Members of the United Nations with a view to such joint action on behalf of the Organization as may be necessary for the purpose of maintaining international peace and security.

Article 107

Nothing in the present *Charter* shall invalidate or preclude action, in relation to any State which during the Second World War has been an enemy of any signatory to the present *Charter*, taken or authorized as a result of that war by the Governments having responsibility for such action.

Chapter XVIII Amendments

Article 108

Amendments to the present *Charter* shall come into force for all Members of the United Nations when they have been adopted by a vote of two thirds of the members of the General Assembly and ratified in accordance with their respective constitutional processes by two thirds of the Members of the United Nations, including all the permanent members of the Security Council.

Article 109

1. A General Conference of the Members of the United Nations for the purpose of reviewing the present *Charter* may be held at a date and place to be fixed by a two-thirds vote of the members of the General Assembly and by a vote of any nine members of the Security Council. Each Member of the United Nations shall have one vote in the conference.

2. Any alteration of the present *Charter* recommended by a two-thirds vote of the conference shall take effect when ratified in accordance with their respective constitutional processes by two thirds of the Members of the United Nations including all the permanent members of the Security Council.

3. If such a conference has not been held before the tenth annual session of the General Assembly following the coming into force of the present *Charter*, the proposal to call such a conference shall be placed on the agenda of that session of the General Assembly, and the conference shall be held if so decided by a majority vote of the members of the General Assembly and by a vote of any seven members of the Security Council.

Chapter XIX Ratification and Signature

Article 110

1. The present *Charter* shall be ratified by the signatory States in accordance with their respective constitutional processes.

2. The ratifications shall be deposited with the Government of the United States of America, which shall notify all the signatory States of each deposit as well as the

Court shall, in the absence of a special agreement, be laid down by the General Assembly upon recommendation of the Security Council.

Article 5

1. At least three months before the date of the election, the Secretary-General of the United Nations shall address a written request to the members of the Permanent Court of Arbitration belonging to the States which are parties to the present *Statute*, and to the members of the national groups appointed under Article 4, paragraph 2, inviting them to undertake, within a given time, by national groups, the nomination of persons in a position to accept the duties of a member of the Court.

2. No group may nominate more than four persons, not more than two of whom shall be of their own nationality. In no case may the number of candidates nominated by a group be more than double the number of seats to be filled.

Article 6

Before making these nominations, each national group is recommended to consult its highest court of justice, its legal faculties and schools of law, and its national academies and national sections of international academies devoted to the study of law.

Article 7

1. The Secretary-General shall prepare a list in alphabetical order of all the persons thus nominated. Save as provided in Article 12, paragraph 2, these shall be the only persons eligible.

2. The Secretary-General shall submit this list to the General Assembly and to the Security Council.

Article 8

The General Assembly and the Security Council shall proceed independently of one another to elect the members of the Court.

Article 9

At every election, the electors shall bear in mind not only that the persons to be elected should individually possess the qualifications required, but also that in the body as a whole the representation of the main forms of civilization and of the principal legal systems of the world should be assured.

Article 10

1. Those candidates who obtain an absolute majority of votes in the General Assembly and in the Security Council shall be considered as elected.

2. Any vote of the Security Council, whether for the election of judges or for the appointment of members of the conference envisaged in Article 12, shall be taken without any distinction between permanent and non-permanent members of the Security Council.

3. In the event of more than one national of the same State obtaining an absolute majority of the votes both of the General Assembly and of the Security Council, the eldest of these only shall be considered as elected.

Article 11

If, after the first meeting held for the purpose of the election, one or more seats remain to be filled, a second and, if necessary, a third meeting shall take place.

Article 12

1. If, after the third meeting, one or more seats still remain unfilled, a joint conference consisting of six members, three appointed by the General Assembly and three by the Security Council, may be formed at any time at the request of either the General Assembly or the Security Council, for the purpose of choosing by the vote of an absolute majority one name for each seat still vacant, to submit to the General Assembly and the Security Council for their respective acceptance.

2. If the joint conference is unanimously agreed upon any person who fulfills the required conditions, he may be included in its list, even though he was not included in the list of nominations referred to in Article 7.

3. If the joint conference is satisfied that it will not be successful in procuring an election, those members of the Court who have already been elected shall, within a period to be fixed by the Security Council, proceed to fill the vacant seats by selection from among those candidates who have obtained votes either in the General Assembly or in the Security Council.

4. In the event of an equality of votes among the judges, the eldest judge shall

have a casting vote.

Article 13

1. The members of the Court shall be elected for nine years and may be re-elected; provided, however, that of the judges elected at the first election, the terms of five judges shall expire at the end of three years and the terms of five more judges shall expire at the end of six years.

2. The judges whose terms are to expire at the end of the above-mentioned initial periods of three and six years shall be chosen by lot to be drawn by the Secretary-General immediately after the first election has been completed.

3. The members of the Court shall continue to discharge their duties until their places have been filled. Though replaced, they shall finish any cases hich they may have begun.

4. In the case of the resignation of a member of the Court, the resignation shall be addressed to the President of the Court for transmission to the Secretary-General. This last notification makes the place vacant.

Article 14

Vacancies shall be filled by the same method as that laid down for the first election, subject to the following provision: the Secretary-General shall, within one month of the occurrence of the vacancy, proceed to issue the invitations provided for in Article 5, and the date of the election shall be fixed by the Security Council.

Article 15

A member of the Court elected to replace a member whose term of office has not expired shall hold office for the remainder of his predecessor's term.

Article 16

1. No member of the Court may exercise any political or administrative function, or engage in any other occupation of a professional nature.

2. Any doubt on this point shall be settled by the decision of the Court.

Article 17

1. No member of the Court may act as agent, counsel, or advocate in any case.

2. No member may participate in the decision of any case in which he has previously taken part as agent, counsel, or advocate for one of the parties, or as a member of a national or international court, or of a commission of enquiry, or in any other capacity.

3. Any doubt on this point shall be settled by the decision of the Court.

Article 18

1. No member of the Court can be dismissed unless, in the unanimous opinion of the other members, he has ceased to fulfill the required conditions.

2. Formal notification thereof shall be made to the Secretary-General by the Registrar.

3. This notification makes the place vacant.

Article 19

The members of the Court, when engaged on the business of the Court, shall enjoy diplomatic privileges and immunities.

Article 20

Every member of the Court shall, before taking up his duties, make a solemn declaration in open court that he will exercise his powers impartially and conscientiously.

Article 21

1. The Court shall elect its President and Vice-President for three years; they may be re-elected.

2. The Court shall appoint its Registrar and may provide for the appointment of such other officers as may be necessary.

Article 22

1. The seat of the Court shall be established at The Hague. This, however, shall not prevent the Court from sitting and exercising its functions elsewhere whenever the Court considers it desirable.

2. The President and the Registrar shall reside at the seat of the Court.

Article 23

1. The Court shall remain permanently in session, except during the judicial vacations, the dates and duration of which shall be fixed by the Court.

2. Members of the Court are entitled to periodic leave, the dates and duration of which shall be fixed by the Court, having in mind the distance between The Hague and the home of each judge.

3. Members of the Court shall be bound, unless they are on leave or prevented from attending by illness or other serious reasons duly explained to the President, to hold themselves permanently at the disposal of the Court.

Article 24

1. If, for some special reason, a member of the Court considers that he should not take part in the decision of a particular case, he shall so inform the President.

2. If the President considers that for some special reason one of the members of the Court should not sit in a particular case, he shall give him notice accordingly.

3. If in any such case the member Court and the President disagree, the matter shall be settled by the decision of the Court.

Article 25

1. The full Court shall sit except when it is expressly provided otherwise in the present *Statute*.

2. Subject to the condition that the number of judges available to constitute the Court is not thereby reduced below eleven, the *Rules of the Court* may provide for allowing one or more judges, according to circumstances and in rotation, to be dispensed from sitting.

3. A quorum of nine judges shall suffice to constitute the Court.

Article 26

1. The Court may from time to time form one or more chambers, composed of three or more judges as the Court may determine, for dealing with particular categories of cases; for example, labour cases and cases relating to transit and communications.

2. The Court may at any time form a chamber for dealing with a particular case. The number of judges to constitute such a chamber shall be determined by the Court

with the approval of the parties.

3. Cases shall be heard and determined by the chambers provided for in this article if the parties so request.

Article 27

A judgment given by any of the chambers provided for in Articles 26 and 29 shall be considered as rendered by the Court.

Article 28

The chambers provided for in Articles 26 and 29 may, with the consent of the parties, sit and exercise their functions elsewhere than at The Hague.

Article 29

With a view to the speedy dispatch of business, the Court shall form annually a chamber composed of five judges which, at the request of the parties, may hear and determine cases by summary procedure. In addition, two judges shall be selected for the purpose of replacing judges who find it impossible to sit.

Article 30

1. The Court shall frame rules for carrying out its functions. In particular, it shall lay down rules of procedure.

2. The Rules of the Court may provide for assessors to sit with the Court or with any of its chambers, without the right to vote.

Article 31

1. Judges of the nationality of each of the parties shall retain their right to sit in the case before the Court.

2. If the Court includes upon the Bench a judge of the nationality of one of the parties, any other party may choose a person to sit as judge. Such person shall be chosen preferably from among those persons who have been nominated as candidates as provided in Articles 4 and 5.

3. If the Court includes upon the Bench no judge of the nationality of the parties, each of these parties may proceed to choose a judge as provided in paragraph 2 of this Article.

(c) the existence of any fact which, if established, would constitute a breach of an international obligation;

(d) the nature or extent of the reparation to be made for the breach of an international obligation.

3. The declarations referred to above may be made unconditionally or on condition of reciprocity on the part of several or certain States, or for a certain time.

4. Such declarations shall be deposited with the Secretary-General of the United Nations, who shall transmit copies thereof to the parties to the Statute and to the Registrar of the Court.

5. Declarations made under Article 36 of the *Statute of the Permanent Court of International Justice* and which are still in force shall be deemed, as between the parties to the present *Statute*, to be acceptances of the compulsory jurisdiction of the International Court of Justice for the period which they still have to run and in accordance with their terms.

6. In the event of a dispute as to whether the Court has jurisdiction, the matter shall be settled by the decision of the Court.

Article 37

Whenever a treaty or convention in force provides for reference of a matter to a tribunal to have been instituted by the League of Nations, or to the Permanent Court of International Justice, the matter shall, as between the parties to the present Statute, be referred to the International Court of Justice.

Article 38

1. The Court, whose function is to decide in accordance with international law such disputes as are submitted to it, shall apply:

(a) international conventions, whether general or particular, establishing rules expressly recognized by the contesting States;

(b) international custom, as evidence of a general practice accepted as law;

(c) the general principles of law recognized by civilized nations;

(d) subject to the provisions of Article 59, judicial decisions and the teachings of the most highly qualified publicists of the various nations, as subsidiary means for the determination of rules of law.

2. This provision shall not prejudice the power of the Court to decide a case *ex*

aequo et bono, if the parties agree thereto.

Chapter III Procedure

Article 39

1. The official languages of the Court shall be French and English. If the parties agree that the case shall be conducted in French, the judgment shall be delivered in French. If the parties agree that the case shall be conducted in English, the judgment shall be delivered in English.

2. In the absence of an agreement as to which language shall be employed, each party may, in the pleadings, use the language which it prefers; the decision of the Court shall be given in French and English. In this case the Court shall at the same time determine which of the two texts shall be considered as authoritative.

3. The Court shall, at the request of any party, authorize a language other than French or English to be used by that party.

Article 40

1. Cases are brought before the Court, as the case may be, either by the notification of the special agreement or by a written application addressed to the Registrar. In either case the subject of the dispute and the parties shall be indicated.

2. The Registrar shall forthwith communicate the application to all concerned.

3. He shall also notify the Members of the United Nations through the Secretary-General, and also any other States entitled to appear before the Court.

Article 41

1. The Court shall have the power to indicate, if it considers that circumstances so require, any provisional measures which ought to be taken to preserve the respective rights of either party.

2. Pending the final decision, notice of the measures suggested shall forthwith be given to the parties and to the Security Council.

Article 42

1. The parties shall be represented by agents.

2. They may have the assistance of counsel or advocates before the Court.

3. The agents, counsel, and advocates of parties before the Court shall enjoy

the privileges and immunities necessary to the independent exercise of their duties.

Article 43

1. The procedure shall consist of two parts: written and oral.

2. The written proceedings shall consist of the communication to the Court and to the parties of memorials, counter-memorials and, if necessary, replies; also all papers and documents in support.

3. These communications shall be made through the Registrar, in the order and within the time fixed by the Court.

4. A certified copy of every document produced by one party shall be communicated to the other party.

5. The oral proceedings shall consist of the hearing by the Court of witnesses, experts, agents, counsel, and advocates.

Article 44

1. For the service of all notices upon persons other than the agents, counsel, and advocates, the Court shall apply direct to the government of the State upon whose territory the notice has to be served.

2. The same provision shall apply whenever steps are to be taken to procure evidence on the spot.

Article 45

The hearing shall be under the control of the President or, if he is unable to preside, of the Vice-President; if neither is able to preside, the senior judge present shall preside.

Article 46

The hearing in Court shall be public, unless the Court shall decide otherwise, or unless the parties demand that the public be not admitted.

Article 47

1. Minutes shall be made at each hearing and signed by the Registrar and the President.

2. These minutes alone shall be authentic.

Article 48

The Court shall make orders for the conduct of the case, shall decide the form and time in which each party must conclude its arguments, and make all arrangements connected with the taking of evidence.

Article 49

The Court may, even before the hearing begins, call upon the agents to produce any document or to supply any explanations. Formal note shall be taken of any refusal.

Article 50

The Court may, at any time, entrust any individual, body, bureau, commission, or other organization that it may select, with the task of carrying out an enquiry or giving an expert opinion.

Article 51

During the hearing any relevant questions are to be put to the witnesses and experts under the conditions laid down by the Court in the rules of procedure referred to in Article 30.

Article 52

After the Court has received the proofs and evidence within the time specified for the purpose, it may refuse to accept any further oral or written evidence that one party may desire to present unless the other side consents.

Article 53

1. Whenever one of the parties does not appear before the Court, or fails to defend its case, the other party may call upon the Court to decide in favour of its claim.

2. The Court must, before doing so, satisfy itself, not only that it has jurisdiction in accordance with Articles 36 and 37, but also that the claim is well founded in fact and law.

Article 54

1. When, subject to the control of the Court, the agents, counsel, and advocates have completed their presentation of the case, the President shall declare the hearing closed.

2. The Court shall withdraw to consider the judgment.

3. The deliberations of the Court shall take place in private and remain secret.

Article 55

1. All questions shall be decided by a majority of the judges present.

2. In the event of an equality of votes, the President or the judge who acts in his place shall have a casting vote.

Article 56

1. The judgment shall state the reasons on which it is based.

2. It shall contain the names of the judges who have taken part in the decision.

Article 57

If the judgment does not represent in whole or in part the unanimous opinion of the judges, any judge shall be entitled to deliver a separate opinion.

Article 58

The judgment shall be signed by the President and by the Registrar. It shall be read in open court, due notice having been given to the agents.

Article 59

The decision of the Court has no binding force except between the parties and in respect of that particular case.

Article 60

The judgment is final and without appeal. In the event of dispute as to the meaning or scope of the judgment, the Court shall construe it upon the request of any party.

Article 61

1. An application for revision of a judgment may be made only when it is based upon the discovery of some fact of such a nature as to be a decisive factor, which fact was, when the judgment was given, unknown to the Court and also to the party claiming revision, always provided that such ignorance was not due to negligence.

2. The proceedings for revision shall be opened by a judgment of the Court expressly recording the existence of the new fact, recognizing that it has such a character as to lay the case open to revision, and declaring the application admissible on this ground.

3. The Court may require previous compliance with the terms of the judgment before it admits proceedings in revision.

4. The application for revision must be made at latest within six months of the discovery of the new fact.

5. No application for revision may be made after the lapse of ten years from the date of the judgment.

Article 62

1. Should a State consider that it has an interest of a legal nature which may be affected by the decision in the case, it may submit a request to the Court to be permitted to intervene.

2. It shall be for the Court to decide upon this request.

Article 63

1. Whenever the construction of a convention to which States other than those concerned in the case are parties is in question, the Registrar shall notify all such States forthwith.

2. Every State so notified has the right to intervene in the proceedings; but if it uses this right, the construction given by the judgment will be equally binding upon it.

Article 64

Unless otherwise decided by the Court, each party shall bear its own costs.

Chapter IV Advisory Opinions

Article 65

1. The Court may give an advisory opinion on any legal question at the request of whatever body may be authorized by or in accordance with the *Charter of the United Nations* to make such a request.

2. Questions upon which the advisory opinion of the Court is asked shall be laid before the Court by means of a written request containing an exact statement of the question upon which an opinion is required, and accompanied by all documents likely to throw light upon the question.

Article 66

1. The Registrar shall forthwith give notice of the request for an advisory opinion to all States entitled to appear before the Court.

2. The Registrar shall also, by means of a special and direct communication, notify any State entitled to appear before the Court or international organization considered by the Court, or, should it not be sitting, by the President, as likely to be able to furnish information on the question, that the Court will be prepared to receive, within a time-limit to be fixed by the President, written statements, or to hear, at a public sitting to be held for the purpose, oral statements relating to the question.

3. Should any such State entitled to appear before the Court have failed to receive the special communication referred to in paragraph 2 of this Article, such State may express a desire to submit a written statement or to be heard; and the Court will decide.

4. States and organizations having presented written or oral statements or both shall be permitted to comment on the statements made by other States or organizations in the form, to the extent, and within the time-limits which the Court, or, should it not be sitting, the President, shall decide in each particular case. Accordingly, the Registrar shall in due time communicate any such written statements to States and organizations having submitted similar statements.

Article 67

The Court shall deliver its advisory opinions in open court, notice having been given to the Secretary-General and to the representatives of Members of the United Nations, of other States and of international organizations immediately concerned.

Article 68

In the exercise of its advisory functions the Court shall further be guided by the provisions of the present *Statute* which apply in contentious cases to the extent to which it recognizes them to be applicable.

Chapter V Amendment

Article 69

Amendments to the present *Statute* shall be effected by the same procedure as is provided by the *Charter of the United Nations* for amendments to that *Charter*, subject however to any provisions which the General Assembly upon recommendation of the Security Council may adopt concerning the participation of States which are parties to the present *Statute* but are not Members of the United Nations.

Article 70

The Court shall have power to propose such amendments to the present *Statute* as it may deem necessary, through written communications to the Secretary-General, for consideration in conformity with the provisions of Article 69.

III. *Universal Declaration of Human Rights (1948)*

General Assembly Resolution 217A (Ⅲ)

Preamble

Whereas recognition of the inherent dignity and of the equal and inalienable rights of all members of the human family is the foundation of freedom, justice and peace in the world,

Whereas disregard and contempt for human rights have resulted in barbarous acts which have outraged the conscience of mankind, and the advent of a world in which human beings shall enjoy freedom of speech and belief and freedom from fear and want has been proclaimed as the highest aspiration of the common people,

Whereas it is essential, if man is not to be compelled to have recourse, as a last resort, to rebellion against tyranny and oppression, that human rights should be protected by the rule of law,

Whereas it is essential to promote the development of friendly relations between nations,

Whereas the peoples of the United Nations have in the *Charter* reaffirmed their faith in fundamental human rights, in the dignity and worth of the human person and in the equal rights of men and women and have determined to promote social progress and better standards of life in larger freedom,

Whereas Member States have pledged themselves to achieve, in co-operation with the United Nations, the promotion of universal respect for and observance of human rights and fundamental freedoms,

Whereas a common understanding of these rights and freedoms is of the greatest importance for the full realization of this pledge,

Now, Therefore **THE GENERAL ASSEMBLY**

Proclaims THIS *UNIVERSAL DECLARATION OF HUMAN RIGHTS* as a common standard of achievement for all peoples and all nations, to the end that every individual and every organ of society, keeping this *Declaration* constantly in mind, shall strive by teaching and education to promote respect for these rights and freedoms and by progressive measures, national and international, to secure their universal and effective recognition and observance, both among the peoples of Member States themselves and among the peoples of territories under their jurisdiction.

Article 1

All human beings are born free and equal in dignity and rights. They are endowed with reason and conscience and should act towards one another in a spirit of brotherhood.

Article 2

Everyone is entitled to all the rights and freedoms set forth in this *Declaration*, without distinction of any kind, such as race, colour, sex, language, religion, political or other opinion, national or social origin, property, birth or other status.

Furthermore, no distinction shall be made on the basis of the political, jurisdictional or international status of the country or territory to which a person belongs, whether it be independent, trust, non-self-governing or under any other limitation of sovereignty.

Article 3

Everyone has the right to life, liberty and security of person.

Article 4

No one shall be held in slavery or servitude; slavery and the slave trade shall be prohibited in all their forms.

Article 5

No one shall be subjected to torture or to cruel, inhuman or degrading treatment or punishment.

Article 6

Everyone has the right to recognition everywhere as a person before the law.

Article 7

All are equal before the law and are entitled without any discrimination to equal protection of the law. All are entitled to equal protection against any discrimination in freedom to hold opinions without interference and to seek, receive and impart information and ideas through any media and regardless of frontiers.

Article 20

(1) Everyone has the right to freedom of peaceful assembly and association.

(2) No one may be compelled to belong to an association.

Article 21

(1) Everyone has the right to take part in the government of his country, directly or through freely chosen representatives.

(2) Everyone has the right of equal access to public service in his country.

(3) The will of the people shall be the basis of the authority of government; this will shall be expressed in periodic and genuine elections which shall be by universal and equal suffrage and shall be held by secret vote or by equivalent free voting procedures.

Article 22

Everyone, as a member of society, has the right to social security and is entitled to realization, through national effort and international co-operation and in accordance with the organization and resources of each State, of the economic, social and cultural rights indispensable for his dignity and the free development of his personality.

Article 23

(1) Everyone has the right to work, to free choice of employment, to just and favourable conditions of work and to protection against unemployment.

(2) Everyone, without any discrimination, has the right to equal pay for equal work.

(3) Everyone who works has the right to just and favourable remuneration ensuring for himself and his family an existence worthy of human dignity, and supplemented, if necessary, by other means of social protection.

(4) Everyone has the right to form and to join trade unions for the protection of his interests.

Article 24

Everyone has the right to rest and leisure, including reasonable limitation of working hours and periodic holidays with pay.

Article 25

(1) Everyone has the right to a standard of living adequate for the health and well-being of himself and of his family, including food, clothing, housing and medical care and necessary social services, and the right to security in the event of unemployment, sickness, disability, widowhood, old age or other lack of livelihood in circumstances beyond his control.

(2) Motherhood and childhood are entitled to special care and assistance. All children, whether born in or out of wedlock, shall enjoy the same social protection.

Article 26

(1) Everyone has the right to education. Education shall be free, at least in the elementary and fundamental stages. Elementary education shall be compulsory. Technical and professional education shall be made generally available and higher education shall be equally accessible to all on the basis of merit.

(2) Education shall be directed to the full development of the human personality and to the strengthening of respect for human rights and fundamental freedoms. It shall promote understanding, tolerance and friendship among all nations, racial or religious groups, and shall further the activities of the United Nations for the maintenance of peace.

(3) Parents have a prior right to choose the kind of education that shall be given to their children.

Article 27

(1) Everyone has the right freely to participate in the cultural life of the community, to enjoy the arts and to share in scientific advancement and its benefits.

(2) Everyone has the right to the protection of the moral and material interests resulting from any scientific, literary or artistic production of which he is the author.

Article 28

Everyone is entitled to a social and international order in which the rights and

Part I Introduction

Article 1 Scope of the present Convention

The present *Convention* applies to treaties between States.

Article 2 Use of terms

1. For the purposes of the present *Convention*:

(a) "treaty" means an international agreement concluded between States in written form and governed by international law, whether embodied in a single instrument or in two or more related instruments and whatever its particular designation;

(b) "ratification", "acceptance", "approval" and "accession" mean in each case the international act so named whereby a State establishes on the international plane its consent to be bound by a treaty;

(c) "full powers" means a document emanating from the competent authority of a State designating a person or persons to represent the State for negotiating, adopting or authenticating the text of a treaty, for expressing the consent of the State to be bound by a treaty, or for accomplishing any other act with respect to a treaty;

(d) "reservation" means a unilateral statement, however phrased or named, made by a State, when signing, ratifying, accepting, approving or acceding to a treaty, whereby it purports to exclude or to modify the legal effect of certain provisions of the treaty in their application to that State;

(e) "negotiating State" means a State which took part in the drawing up and adoption of the text of the treaty;

(f) "contracting State" means a State which has consented to be bound by the treaty, whether or not the treaty has entered into force;

(g) "party" means a State which has consented to be bound by the treaty and for which the treaty is in force;

(h) "third State" means a State not a party to the treaty;

(i) "international organization" means an intergovernmental organization.

2. The provisions of paragraph 1 regarding the use of terms in the present *Convention* are without prejudice to the use of those terms or to the meanings which may be given to them in the internal law of any State.

Article 3 International agreements not within the scope of the present Convention

The fact that the present *Convention* does not apply to international agreements concluded between States and other subjects of international law or between such other subjects of international law, or to international agreements not in written form, shall not affect:

(a) the legal force of such agreements;

(b) the application to them of any of the rules set forth in the present *Convention* to which they would be subject under international law independently of the *Convention*;

(c) the application of the *Convention* to the relations of States as between themselves under international agreements to which other subjects of international law are also parties.

Article 4 Non-retroactivity of the present Convention

Without prejudice to the application of any rules set forth in the present *Convention* to which treaties would be subject under international law independently of the *Convention*, the *Convention* applies only to treaties which are concluded by States after the entry into force of the present *Convention* with regard to such States.

Article 5 Treaties constituting international organizations and treaties adopted within an international organization

The present *Convention* applies to any treaty which is the constituent instrument of an international organization and to any treaty adopted within an international organization without prejudice to any relevant rules of the organization.

Part II Conclusion and Entry into Force of Treaties

Section I Conclusion of Treaties

Article 6 Capacity of States to conclude treaties

Every State possesses capacity to conclude treaties.

Article 7 Full powers

1. A person is considered as representing a State for the purpose of adopting or

authenticating the text of a treaty or for the purpose of expressing the consent of the State to be bound by a treaty if:

(a) he produces appropriate full powers; or

(b) it appears from the practice of the States concerned or from other circumstances that their intention was to consider that person as representing the State for such purposes and to dispense with full powers.

2. In virtue of their functions and without having to produce full powers, the following are considered as representing their State:

(a) Heads of State, Heads of Government and Ministers for Foreign Affairs, for the purpose of performing all acts relating to the conclusion of a treaty;

(b) heads of diplomatic missions, for the purpose of adopting the text of a treaty between the accrediting State and the State to which they are accredited;

(c) representatives accredited by States to an international conference or to an international organization or one of its organs, for the purpose of adopting the text of a treaty in that conference, organization or organ.

Article 8 Subsequent confirmation of an act performed without authorization

An act relating to the conclusion of a treaty performed by a person who cannot be considered under article 7 as authorized to represent a State for that purpose is without legal effect unless afterwards confirmed by that State.

Article 9 Adoption of the text

1. The adoption of the text of a treaty takes place by the consent of all the States participating in its drawing up except as provided in paragraph 2.

2. The adoption of the text of a treaty at an international conference takes place by the vote of two thirds of the States present and voting, unless by the same majority they shall decide to apply a different rule.

Article 10 Authentication of the text

The text of a treaty is established as authentic and definitive:

(a) by such procedure as may be provided for in the text or agreed upon by the States participating in its drawing up; or

(b) failing such procedure, by the signature, signature ad referendum or initialling by the representatives of those States of the text of the treaty or of the Final

Act of a conference incorporating the text.

Article 11 Means of expressing consent to be bound by a treaty

The consent of a State to be bound by a treaty may be expressed by signature, exchange of instruments constituting a treaty, ratification, acceptance, approval or accession, or by any other means if so agreed.

Article 12 Consent to be bound by a treaty expressed by signature

1. The consent of a State to be bound by a treaty is expressed by the signature of its representative when:

(a) the treaty provides that signature shall have that effect;

(b) it is otherwise established that the negotiating States were agreed that signature should have that effect; or

(c) the intention of the State to give that effect to the signature appears from the full powers of its representative or was expressed during the negotiation.

2. For the purposes of paragraph 1:

(a) the initialling of a text constitutes a signature of the treaty when it is established that the negotiating States so agreed;

(b) the signature ad referendum of a treaty by a representative, if confirmed by his State, constitutes a full signature of the treaty.

Article 13 Consent to be bound by a treaty expressed by an exchange of instruments constituting a treaty

The consent of States to be bound by a treaty constituted by instruments exchanged between them is expressed by that exchange when:

(a) the instruments provide that their exchange shall have that effect; or

(b) it is otherwise established that those States were agreed that the exchange of instruments should have that effect.

Article 14 Consent to be bound by a treaty expressed by ratification, acceptance or approval

1. The consent of a State to be bound by a treaty is expressed by ratification when:

(a) the treaty provides for such consent to be expressed by means of ratification;

(b) it is otherwise established that the negotiating States were agreed that ratification should be required;

(c) the representative of the State has signed the treaty subject to ratification; or

(d) the intention of the State to sign the treaty subject to ratification appears from the full powers of its representative or was expressed during the negotiation.

2. The consent of a State to be bound by a treaty is expressed by acceptance or approval under conditions similar to those which apply to ratification.

Article 15 Consent to be bound by a treaty expressed by accession

The consent of a State to be bound by a treaty is expressed by accession when:

(a) the treaty provides that such consent may be expressed by that State by means of accession;

(b) it is otherwise established that the negotiating States were agreed that such consent may be expressed by that State by means of accession; or

(c) all the parties have subsequently agreed that such consent may be expressed by that State by means of accession.

Article 16 Exchange or deposit of instruments of ratification, acceptance, approval or accession

Unless the treaty otherwise provides, instruments of ratification, acceptance, approval or accession establish the consent of a State to be bound by a treaty upon:

(a) their exchange between the contracting States;

(b) their deposit with the depositary; or

(c) their notification to the contracting States or to the depositary, if so agreed.

Article 17 Consent to be bound by part of a treaty and choice of differing provisions

1. Without prejudice to articles 19 to 23, the consent of a State to be bound by part of a treaty is effective only if the treaty so permits or the other contracting States so agree.

2. The consent of a State to be bound by a treaty which permits a choice between differing provisions is effective only if it is made clear to which of the

provisions the consent relates.

Article 18 Obligation not to defeat the object and purpose of a treaty prior to its entry into force

A State is obliged to refrain from acts which would defeat the object and purpose of a treaty when:

(a) it has signed the treaty or has exchanged instruments constituting the treaty subject to ratification, acceptance or approval, until it shall have made its intention clear not to become a party to the treaty; or

(b) it has expressed its consent to be bound by the treaty, pending the entry into force of the treaty and provided that such entry into force is not unduly delayed.

Section II Reservations

Article 19 Formulation of reservations

A State may, when signing, ratifying, accepting, approving or acceding to a treaty, formulate a reservation unless:

(a) the reservation is prohibited by the treaty;

(b) the treaty provides that only specified reservations, which do not include the reservation in question, may be made; or

(c) in cases not failing under subparagraphs (a) and (b), the reservation is incompatible with the object and purpose of the treaty.

Article 20 Acceptance of and objection to reservations

1. A reservation expressly authorized by a treaty does not require any subsequent acceptance by the other contracting States unless the treaty so provides.

2. When it appears from the limited number of the negotiating States and the object and purpose of a treaty that the application of the treaty in its entirety between all the parties is an essential condition of the consent of each one to be bound by the treaty, a reservation requires acceptance by all the parties.

3. When a treaty is a constituent instrument of an international organization and unless it otherwise provides, a reservation requires the acceptance of the competent organ of that organization.

4. In cases not falling under the preceding paragraphs and unless the treaty otherwise provides:

(a) acceptance by another contracting State of a reservation constitutes the reserving State a party to the treaty in relation to that other State if or when the treaty is in force for those States;

(b) an objection by another contracting State to a reservation does not preclude the entry into force of the treaty as between the objecting and reserving States unless a contrary intention is definitely expressed by the objecting State;

(c) an act expressing a State's consent to be bound by the treaty and containing a reservation is effective as soon as at least one other contracting State has accepted the reservation.

5. For the purposes of paragraphs 2 and 4 and unless the treaty otherwise provides, a reservation is considered to have been accepted by a State if it shall have raised no objection to the reservation by the end of a period of twelve months after it was notified of the reservation or by the date on which it expressed its consent to be bound by the treaty, whichever is later.

Article 21 Legal effects of reservations and of objections to reservations

1. A reservation established with regard to another party in accordance with articles 19, 20 and 23:

(a) modifies for the reserving State in its relations with that other party the provisions of the treaty to which the reservation relates to the extent of the reservation; and

(b) modifies those provisions to the same extent for that other party in its relations with the reserving State.

2. The reservation does not modify the provisions of the treaty for the other parties to the treaty inter se.

3. When a State objecting to a reservation has not opposed the entry into force of the treaty between itself and the reserving State, the provisions to which the reservation relates do not apply as between the two States to the extent of the reservation.

Article 22 Withdrawal of reservations and of objections to reservations

1. Unless the treaty otherwise provides, a reservation may be withdrawn at any time and the consent of a State which has accepted the reservation is not required for its withdrawal.

2. Unless the treaty otherwise provides, an objection to a reservation may be withdrawn at any time.

3. Unless the treaty otherwise provides, or it is otherwise agreed:

(a) the withdrawal of a reservation becomes operative in relation to another contracting State only when notice of it has been received by that State;

(b) the withdrawal of an objection to a reservation becomes operative only when notice of it has been received by the State which formulated the reservation.

Article 23 Procedure regarding reservations

1. A reservation, an express acceptance of a reservation and an objection to a reservation must be formulated in writing and communicated to the contracting States and other States entitled to become parties to the treaty.

2. If formulated when signing the treaty subject to ratification, acceptance or approval, a reservation must be formally confirmed by the reserving State when expressing its consent to be bound by the treaty. In such a case the reservation shall be considered as having been made on the date of its confirmation.

3. An express acceptance of, or an objection to, a reservation made previously to confirmation of the reservation does not itself require confirmation.

4. The withdrawal of a reservation or of an objection to a reservation must be formulated in writing.

Section Ⅲ Entry into Force and Provisional, Application of Treaties

Article 24 Entry into force

1. A treaty enters into force in such manner and upon such date as it may provide or as the negotiating States may agree.

2. Failing any such provision or agreement, a treaty enters into force as soon as consent to be bound by the treaty has been established for all the negotiating States.

3. When the consent of a State to be bound by a treaty is established on a date after the treaty has come into force, the treaty enters into force for that State on that date, unless the treaty otherwise provides.

4. The provisions of a treaty regulating the authentication of its text, the establishment of the consent of States to be bound by the treaty, the manner or date of its entry into force, reservations, the functions of the depositary and other matters arising necessarily before the entry into force of the treaty apply from the time of the

adoption of its text.

Article 25 Provisional application

1. A treaty or a part of a treaty is applied provisionally pending its entry into force if:

(a) the treaty itself so provides; or

(b) the negotiating States have in some other manner so agreed.

2. Unless the treaty otherwise provides or the negotiating States have otherwise agreed, the provisional application of a treaty or a part of a treaty with respect to a State shall be terminated if that State notifies the other States between which the treaty is being applied provisionally of its intention not to become a party to the treaty.

Part III Observance, Application and Interpretation of Treaties

Section I Observance of Treaties

Article 26 "*Pacta sunt servanda*"

Every treaty in force is binding upon the parties to it and must be performed by them in good faith.

Article 27 Internal law and observance of treaties

A party may not invoke the provisions of its internal law as justification for its failure to perform a treaty. This rule is without prejudice to article 46.

Section II Application of Treaties

Article 28 Non-retroactivity of treaties

Unless a different intention appears from the treaty or is otherwise established, its provisions do not bind a party in relation to any act or fact which took place or any situation which ceased to exist before the date of the entry into force of the treaty with respect to that party.

Article 29 Territorial scope of treaties

Unless a different intention appears from the treaty or is otherwise established, a treaty is binding upon each party in respect of its entire territory.

Article 30 Application of successive treaties relating to the same subject matter

1. Subject to Article 103 of the *Charter of the United Nations*, the rights and obligations of States Parties to successive treaties relating to the same subject matter shall be determined in accordance with the following paragraphs.

2. When a treaty specifies that it is subject to, or that it is not to be considered as incompatible with, an earlier or later treaty, the provisions of that other treaty prevail.

3. When all the parties to the earlier treaty are parties also to the later treaty but the earlier treaty is not terminated or suspended in operation under article 59, the earlier treaty applies only to the extent that its provisions are compatible with those of the later treaty.

4. When the parties to the later treaty do not include all the parties to the earlier one:

(a) as between States Parties to both treaties the same rule applies as in paragraph 3;

(b) as between a State party to both treaties and a State party to only one of the treaties, the treaty to which both States are parties governs their mutual rights and obligations.

5. Paragraph 4 is without prejudice to article 41, or to any question of the termination or suspension of the operation of a treaty under article 60 or to any question of responsibility which may arise for a State from the conclusion or application of a treaty the provisions of which are incompatible with its obligations towards another State under another treaty.

Section Ⅲ Interpretation of Treaties

Article 31 General rule of interpretation

1. A treaty shall be interpreted in good faith in accordance with the ordinary meaning to be given to the terms of the treaty in their context and in the light of its object and purpose.

2. The context for the purpose of the interpretation of a treaty shall comprise, in

addition to the text, including its preamble and annexes:

(a) any agreement relating to the treaty which was made between all the parties in connection with the conclusion of the treaty;

(b) any instrument which was made by one or more parties in connection with the conclusion of the treaty and accepted by the other parties as an instrument related to the treaty.

3. There shall be taken into account, together with the context:

(a) any subsequent agreement between the parties regarding the interpretation of the treaty or the application of its provisions;

(b) any subsequent practice in the application of the treaty which establishes the agreement of the parties regarding its interpretation;

(c) any relevant rules of international law applicable in the relations between the parties.

4. A special meaning shall be given to a term if it is established that the parties so intended.

Article 32 Supplementary means of interpretation

Recourse may be had to supplementary means of interpretation, including the preparatory work of the treaty and the circumstances of its conclusion, in order to confirm the meaning resulting from the application of article 31, or to determine the meaning when the interpretation according to article 31:

(a) leaves the meaning ambiguous or obscure; or

(b) leads to a result which is manifestly absurd or unreasonable.

Article 33 Interpretation of treaties authenticated in two or more languages

1. When a treaty has been authenticated in two or more languages, the text is equally authoritative in each language, unless the treaty provides or the parties agree that, in case of divergence, a particular text shall prevail.

2. A version of the treaty in a language other than one of those in which the text was authenticated shall be considered an authentic text only if the treaty so provides or the parties so agree.

3. The terms of the treaty are presumed to have the same meaning in each

authentic text.

4. Except where a particular text prevails in accordance with paragraph 1, when a comparison of the authentic texts discloses a difference of meaning which the application of articles 31 and 32 does not remove, the meaning which best reconciles the texts, having regard to the object and purpose of the treaty, shall be adopted.

Section Ⅳ Treaties and Third States

Article 34 General rule regarding third States

A treaty does not create either obligations or rights for a third State without its consent.

Article 35 Treaties providing for obligations for third States

An obligation arises for a third State from a provision of a treaty if the parties to the treaty intend the provision to be the means of establishing the obligation and the third State expressly accepts that obligation in writing.

Article 36 Treaties providing for rights for third States

1. A right arises for a third State from a provision of a treaty if the parties to the treaty intend the provision to accord that right either to the third State, or to a group of States to which it belongs, or to all States, and the third State assents thereto. Its assent shall be presumed so long as the contrary is not indicated, unless the treaty otherwise provides.

2. A State exercising a right in accordance with paragraph 1 shall comply with the conditions for its exercise provided for in the treaty or established in conformity with the treaty.

Article 37 Revocation or modification of obligations or rights of third States

1. When an obligation has arisen for a third State in conformity with article 35, the obligation may be revoked or modified only with the consent of the parties to the treaty and of the third State, unless it is established that they had otherwise agreed.

2. When a right has arisen for a third State in conformity with article 36, the right may not be revoked or modified by the parties if it is established that the right

was intended not to be revocable or subject to modification without the consent of the third State.

Article 38 Rules in a treaty becoming binding on third States through international custom

Nothing in articles 34 to 37 precludes a rule set forth in a treaty from becoming binding upon a third State as a customary rule of international law, recognized as such.

Part Ⅳ Amendment and Modification of Treaties

Article 39 General rule regarding the amendment of treaties

A treaty may be amended by agreement between the parties. The rules laid down in Part II apply to such an agreement except insofar as the treaty may otherwise provide.

Article 40 Amendment of multilateral treaties

1. Unless the treaty otherwise provides, the amendment of multilateral treaties shall be governed by the following paragraphs.

2. Any proposal to amend a multilateral treaty as between all the parties must be notified to all the contracting States, each one of which shall have the right to take part in:

(a) the decision as to the action to be taken in regard to such proposal;

(b) the negotiation and conclusion of any agreement for the amendment of the treaty.

3. Every State entitled to become a party to the treaty shall also be entitled to become a party to the treaty as amended.

4. The amending agreement does not bind any State already a party to the treaty which does not become a party to the amending agreement; article 30, paragraph 4 (b), applies in relation to such State.

5. Any State which becomes a party to the treaty after the entry into force of the amending agreement shall, failing an expression of a different intention by that State:

(a) be considered as a party to the treaty as amended; and

(b) be considered as a party to the unamended treaty in relation to any party to the treaty not bound by the amending agreement.

Article 41 Agreements to modify multilateral treaties between certain of the parties only

1. Two or more of the parties to a multilateral treaty may conclude an agreement to modify the treaty as between themselves alone if:

(a) the possibility of such a modification is provided for by the treaty; or

(b) the modification in question is not prohibited by the treaty and:

(i) does not affect the enjoyment by the other parties of their rights under the treaty or the performance of their obligations;

(ii) does not relate to a provision, derogation from which is incompatible with the effective execution of the object and purpose of the treaty as a whole.

2. Unless in a case falling under paragraph 1 (a) the treaty otherwise provides, the parties in question shall notify the other parties of their intention to conclude the agreement and of the modification to the treaty for which it provides.

Part V Invalidity, Termination and Suspension of the Operation of Treaties

Section I General Provisions

Article 42 Validity and continuance in force of treaties

1. The validity of a treaty or of the consent of a State to be bound by a treaty may be impeached only through the application of the present *Convention*.

2. The termination of a treaty, its denunciation or the withdrawal of a party, may take place only as a result of the application of the provisions of the treaty or of the present *Convention*. The same rule applies to suspension of the operation of a treaty.

Article 43 Obligations imposed by international law independently of a treaty

The invalidity, termination or denunciation of a treaty, the withdrawal of a party from it, or the suspension of its operation, as a result of the application of the present *Convention* or of the provisions of the treaty, shall not in any way impair the duty of any State to fulfil any obligation embodied in the treaty to which it would be subject under international law independently of the treaty.

Article 44 Separability of treaty provisions

1. A right of a party, provided for in a treaty or arising under article 56, to denounce, withdraw from or suspend the operation of the treaty may be exercised only with respect to the whole treaty unless the treaty otherwise provides or the parties otherwise agree.

2. A ground for invalidating, terminating, withdrawing from or suspending the operation of a treaty recognized in the present *Convention* may be invoked only with respect to the whole treaty except as provided in the following paragraphs or in article 60.

3. If the ground relates solely to particular clauses, it may be invoked only with respect to those clauses where:

(a) the said clauses are separable from the remainder of the treaty with regard to their application;

(b) it appears from the treaty or is otherwise established that acceptance of those clauses was not an essential basis of the consent of the other party or parties to be bound by the treaty as a whole; and

(c) continued performance of the remainder of the treaty would not be unjust.

4. In cases falling under articles 49 and 50, the State entitled to invoke the fraud or corruption may do so with respect either to the whole treaty or, subject to paragraph 3, to the particular clauses alone.

5. In cases falling under articles 51, 52 and 53, no separation of the provisions of the treaty is permitted.

Article 45 Loss of a right to invoke a ground for invalidating, terminating, withdrawing from or suspending the operation of a treaty

A State may no longer invoke a ground for invalidating, terminating, withdrawing from or suspending the operation of a treaty under articles 46 to 50 or articles 60 and 62 if, after becoming aware of the facts:

(a) it shall have expressly agreed that the treaty is valid or remains in force or continues in operation, as the case may be; or

(b) it must by reason of its conduct be considered as having acquiesced in the validity of the treaty or in its maintenance in force or in operation, as the case may be.

Section II Invalidity of Treaties

Article 46 Provisions of internal law regarding competence to conclude treaties

1. A State may not invoke the fact that its consent to be bound by a treaty has been expressed in violation of a provision of its internal law regarding competence to conclude treaties as invalidating its consent unless that violation was manifest and concerned a rule of its internal law of fundamental importance.

2. A violation is manifest if it would be objectively evident to any State conducting itself in the matter in accordance with normal practice and in good faith.

Article 47 Specific restrictions on authority to express the consent of a State

If the authority of a representative to express the consent of a State to be bound by a particular treaty has been made subject to a specific restriction, his omission to observe that restriction may not be invoked as invalidating the consent expressed by him unless the restriction was notified to the other negotiating States prior to his expressing such consent.

Article 48 Error

1. A State may invoke an error in a treaty as invalidating its consent to be bound by the treaty if the error relates to a fact or situation which was assumed by that State to exist at the time when the treaty was concluded and formed an essential basis of its consent to be bound by the treaty.

2. Paragraph 1 shall not apply if the State in question contributed by its own conduct to the error or if the circumstances were such as to put that State on notice of a possible error.

3. An error relating only to the wording of the text of a treaty does not affect its validity; article 79 then applies.

Article 49 Fraud

If a State has been induced to conclude a treaty by the fraudulent conduct of another negotiating State, the State may invoke the fraud as invalidating its consent to be bound by the treaty.

Article 50 Corruption of a representative of a State

If the expression of a State's consent to be bound by a treaty has been procured through the corruption of its representative directly or indirectly by another negotiating State, the State may invoke such corruption as invalidating its consent to be bound by the treaty.

Article 51 Coercion of a representative of a State

The expression of a State's consent to be bound by a treaty which has been procured by the coercion of its representative through acts or threats directed against him shall be without any legal effect.

Article 52 Coercion of a State by the threat or use of force

A treaty is void if its conclusion has been procured by the threat or use of force in violation of the principles of international law embodied in the Charter of the *United Nations*.

Article 53 Treaties conflicting with a peremptory norm of general international law ("*jus cogens*")

A treaty is void if, at the time of its conclusion, it conflicts with a peremptory norm of general international law. For the purposes of the present *Convention*, a peremptory norm of general international law is a norm accepted and recognized by the international community of States as a whole as a norm from which no derogation is permitted and which can be modified only by a subsequent norm of general international law having the same character.

Section Ⅲ Termination and Suspension of the Operation of Treaties

Article 54 Termination of or withdrawal from a treaty under its provisions or by consent of the parties

The termination of a treaty or the withdrawal of a party may take place:

(a) in conformity with the provisions of the treaty; or

(b) at any time by consent of all the parties after consultation with the other contracting States.

Article 55 Reduction of the parties to a multilateral treaty below the number necessary for its entry into force

Unless the treaty otherwise provides, a multilateral treaty does not terminate by reason only of the fact that the number of the parties falls below the number necessary for its entry into force.

Article 56 Denunciation of or withdrawal from a treaty containing no provision regarding termination, denunciation or withdrawal

1. A treaty which contains no provision regarding its termination and which does not provide for denunciation or withdrawal is not subject to denunciation or withdrawal unless:

(a) it is established that the parties intended to admit the possibility of denunciation or withdrawal; or

(b) a right of denunciation or withdrawal may be implied by the nature of the treaty.

2. A party shall give not less than twelve months' notice of its intention to denounce or withdraw from a treaty under paragraph 1.

Article 57 Suspension of the operation of a treaty under its provisions or by consent of the parties

The operation of a treaty in regard to all the parties or to a particular party may be suspended:

(a) in conformity with the provisions of the treaty; or

(b) at any time by consent of all the parties after consultation with the other contracting States.

Article 58 Suspension of the operation of a multilateral treaty by agreement between certain of the parties only

1. Two or more parties to a multilateral treaty may conclude an agreement to suspend the operation of provisions of the treaty, temporarily and as between themselves alone, if:

(a) the possibility of such a suspension is provided for by the treaty; or

(b) the suspension in question is not prohibited by the treaty and:

(i) does not affect the enjoyment by the other parties of their rights under the treaty or the performance of their obligations;

(ii) is not incompatible with the object and purpose of the treaty.

2. Unless in a case falling under paragraph 1 (a) the treaty otherwise provides, the parties in question shall notify the other parties of their intention to conclude the agreement and of those provisions of the treaty the operation of which they intend to suspend.

Article 59 Termination or suspension of the operation of a treaty implied by conclusion of a later treaty

1. A treaty shall be considered as terminated if all the parties to it conclude a later treaty relating to the same subject matter and:

(a) it appears from the later treaty or is otherwise established that the parties intended that the matter should be governed by that treaty; or

(b) the provisions of the later treaty are so far incompatible with those of the earlier one that the two treaties are not capable of being applied at the same time.

2. The earlier treaty shall be considered as only suspended in operation if it appears from the later treaty or is otherwise established that such was the intention of the parties.

Article 60 Termination or suspension of the operation of a treaty as a consequence of its breach

1. A material breach of a bilateral treaty by one of the parties entitles the other to invoke the breach as a ground for terminating the treaty or suspending its operation in whole or in part.

2. A material breach of a multilateral treaty by one of the parties entitles:

(a) the other parties by unanimous agreement to suspend the operation of the treaty in whole or in part or to terminate it either:

(i) in the relations between themselves and the defaulting State; or

(ii) as between all the parties;

(b) a party specially affected by the breach to invoke it as a ground for suspending the operation of the treaty in whole or in part in the relations between itself and the defaulting State;

(c) any party other than the defaulting State to invoke the breach as a ground for suspending the operation of the treaty in whole or in part with respect to itself if the treaty is of such a character that a material breach of its provisions by one party radically changes the position of every party with respect to the further performance of its obligations under the treaty.

3. A material breach of a treaty, for the purposes of this article, consists in:

(a) a repudiation of the treaty not sanctioned by the present *Convention*; or

(b) the violation of a provision essential to the accomplishment of the object or purpose of the treaty.

4. The foregoing paragraphs are without prejudice to any provision in the treaty applicable in the event of a breach.

5. Paragraphs 1 to 3 do not apply to provisions relating to the protection of the human person contained in treaties of a humanitarian character, in particular to provisions prohibiting any form of reprisals against persons protected by such treaties.

Article 61 Supervening impossibility of performance

1. A party may invoke the impossibility of performing a treaty as a ground for terminating or withdrawing from it if the impossibility results from the permanent disappearance or destruction of an object indispensable for the execution of the treaty. If the impossibility is temporary, it may be invoked only as a ground for suspending the operation of the treaty.

2. Impossibility of performance may not be invoked by a party as a ground for terminating, withdrawing from or suspending the operation of a treaty if the impossibility is the result of a breach by that party either of an obligation under the treaty or of any other international obligation owed to any other party to the treaty.

Article 62 Fundamental change of circumstances

1. A fundamental change of circumstances which has occurred with regard to those existing at the time of the conclusion of a treaty, and which was not foreseen by the parties, may not be invoked as a ground for terminating or withdrawing from the treaty unless:

(a) the existence of those circumstances constituted an essential basis of the consent of the parties to be bound by the treaty; and

(b) the effect of the change is radically to transform the extent of obligations still to be performed under the treaty.

2. A fundamental change of circumstances may not be invoked as a ground for

65 and 67

A notification or instrument provided for in article 65 or 67 may be revoked at any time before it takes effect.

Section V Consequences of the Invalidity, Termination or Suspension of the Operation of a Treaty

Article 69 Consequences of the invalidity of a treaty

1. A treaty the invalidity of which is established under the present *Convention* is void. The provisions of a void treaty have no legal force.

2. If acts have nevertheless been performed in reliance on such a treaty:

(a) each party may require any other party to establish as far as possible in their mutual relations the position that would have existed if the acts had not been performed;

(b) acts performed in good faith before the invalidity was invoked are not rendered unlawful by reason only of the invalidity of the treaty.

3. In cases falling under Articles 49, 50, 51 or 52, paragraph 2 does not apply with respect to the party to which the fraud, the act of corruption or the coercion is imputable.

4. In the case of the invalidity of a particular State's consent to be bound by a multilateral treaty, the foregoing rules apply in the relations between that State and the parties to the treaty.

Article 70 Consequences of the termination of a treaty

1. Unless the treaty otherwise provides or the parties otherwise agree, the termination of a treaty under its provisions or in accordance with the present *Convention*:

(a) releases the parties from any obligation further to perform the treaty;

(b) does not affect any right, obligation or legal situation of the parties created through the execution of the treaty prior to its termination.

2. If a State denounces or withdraws from a multilateral treaty, paragraph 1 applies in the relations between that State and each of the other parties to the treaty from the date when such denunciation or withdrawal takes effect.

Article 71 Consequences of the invalidity of a treaty which conflicts with a

peremptory norm of general international law

1. In the case of a treaty which is void under article 53 the parties shall:

(a) eliminate as far as possible the consequences of any act performed in reliance on any provision which conflicts with the peremptory norm of general international law; and

(b) bring their mutual relations into conformity with the peremptory norm of general international law.

2. In the case of a treaty which becomes void and terminates under article 64, the termination of the treaty:

(a) releases the parties from any obligation further to perform the treaty;

(b) does not affect any right, obligation or legal situation of the parties created through the execution of the treaty prior to its termination, provided that those rights, obligations or situations may thereafter be maintained only to the extent that their maintenance is not in itself in conflict with the new peremptory norm of general international law.

Article 72 Consequences of the suspension of the operation of a treaty

1. Unless the treaty otherwise provides or the parties otherwise agree, the suspension of the operation of a treaty under its provisions or in accordance with the present *Convention*:

(a) releases the parties between which the operation of the treaty is suspended from the obligation to perform the treaty in their mutual relations during the period of the suspension;

(b) does not otherwise affect the legal relations between the parties established by the treaty.

2. During the period of the suspension the parties shall refrain from acts tending to obstruct the resumption of the operation of the treaty.

Part Ⅵ Miscellaneous Provisions

Article 73 Cases of State succession, State responsibility and outbreak of hostilities

The provisions of the present *Convention* shall not prejudge any question that may arise in regard to a treaty from a succession of States or from the international responsibility of a State or from the outbreak of hostilities between States.

Article 74 Diplomatic and consular relations and the conclusion of treaties

The severance or absence of diplomatic or consular relations between two or more States does not prevent the conclusion of treaties between those States. The conclusion of a treaty does not in itself affect the situation in regard to diplomatic or consular relations.

Article 75 Case of an aggressor State

The provisions of the present *Convention* are without prejudice to any obligation in relation to a treaty which may arise for an aggressor State in consequence of measures taken in conformity with the *Charter of the United Nations* with reference to that State's aggression.

Part VII Depositaries, Notifications, Corrections and Registration

Article 76 Depositaries of treaties

1. The designation of the depositary of a treaty may be made by the negotiating States, either in the treaty itself or in some other manner. The depositary may be one or more States, an international organization or the chief administrative officer of the organization.

2. The functions of the depositary of a treaty are international in character and the depositary is under an obligation to act impartially in their performance. In particular, the fact that a treaty has not entered into force between certain of the parties or that a difference has appeared between a State and a depositary with regard to the performance of the latter's functions shall not affect that obligation.

Article 77 Functions of depositaries

1. The functions of a depositary, unless otherwise provided in the treaty or agreed by the contracting States, comprise in particular:

(a) keeping custody of the original text of the treaty and of any full powers delivered to the depositary;

(b) preparing certified copies of the original text and preparing any further text of the treaty in such additional languages as may be required by the treaty and transmitting them to the parties and to the States entitled to become parties to the treaty;

(c) receiving any signatures to the treaty and receiving and keeping custody of any instruments, notifications and communications relating to it;

(d) examining whether the signature or any instrument, notification or communication relating to the treaty is in due and proper form and, if need be, bringing the matter to the attention of the State in question;

(e) informing the parties and the States entitled to become parties to the treaty of acts, notifications and communications relating to the treaty;

(f) informing the States entitled to become parties to the treaty when the number of signatures or of instruments of ratification, acceptance, approval or accession required for the entry into force of the treaty has been received or deposited;

(g) registering the treaty with the Secretariat of the United Nations;

(h) performing the functions specified in other provisions of the present *Convention*.

2. In the event of any difference appearing between a State and the depositary as to the performance of the latter's functions, the depositary shall bring the question to the attention of the signatory States and the contracting States or, where appropriate, of the competent organ of the international organization concerned.

Article 78 Notifications and communications

Except as the treaty or the present *Convention* otherwise provide, any notification or communication to be made by any State under the present *Convention* shall:

(a) if there is no depositary, be transmitted direct to the States for which it is intended, or if there is a depositary, to the latter;

(b) be considered as having been made by the State in question only upon its receipt by the State to which it was transmitted or, as the case may be, upon its receipt by the depositary;

(c) if transmitted to a depositary, be considered as received by the State for which it was intended only when the latter State has been informed by the depositary in accordance with article 77, paragraph 1 (e).

Article 79 Correction of errors in texts or in certified copies of treaties

1. Where, after the authentication of the text of a treaty, the signatory States and the contracting States are agreed that it contains an error, the error shall, unless

they decide upon some other means of correction, be corrected:

(a) by having the appropriate correction made in the text and causing the correction to be initialled by duly authorized representatives;

(b) by executing or exchanging an instrument or instruments setting out the correction which it has been agreed to make; or

(c) by executing a corrected text of the whole treaty by the same procedure as in the case of the original text.

2. Where the treaty is one for which there is a depositary, the latter shall notify the signatory States and the contracting States of the error and of the proposal to correct it and shall specify an appropriate time-limit within which objection to the proposed correction may be raised. If, on the expiry of the time-limit:

(a) no objection has been raised, the depositary shall make and initial the correction in the text and shall execute a procès-verbal of the rectification of the text and communicate a copy of it to the parties and to the States entitled to become parties to the treaty;

(b) an objection has been raised, the depositary shall communicate the objection to the signatory States and to the contracting States.

3. The rules in paragraphs 1 and 2 apply also where the text has been authenticated in two or more languages and it appears that there is a lack of concordance which the signatory States and the contracting States agree should be corrected.

4. The corrected text replaces the defective text ab initio, unless the signatory States and the contracting States otherwise decide.

5. The correction of the text of a treaty that has been registered shall be notified to the Secretariat of the United Nations.

6. Where an error is discovered in a certified copy of a treaty, the depositary shall execute a procès-verbal specifying the rectification and communicate a copy of it to the signatory States and to the contracting States.

Article 80 Registration and publication of treaties

1. Treaties shall, after their entry into force, be transmitted to the Secretariat of the United Nations for registration or filing and recording, as the case may be, and for publication.

2. The designation of a depositary shall constitute authorization for it to perform

the acts specified in the preceding paragraph.

Part VIII Final Provisions

Article 81 Signature

The present *Convention* shall be open for signature by all States Members of the United Nations or of any of the specialized agencies or of the International Atomic Energy Agency or parties to the Statute of the International Court of Justice, and by any other State invited by the General Assembly of the United Nations to become a party to the *Convention*, as follows: until 30 November, 1969, at the Federal Ministry for Foreign Affairs of the Republic of Austria, and subsequently, until 30 April, 1970, at United Nations Headquarters, New York.

Article 82 Ratification

The present *Convention* is subject to ratification. The instruments of ratification shall be deposited with the Secretary-General of the United Nations.

Article 83 Accession

The present *Convention* shall remain open for accession by any State belonging to any of the categories mentioned in article 81. The instruments of accession shall be deposited with the Secretary-General of the United Nations.

Article 84 Entry into force

1. The present *Convention* shall enter into force on the thirtieth day following the date of deposit of the thirty-fifth instrument of ratification or accession.

2. For each State ratifying or acceding to the *Convention* after the deposit of the thirty-fifth instrument of ratification or accession, the *Convention* shall enter into force on the thirtieth day after deposit by such State of its instrument of ratification or accession.

Article 85 Authentic texts

The original of the present *Convention*, of which the Chinese, English, French, Russian and Spanish texts are equally authentic, shall be deposited with the Secretary-General of the United Nations.

IN WITNESS WHEREOF the undersigned Plenipotentiaries, being duly authorized thereto by their respective Governments, have signed the present *Convention.*

DONE at Vienna, 23 May, 1969.

V. *Declaration on Principles of International Law Concerning Friendly Relations and Co-Operation Among States in Accordance with the Charter of the United Nations* (*1970*)

General Assembly Resolution 2625 (XXV)

The General Assembly,

Recalling its resolutions 1815 (XVII) of 18 December, 1962, 1966 (XVIII) of 16 December, 1963, 2103 (XX) of 20 December, 1965, 2181 (XXI) of 12 December, 1966, 2327 (XXII) of 18 December 1967, 2463 (XXIII) of 20 December, 1968 and 2533 (XXIV) of 8 December, 1969, in which it affirmed the importance of the progressive development and codification of the principles of international law concerning friendly relations and co-operation among States,

Having considered the report of the Special Committee on Principles of International Law concerning Friendly Relations and Co-operation among States, which met in Geneva from 31 March to 1 May, 1970,

Emphasizing the paramount importance of the *Charter of the United Nations* for the maintenance of international peace and security and for the development of Friendly relations and Co-operation among States,

Deeply convinced that the adoption of the *Declaration on Principles of International Law Concerning Friendly Relations and Co-operation Among States in Accordance with the Charter of the United Nations* on the occasion of the twenty-fifth anniversary of the United Nations would contribute to the strengthening of world peace and constitute a landmark in the development of international law and of relations among States, in promoting the rule of law among nations and particularly the universal application of the principles embodied in the *Charter*,

Considering the desirability of the wide dissemination of the text of the *Declaration*,

1. *Approves* the *Declaration on Principles of International Law Concerning Friendly Relations and Co-operation Among States in Accordance with the Charter of the United Nations*, the text of which is annexed to the present resolution;

2. *Expresses its appreciation* to the Special Committee on Principles of International Law concerning Friendly Relations and Co-operation among States for its work resulting in the elaboration of the *Declaration*;

3. *Recommends* that all efforts be made so that the *Declaration* becomes generally known.

Annex

Declaration on Principles of International Law Concerning Friendly Relations and Co-Operation Among States in Accordance with the Charter of the United Nations

Preamble

The General Assembly,

Reaffirming in the terms of the *Charter of the United Nations* that the maintenance of international peace and security and the development of friendly relations and co-operation between nations are among the fundamental purposes of the United Nations,

Recalling that the peoples of the United Nations are determined to practise tolerance and live together in peace with one another as good neighbours,

Bearing in mind the importance of maintaining and strengthening international peace founded upon freedom, equality, justice and respect for fundamental human rights and of developing friendly relations among nations irrespective of their political, economic and social systems or the levels of their development,

Bearing in mind also the paramount importance of the *Charter of the United Nations* in the promotion of the rule of law among nations,

Considering that the faithful observance of the principles of international law concerning friendly relations and co-operation among States and the fulfillment in good faith of the obligations assumed by States, in accordance with the *Charter*, is of the greatest importance for the maintenance of international peace and security and for the implementation of the other purposes of the United Nations,

Noting that the great political, economic and social changes and scientific progress which have taken place in the world since the adoption of the *Charter* give increased importance to these principles and to the need for their more effective application in the conduct of States wherever carried on,

Recalling the established principle that outer space, including the Moon and other celestial bodies, is not subject to national appropriation by claim of sovereignty, by means of use or occupation, or by any other means, and mindful of the fact that consideration is being given in the United Nations to the question of establishing other appropriate provisions similarly inspired,

Convinced that the strict observance by States of the obligation not to intervene in the affairs of any other State is an essential condition to ensure that nations live together in peace with one another, since the practice of any form of intervention not only violates the spirit and letter of the *Charter*, but also leads to the creation of situations which threaten international peace and security,

Recalling the duty of States to refrain in their international relations from military, political, economic or any other form of coercion aimed against the political independence or territorial integrity of any State,

Considering it essential that all States shall refrain in their international relations from the threat or use of force against the territorial integrity or political independence of any State, or in any other manner inconsistent with the purposes of the United Nations,

Considering it equally essential that all States shall settle their international disputes by peaceful means in accordance with the *Charter*,

Reaffirming, in accordance with the *Charter*, the basic importance of sovereign equality and stressing that the purposes of the United Nations can be implemented only if States enjoy sovereign equality and comply fully with the requirements of this principle in their international relations,

Convinced that the subjection of peoples to alien subjugation, domination and exploitation constitutes a major obstacle to the promotion of international peace and security,

Convinced that the principle of equal rights and self-determination of peoples constitutes a significant contribution to contemporary international law, and that its effective application is of paramount importance for the promotion of friendly relations among States, based on respect for the principle of sovereign equality,

Convinced in consequence that any attempt aimed at the partial or total disruption of the national unity and territorial integrity of a State or country or at its political independence is incompatible with the purposes and principles of the

Charter,

Considering the provisions of the *Charter* as a whole and taking into account the role of relevant resolutions adopted by the competent organs of the United Nations relating to the content of the principles,

Considering that the progressive development and codification of the following principles:

(a) The principle that States shall refrain in their international relations from the threat or use of force against the territorial integrity or political independence of any State, or in any other manner inconsistent with the purposes of the United Nations,

(b) The principle that States shall settle their international disputes by peaceful means in such a manner that international peace and security and justice are not endangered,

(c) The duty not to intervene in matters within the domestic jurisdiction of any State, in accordance with the *Charter*,

(d) The duty of States to co-operate with one another in accordance with the *Charter*,

(e) The principle of equal rights and self-determination of peoples,

(f) The principle of sovereign equality of States,

(g) The principle that States shall fulfil in good faith the obligations assumed by them in accordance with the *Charter*, so as to secure their more effective application within the international community, would promote the realization of the purposes of the United Nations,

Having considered the principles of international law relating to friendly relations and co-operation among States,

***1. Solemnly proclaims the following principles*:**

The principle that States shall refrain in their international relations from the threat or use of force against the territorial integrity or political independence of any State or in any other manner inconsistent with the purposes of the United Nations

Every State has the duty to refrain in its international relations from the threat or use of force against the territorial integrity or political independence of any State, or in any other manner inconsistent with the purposes of the United Nations. Such a threat or use of force constitutes a violation of international law and the *Charter of the United Nations* and shall never be employed as a means of settling international issues.

A war of aggression constitutes a crime against the peace, for which there is responsibility under international law.

In accordance with the purposes and principles of the United Nations, States have the duty to refrain from propaganda for wars of aggression.

Every State has the duty to refrain from the threat or use of force to violate the existing international boundaries of another State or as a means of solving international disputes, including territorial disputes and problems concerning frontiers of States.

Every State likewise has the duty to refrain from the threat or use of force to violate international lines of demarcation, such as armistice lines, established by or pursuant to an international agreement to which it is a party or which it is otherwise bound to respect. Nothing in the foregoing shall be construed as prejudicing the positions of the parties concerned with regard to the status and effects of such lines under their special regimes or as affecting their temporary character.

States have a duty to refrain from acts of reprisal involving the use of force.

Every State has the duty to refrain from any forcible action which deprives peoples referred to in the elaboration of the principle of equal rights and self-determination of their right to self-determination and freedom and independence.

Every State has the duty to refrain from organizing or encouraging the organization of irregular forces or armed bands including mercenaries, for incursion into the territory of another State.

Every State has the duty to refrain from organizing, instigating, assisting or participating in acts of civil strife or terrorist acts in another State or acquiescing in organized activities within its territory directed towards the commission of such acts, when the acts referred to in the present paragraph involve a threat or use of force.

The territory of a State shall not be the object of military occupation resulting from the use of force in contravention of the provisions of the *Charter*. The territory of a State shall not be the object of acquisition by another State resulting from the threat or use of force. No territorial acquisition resulting from the threat or use of force shall be recognized as legal. Nothing in the foregoing shall be construed as affecting:

(a) Provisions of the *Charter* or any international agreement prior to the

Charter regime and valid under international law; or

(b) The powers of the Security Council under the *Charter*.

All States shall pursue in good faith negotiations for the early conclusion of a universal treaty on general and complete disarmament under effective international control and strive to adopt appropriate measures to reduce international tensions and strengthen confidence among States.

All States shall comply in good faith with their obligations under the generally recognized principles and rules of international law with respect to the maintenance of international peace and security, and shall endeavour to make the United Nations security system based on the *Charter* more effective.

Nothing in the foregoing paragraphs shall be construed as enlarging or diminishing in any way the scope of the provisions of the *Charter* concerning cases in which the use of force is lawful.

The principle that States shall settle their international disputes by peaceful means in such a manner that international peace and security and justice are not endangered

Every State shall settle its international disputes with other States by peaceful means in such a manner that international peace and security and justice are not endangered.

States shall accordingly seek early and just settlement of their international disputes by negotiation, inquiry, mediation, conciliation, arbitration, judicial settlement, resort to regional agencies or arrangements or other peaceful means of their choice. In seeking such a settlement the parties shall agree upon such peaceful means as may be appropriate to the circumstances and nature of the dispute.

The parties to a dispute have the duty, in the event of failure to reach a solution by any one of the above peaceful means, to continue to seek a settlement of the dispute by other peaceful means agreed upon by them.

States parties to an international dispute, as well as other States shall refrain from any action which may aggravate the Situation so as to endanger the maintenance of international peace and security, and shall act in accordance with the purposes and principles of the United Nations.

International disputes shall be settled on the basis of the Sovereign equality of

States and in accordance with the Principle of free choice of means. Recourse to, or acceptance of, a settlement procedure freely agreed to by States with regard to existing or future disputes to which they are parties shall not be regarded as incompatible with sovereign equality.

Nothing in the foregoing paragraphs prejudices or derogates from the applicable provisions of the *Charter*, in particular those relating to the pacific settlement of international disputes.

The principle concerning the duty not to intervene in matters within the domestic jurisdiction of any State, in accordance with the *Charter*

No State or group of States has the right to intervene, directly or indirectly, for any reason whatever, in the internal or external affairs of any other State. Consequently, armed intervention and all other forms of interference or attempted threats against the personality of the State or against its political, economic and cultural elements, are in violation of international law.

No State may use or encourage the use of economic political or any other type of measures to coerce another State in order to obtain from it the subordination of the exercise of its sovereign rights and to secure from it advantages of any kind. Also, no State shall organize, assist, foment, finance, incite or tolerate subversive, terrorist or armed activities directed towards the violent overthrow of the regime of another State, or interfere in civil strife in another State.

The use of force to deprive peoples of their national identity constitutes a violation of their inalienable rights and of the principle of non-intervention.

Every State has an inalienable right to choose its political, economic, social and cultural systems, without interference in any form by another State.

Nothing in the foregoing paragraphs shall be construed as reflecting the relevant provisions of the *Charter* relating to the maintenance of international peace and security.

The duty of States to co-operate with one another in accordance with the *Charter*

States have the duty to co-operate with one another, irrespective of the differences in their political, economic and social systems, in the various spheres of international relations, in order to maintain international peace and security and to promote international economic stability and progress, the general welfare of nations and international co-operation free from discrimination based on such differences.

To this end:

(a) States shall co-operate with other States in the maintenance of international peace and security;

(b) States shall co-operate in the promotion of universal respect for, and observance of, human rights and fundamental freedoms for all, and in the elimination of all forms of racial discrimination and all forms of religious intolerance;

(c) States shall conduct their international relations in the economic, social, cultural, technical and trade fields in accordance with the principles of sovereign equality and non-intervention;

(d) States Members of the United Nations have the duty to take joint and separate action in co-operation with the United Nations in accordance with the relevant provisions of the *Charter*.

States should co-operate in the economic, social and cultural fields as well as in the field of science and technology and for the promotion of international cultural and educational progress. States should co-operate in the promotion of economic growth throughout the world, especially that of the developing countries.

The principle of equal rights and self-determination of peoples

By virtue of the principle of equal rights and self-determination of peoples enshrined in the *Charter of the United Nations*, all peoples have the right freely to determine, without external interference, their political status and to pursue their economic, social and cultural development, and every State has the duty to respect this right in accordance with the provisions of the *Charter*.

Every State has the duty to promote, through joint and separate action, realization of the principle of equal rights and self-determination of peoples, in accordance with the provisions of the *Charter*, and to render assistance to the United Nations in carrying out the responsibilities entrusted to it by the *Charter* regarding the implementation of the principle, in order:

(a) To promote friendly relations and co-operation among States; and

(b) To bring a speedy end to colonialism, having due regard to the freely expressed will of the peoples concerned;

and bearing in mind that subjection of peoples to alien subjugation, domination and exploitation constitutes a violation of the principle, as well as a denial of fundamental human rights, and is contrary to the *Charter*.

Every State has the duty to promote through joint and separate action universal respect for and observance of human rights and fundamental freedoms in accordance with the *Charter*.

The establishment of a sovereign and independent State, the free association or integration with an independent State or the emergence into any other political status freely determined by a people constitute modes of implementing the right of self-determination by that people.

Every State has the duty to refrain from any forcible action which deprives peoples referred to above in the elaboration of the present principle of their right to self-determination and freedom and independence. In their actions against, and resistance to, such forcible action in pursuit of the exercise of their right to self-determination, such peoples are entitled to seek and to receive support in accordance with the purposes and principles of the *Charter*.

The territory of a colony or other Non-Self-Governing Territory has, under the *Charter*, a status separate and distinct from the territory of the State administering it; and such separate and distinct status under the *Charter* shall exist until the people of the colony or Non-Self-Governing Territory have exercised their right of self-determination in accordance with the *Charter*, and particularly its purposes and principles.

Nothing in the foregoing paragraphs shall be construed as authorizing or encouraging any action which would dismember or impair, totally or in part, the territorial integrity or political unity of sovereign and independent States conducting themselves in compliance with the principle of equal rights and self-determination of peoples as described above and thus possessed of a government representing the whole people belonging to the territory without distinction as to race, creed or colour.

Every State shall refrain from any action aimed at the partial or total disruption of the national unity and territorial integrity of any other State or country.

The principle of sovereign equality of States

All States enjoy sovereign equality. They have equal rights and duties and are equal members of the international community, notwithstanding differences of an economic, social, political or other nature.

In particular, sovereign equality includes the following elements:

(a) States are judicially equal;

(b) Each State enjoys the rights inherent in full sovereignty;

(c) Each State has the duty to respect the personality of other States;

(d) The territorial integrity and political independence of the State are inviolable;

(e) Each State has the right freely to choose and develop its political, social, economic and cultural systems;

(f) Each State has the duty to comply fully and in good faith with its international obligations and to live in peace with other States.

The principle that States shall fulfil in good faith the obligations assumed by them in accordance with the *Charter*

Every State has the duty to fulfil in good faith the obligations assumed by it in accordance with the *Charter of the United Nations*.

Every State has the duty to fulfil in good faith its obligations under the generally recognized principles and rules of international law.

Every State has the duty to fulfil in good faith its obligations under international agreements valid under the generally recognized principles and rules of international law.

Where obligations arising under international agreements are in conflict with the obligations of Members of the United Nations under the *Charter of the United Nations*, the obligations under the *Charter* shall prevail.

General Part

***2. Declares that*:**

In their interpretation and application the above principles are interrelated and each principle should be construed in the context of the other principles. Nothing in this *Declaration* shall be construed as prejudicing in any manner the provisions of *the Charter* or the rights and duties of Member States under the *Charter* or the rights of peoples under the *Charter*, taking into account the elaboration of these rights in this *Declaration*.

***3. Declares further that*:**

The principles of the *Charter* which *are embodied in this Declaration* constitute basic principles of international law, and consequently appeals to all States to be guided by these principles in their international conduct and to develop their mutual relations on the basis of the strict observance of these principles.

VI. *Definition of Aggression* (*1974*)

General Assembly Resolution 3314 (XXIX)

The General Assembly,

Having considered the report of the Special Committee on the Question of Defining Aggression, established pursuant to its resolution 2330 (XXII) of 18 December, 1967, covering the work of its seventh session held from 11 March to 12 April, 1974, including the draft *Definition of Aggression* adopted by the Special Committee by consensus and recommended for adoption by the General Assembly, */1*

Deeply convinced that the adoption of the *Definition of Aggression* would contribute to the strengthening of international peace and security,

1. Approves the *Definition of Aggression*, the text of which is annexed to the present resolution;

2. Expresses its appreciation to the Special Committee on the Question of Defining Aggression for its work which resulted in the elaboration of the *Definition of Aggression*;

3. Calls upon all States to refrain from all acts of aggression and other uses of force contrary to the *Charter of the United Nations* and the *Declaration on Principles of International Law Concerning Friendly Relations and Co-Operation Among States in Accordance with the Charter of the United Nations*; /2

4. Calls the attention of the Security Council to the *Definition of Aggression*, as set out below, and recommends that it should, as appropriate, take account of that *Definition as guidance* in determination, in accordance with the *Charter*, the existence of an act of aggression.

Annex

Definition of Aggression

The General Assembly,

Basing itself on the fact that one of the fundamental purposes of the United

Nations is to maintain international peace and security and to take effective collective measures for the prevention and removal of threats to the peace, and for the suppression of acts of aggression or other breaches of the peace,

Recalling that the Security Council, in accordance with *Article 39* of the *Charter of the United Nations*, shall determine the existence of any threat to the peace, breach of the peace or act of aggression and shall make recommendations, or decide what measures shall be taken in accordance with *Articles 41 and 42*, to maintain or restore international peace and security,

Recalling also the duty of States under the *Charter* to settle their international disputes by peaceful means in order not to endanger international peace, security and justice,

Bearing in mind that nothing in this *Definition* shall be interpreted as in any way affecting the scope of the provisions of the *Charter* with respect to the functions and powers of the organs of the United Nations,

Considering also that, since aggression is the most serious and dangerous form of the illegal use of force, being fraught, in the conditions created by the existence of all types of weapons of mass destruction, with the possible threat of a world conflict and all its catastrophic consequences, aggression should be defined at the present stage,

Reaffirming the duty of States not to use armed force to deprive peoples of their right to self-determination, freedom and independence, or to disrupt territorial Integrity,

Reaffirming also that the territory of a State shall not be violated by being the object, even temporarily, of military occupation or of other measures of force taken by another State in contravention of the *Charter*, and that it shall not be the object of acquisition by another State resulting from such measures or the threat thereof,

Reaffirming also the provisions of the *Declaration on Principles of International Law Concerning Friendly Relations and Co-Operation Among States in Accordance with the Charter of the United Nations*,

Convinced that the adoption of a definition of aggression ought to have the effect of deterring a potential aggressor, would simplify the determination of acts of aggression and the implementation of measures to suppress them and would also facilitate the protection of the rights and lawful interests of, and the rendering of assistance to, the victim,

Believing that, although the question whether an act of aggression has been committed must be considered in the light of all the circumstances of each particular case, it is nevertheless desirable to formulate basic principles as guidance for such determination,

Adopts the following *Definition of Agression* :

Article 1

Aggression is the use of armed force by a State against the sovereignty, territorial integrity or political independence of another State, or in any other manner inconsistent with the *Charter of the United Nations*, as set out in this *Definition*.

Explanatory note: In this *Definition* the term "State":

(a) is used without prejudice to questions of recognition or to whether a State is a member of the United Nations;

(b) includes the concept of a "group of States" where appropriate.

Article 2

The First use of armed force by a State in contravention of the *Charter* shall constitute prima facie evidence of an act of aggression although the Security Council may, in conformity with the *Charter*, conclude that a determination that an act of aggression has been committed would not be justified in the light of other relevant circumstances, including the fact that the acts concerned or their consequences are not of sufficient gravity.

Article 3

Any of the following acts, regardless of a declaration of war, shall, subject to and in accordance with the provisions of Article 2, qualify as an act of aggression:

(a) the invasion or attack by the armed forces of a State of the territory of another State, or any military occupation, however temporary, resulting from such invasion or attack, or any annexation by the use of force of the territory of another State or part thereof,

(b) bombardment by the armed forces of a State against the territory of another State or the use of any weapons by a State against the territory of another State;

(c) the blockade of the ports or coasts of a State by the armed forces of another State;

(d) an attack by the armed forces of a State on the land, sea or air forces, or marine and air fleets of another State;

(e) the use of armed forces of one State which are within the territory of another State with the agreement of the receiving State, in contravention of the conditions provided for in the agreement or any extension of their presence in such territory beyond the termination of the agreement;

(f) the action of a State in allowing its territory, which it has placed at the disposal of another State, to be used by that other State for perpetrating an act of aggression against a third State;

(g) the sending by or on behalf of a State of armed bands, groups, irregulars or mercenaries, which carry out acts of armed force against another State of such gravity as to amount to the acts listed above, or its substantial involvement therein.

Article 4

The acts enumerated above are not exhaustive and the Security Council may determine that other acts constitute aggression under the provisions of the *Charter*.

Article 5

1. No consideration of whatever nature, whether political, economic, military or otherwise, may serve as a justification for aggression.

2. A war of aggression is a crime against international peace. Aggression gives rise to international responsibility.

3. No territorial acquisition or special advantage resulting from aggression is or shall be recognized as lawful.

Article 6

Nothing in this *Definition* shall be construed as in any way enlarging or diminishing the scope of the *Charter*, including its provisions concerning cases in which the use of force is lawful.

Article 7

Nothing in this *Definition*, and in particular article 3, could in any way prejudice the right to self-determination, freedom and independence, as derived from the *Charter*, of peoples forcibly deprived of that right and referred to in the

Declaration on Principles of International Law Concerning Friendly Relations and Co-Operation Among States in Accordance with the Charter of the United Nations, particularly peoples under colonial and racist regimes or other forms of alien domination; nor the right of these peoples to struggle to that end and to seek and receive support, in accordance with the principles of the *Charter* and in conformity with the above-mentioned *Declaration*.

Article 8

In their interpretation and application the above provisions are interrelated and each provision should be construed in the context of the other provisions.

VII. *ILC Draft Articles on Responsibility of States for Internationally Wrongful Acts* (*2001*)

(Adopted on *9* August, *2001*)

Part I The Internationally Wrongful Act of a State

Chapter I General Principles

Article 1 Responsibility of a State for its internationally wrongful acts

Every internationally wrongful act of a State entails the international responsibility of that State.

Article 2 Elements of internationally wrongful act of a State

There is an internationally wrongful act of a State when conduct consisting of an action or omission:

(a) is attributable to the State under international law; and

(b) constitutes a breach of an international obligation of the State.

Article 3 Characterisation of an act of a State as internationally wrongful

The characterisation of an act of a State as internationally wrongful is governed by international law. Such characterisation is not affected by the characterisation of the same act as lawful by internal law.

Chapter II Attribution of Conduct to a State

Article 4 Conduct of organs of a State

1. The conduct of any State organ shall be considered an act of that State under international law, whether the organ exercises legislative, executive, judicial or any other functions, whatever position it holds in the organization of the State, and whatever its character as an organ of the central government or of a territorial unit of the State.

2. An organ includes any person or entity which has that status in accordance with the internal law of the State.

Article 5 Conduct of persons or entities exercising elements of governmental authority

The conduct of a person or entity which is not an organ of the State under Article 4 but which is empowered by the law of that State to exercise the elements of the governmental authority shall be considered as an act of the State under international law, provided the person or entity is acting in that capacity in the particular instance.

Article 6 Conduct of organs placed at the disposal of a State by another State

The conduct of an organ placed at the disposal of a State by another State shall be considered an act of the former State under international law if the organ is acting in the exercise of elements of the governmental authority of the State at whose disposal it is placed.

Article 7 Excess of authority or contraventions of instructions

The conduct of an organ of a State or of a person or entity empowered to exercise elements of the governmental authority shall be considered an act of the State under international law if the organ, person or entity acts in that capacity, even if it exceeds its authority or contravenes instructions.

Article 8 Conduct directed or controlled by a State

The conduct of a person or group of persons shall be considered an act of a State under international law if the person or group of persons is in fact acting on the instructions of, or under the direction or control of that State in carrying out the conduct.

Article 9 Conduct carried out in the absence or default of the official authorities

The conduct of a person or group of persons shall be considered an act of a State under international law if the person or group of persons is in fact exercising elements of the governmental authority in the absence or default of the official authorities and in circumstances such as to call for the exercise of those elements of authority.

Article 10 Conduct of an insurrectional or other movement

1. The conduct of an insurrectional movement which becomes the new government of a State shall be considered as an act of that State under international law.

2. The conduct of a movement, insurrectional or other, which succeeds in establishing a new State in part of the territory of a pre-existing State or in a territory under its administration, shall be considered an act of the new State under international law.

3. This Article is without prejudice to the attribution to a State of any conduct, however related to that of the movement concerned, which is to be considered an act of that State by virtue of Articles 4 to 9.

Article 11 Conduct acknowledged and adopted by a State as its own

Conduct which is not attributed to a State under the preceding Articles shall nevertheless be considered an act of that State under international law if and to the extent that the State acknowledges and adopts the conduct in question as its own.

Chapter III Breach of an International Obligation

Article 12 Existence of a breach of an international obligation

There is a breach of an international obligation by a State when an act of that State is not in conformity with what is required of it by that obligation, regardless of its origin or character.

Article 13 International obligation in force for a State

An act of a State does not constitute a breach of an international obligation unless the State is bound by the obligation in question at the time of the act.

Article 14 Extension in time of the breach of an international obligation

1. The breach of an international obligation by an act of a State not having a continuing character occurs at the moment when the act is performed even if its effects continue.

2. The breach of an international obligation by an act of a State having a continuing character extends over the entire period during which the act continues and

remains not in conformity with the international obligation.

3. The breach of an international obligation requiring a State to prevent a given event occurs when the event occurs and extends over the entire period during which the event continues and remains not in conformity with that obligation.

Article 15 Breach consisting of a composite act

1. The breach of an international obligation by a State through a series of actions or omissions defined in aggregate as wrongful,① occurs when the action or omission occurs which, taken with the other actions or omissions, is sufficient to constitute the wrongful act.

2. In such a case, the breach extends over the entire period starting with the first of the actions or omissions of the series and lasts for as long as these actions or omissions are repeated and remain not in conformity with the international obligation.

Chapter IV Responsibility of a State in Connection with the Act of Another State

Article 16 Aid or assistance in the commission of an internationally wrongful act

A State which aids or assists another State in the commission of an internationally wrongful act by the latter is internationally responsible for doing so if:

(a) that State does so with knowledge of the circumstances of the internationally wrongful act; and

(b) the act would be internationally wrongful if committed by that State.

Article 17 Direction and control exercised over the commission of an internationally wrongful act

A State which directs and controls another State in the commission of an internationally wrongful act by the latter is internationally responsible for that act if:

(a) that State does so with knowledge of the circumstances of the internationally wrongful act; and

(b) the act would be internationally wrongful if committed by that State.

---

① In the French text these words are expressed as follows: "*d' une série d' actions ou d'omissions, définie dans son ensemble comme illicite.*"

Article 18 Coercion of another State

A State which coerces another State to commit an act is internationally responsible for that act if:

(a) the act would, but for the coercion, be an internationally wrongful act of the coerced State; and

(b) the coercing State does so with knowledge of the circumstances of the act.

Article 19 Effect of this Chapter

This Chapter is without prejudice to the international responsibility, under other provisions of these Articles, of the State which commits the act in question, or of any other State.

Chapter V Circumstances Precluding Wrongfulness

Article 20 Consent

Valid consent by a State to the commission of a given act by another State precludes the wrongfulness of that act in relation to the former State to the extent that the act remains within the limits of that consent.

Article 21 Self-defence

The wrongfulness of an act of a State is precluded if the act constitutes a lawful measure of self-defence taken in conformity with the *Charter of the United Nations*.

Article 22 Countermeasures in respect of an internationally wrongful act

The wrongfulness of an act of a State not in conformity with an international obligation towards another State is precluded if and to the extent that the act constitutes a countermeasure taken against the latter State in accordance with Chapter II of Part Three.

Article 23 *Force majeure*

1. The wrongfulness of an act of a State not in conformity with an international obligation of that State is precluded if the act is due to *force majeure*, that is the

occurrence of an irresistible force or of an unforeseen event, beyond the control of the State, making it materially impossible in the circumstances to perform the obligation.

2. Paragraph 1 does not apply if:

(a) the situation of *force majeure* is due, either alone or in combination with other factors, to the conduct of the State invoking it; or

(b) the State has assumed the risk of that situation occurring.

Article 24 Distress

1. The wrongfulness of an act of a State not in conformity with an international obligation of that State is precluded if the author of the act in question has no other reasonable way, in a situation of distress, of saving the author's life or the lives of other persons entrusted to the author's care.

2. Paragraph 1 does not apply if:

(a) the situation of distress is due, either alone or in combination with other factors, to the conduct of the State invoking it; or

(b) the act in question is likely to create a comparable or greater peril.

Article 25 Necessity

1. Necessity may not be invoked by a State as a ground for precluding the wrongfulness of an act not in conformity with an international obligation of that State unless the act

(a) is the only way for the State to safeguard an essential interest against a grave and imminent peril; and

(b) does not seriously impair an essential interest of the State or States towards which the obligation exists, or of the international community as a whole.

2. In any case, necessity may not be invoked by a State as a ground for precluding wrongfulness if:

(a) the international obligation in question excludes the possibility of invoking necessity; or

(b) the State has contributed to the situation of necessity.

Article 26 Compliance with peremptory norms

Nothing in the present Chapter precludes the wrongfulness of any act of a State which is not in conformity with an obligation arising under a peremptory norm of general international law.

Article 27 Consequences of invoking a circumstance precluding wrongfulness

The invocation of a circumstance precluding wrongfulness in accordance with this Chapter is without prejudice to:

(a) compliance with the obligation in question, if and to the extent that the circumstance precluding wrongfulness no longer exists;

(b) the question of compensation for any material loss caused by the act in question.

Part II Content of the International Responsibility of a State

Chapter I General Principles

Article 28 Legal consequences of an internationally wrongful act

The international responsibility of a State which is entailed by an internationally wrongful act in accordance with the provisions of Part I involve legal consequences as set out in this Part.

Article 29 Continued duty of performance

The legal consequences of an internationally wrongful act under this Part do not affect the continued duty of the responsible State to perform the obligation breached.

Article 30 Cessation and non-repetition

The State responsible for the internationally wrongful act is under an obligation:

(a) to cease that act, if it is continuing;

(b) to offer appropriate assurances and guarantees of non-repetition, if circumstances so require.

Article 31 Reparation

1. The responsible State is under an obligation to make full reparation for the

injury caused by the internationally wrongful act.

2. Injury includes any damage, whether material or moral, caused by the internationally wrongful act of a State.

Article 32 Irrelevance of internal law

The responsible State may not rely on the provisions of its internal law as justification for failure to comply with the obligations under this Part.

Article 33 Scope of obligations set out in this Part

1. The obligations of the responsible State set out in this Part may be owed to another State, to several States, or to the international community as a whole, depending in particular of the character and content of the international obligation and on the circumstances of the breach.

2. This Part is without prejudice to any right, arising from the international responsibility of a State, which may accrue directly to any person or entity other than a State.

Chapter II Reparation for Injury

Article 34 Forms of reparation

Full reparation for the injury caused by the internationally wrongful act shall take the form of restitution, compensation and satisfaction, either singly or in combination, in accordance with the provisions of this Chapter.

Article 35 Restitution

A State responsible for an internationally wrongful act is under an obligation to make restitution, that is, to re-establish the situation which existed before the wrongful act was committed, provided and to the extent that restitution:

(a) is materially impossible;

(b) does not involve a burden out of all proportion to the benefit deriving from restitution instead of compensation.

Article 36 Compensation

1. The State responsible for an internationally wrongful act is under an obligation to compensate for the damage caused thereby, insofar as such damage is not made

good by restitution.

2. The compensation shall cover any financially assessable damage including loss of profit insofar as it is established.

Article 37 Satisfaction

1. The State responsible for an internationally wrongful act is under an obligation to give satisfaction for the injury caused by that act in so far as it cannot be made good for restitution or compensation.

2. Satisfaction may consist in an acknowledgement of the breach, an expression of regret, a formal apology or another appropriate modality.

3. Satisfaction shall not be out of proportion to the injury and may not take a form humiliation to the responsible State.

Article 38 Interest

1. Interest on any principal sum due under this Chapter shall be payable when necessary in order to ensure full reparation. The interest rate and mode of calculation shall be set so as to achieve that result.

2. Interest runs from the time when the principal sum should have been paid until the date the obligation to pay is fulfilled.

Article 39 Contribution to the injury

In the determination of reparation, account shall be taken of the contribution to the injury by willful or neglected action or commission of the injured State or any person or entity in relation to whom reparation is sought.

Chapter III Serious Breaches of Obligations Under Peremptory Norms of General International Law

Article 40 Application of this Chapter

1. This Chapter applies to the international responsibility which is entailed by a serious breach by a State of an obligation arising under a peremptory norm of general international law.

2. A breach of such an obligation is serious if it involves a gross or systematic failure by the responsible State to fulfill the obligation.

Article 41 Particular consequences of a serious breach of an obligation under this Chapter

1. States shall co-operate to bring to an end through lawful means any serious breach within the meaning of Article 40.

2. No State shall recognize as lawful a situation created by a serious breach within the meaning of Article 40, nor render aid or assistance in maintaining that situation.

3. This Article is without prejudice to the other consequences referred to in this Part and to such further consequences that a breach to which this Chapter applies may entail under international law.

Part III The Implementation of the International Responsibility of a State

Chapter I Invocation of the Responsibility of a State

Article 42 Invocation of responsibility by an injured State

A State is entitled as an injured State to invoke the responsibility of another State if the obligation breached is owed to:

(a) that State individually; or

(b) a group of States including that State, or the international community as a whole, and the breach of the obligation:

(i) specially affect that State; or

(ii) is of such a character as radically to change the position of all the other States to which the obligation is owed with respect to the further performance of the obligation.

Article 43 Notice of claim by an injured State

1. An injured State which invokes the responsibility of another States shall give notice of its claim to that State.

2. The injured State may specify in particular:

(a) the conduct that the responsible State should take in order to cease the wrongful act, if it is continuing;

(b) what form of reparation should take in accordance with the provisions of Part Two.